JOURNEY THROUGH YORKSHIRE:
its history, customs and beauty

Kenneth Fields

'Give me the clear sky above my head, and the green turf beneath my feet, a winding road before me and a three hour march to dinner.'

(William Hazlitt, 1778-1830)

Published by Sigma Leisure – an imprint of
Sigma Press, 1 South Oak Lane, Wilmslow, Cheshire SK9 6AR, England.

British Library Cataloguing in Publication Data
A CIP record for this book is available from the British Library.

ISBN: 1-85058-499-0

Typesetting and Design by: Sigma Press, Wilmslow, Cheshire.

Cover photographs: set against a background of the River Wharfe, from top to bottom – St Mary's abbey (York); the approach to Malham Cove; York Minster from the city walls *(Graham Beech)*

Photographs: the author, except where indicated

Sketches: Mike Ince and the author

Printed by: MFP Design & Print

Preface

In these pages you will find a record of the haphazard wanderings of a Lancastrian through one of England's most fascinating corners – Yorkshire! It is a journey which began with grey overcast skies, but happily these quickly turned to blue. Soon I was privileged to continue my exploration during the hottest and driest summer we have ever seen. It was a unique experience that was truly unforgettable for I saw this splendid landscape at its very best.

It was once a proud boast that Yorkshire contains more acres of land than there are letters in the bible and I have no reason to doubt this. For as I continued my journey it soon became apparent that it was not a mere county that I was exploring but more a self-contained kingdom. For such is its size, that Yorkshire could quite easily declare unilateral independence and, I believe, survive quite happily.

As you will read, I began my journey at the northern tip of the Peak District in a landscape of windswept hills which, due to a popular TV series, has become known as the Summer Wine Country. I then continued into the softer limestone landscape of the Yorkshire Dales; a region which is regarded by many as being the most beautiful in all of England. After descending into that huge green vale which spreads northwards from York, I found myself once more in a wide horizon of high hills; the North York Moors. Then in complete contrast I reached the magnificent Yorkshire coast; a place of thundering waves, shrieking gulls and towering cliffs. Turning to the west, my homeward path now lay through the timeless villages of the Yorkshire Wolds; an ancient pastoral land that could quite easily be mistaken for Sussex.

But I discovered that this amazing diversity of countryside which lies in Yorkshire is more than equalled by the vast differences of its cities, towns and villages. Huddersfield, Skipton, Hawes, Richmond, Thirsk, Whitby, Beverley, York, Harrogate and scores more, are splendidly unique. Each possesses a striking individuality which makes them all a real joy to explore. However, let me warn you that a stranger venturing here can quite easily become the victim of an inferiority complex. For in this land of ancient abbeys, stately homes, bustling towns and rugged mountains, one is constantly being reminded of Yorkshire's superiority. On my travels I came across England's deepest cave, highest waterfall, highest pub, largest cathedral and oldest chemist shop!

Finally let me say that for a Lancastrian to attempt to write a book about Yorkshire may seem on the face of it to be foolhardy, for the rivalry between the white and red rose counties is legendary. However on close examination this rivalry is revealed as being of the type found in families; it is perfectly acceptable for a Yorkshireman to remind a Lancastrian of his shortcomings, and for a Lancastrian to point out the weak points of his Pennine neighbour. However should any other person be foolish enough to criticise either let him do so at his own peril!

So bearing this in mind, nowhere in these pages do I repeat those old retorts such as: 'The only good thing to come out of Yorkshire is the road into Lancashire' or 'You can always tell a Yorkshireman, but you can't tell him much' or 'A Yorkshireman is the only person who can buy from a Scotsman and sell to a Jew, and make a profit . . .'

Acknowledgements

Good maps are essential companions for every traveller. It was the Official Tourist Map of Yorkshire and Humberside by Estate Publications, together with my faithful Ordnance Survey map which guided me on my journey.

Much of the up-to-date information which I required was freely given by the staff of the many excellent Tourist Information Centres which exist in Yorkshire; to these I extend my thanks.

Most of the sketches found in the book are the work of Mike Ince of Croston in Lancashire, to whom I am particularly grateful. I would also like to thank The Sutcliffe Gallery in Whitby, Valerie Weyland and Neil Heaton for permission to reproduce their photographs.

Finally, as always, my special thanks to my wife Wynne, who read, criticised and suggested improvements to the manuscript and gave me support and motivation during my journey.

This book is dedicated to the memory of my father, James William Fields, who enjoyed many a happy day fishing on the waterways of Yorkshire.

Kenneth Fields

Contents

1. Holmfirth to Todmorden   1

2. Todmorden to Ilkley   23

3. Ilkley to the Yorkshire Dales   42

4. The Yorkshire Dales to Richmond   64

5. Richmond to the North York Moors   89

6. North York Moors to Whitby   110

7. Whitby to Flamborough Head   130

8. Flamborough Head to York   148

9. York to Harrogate   170

Index   193

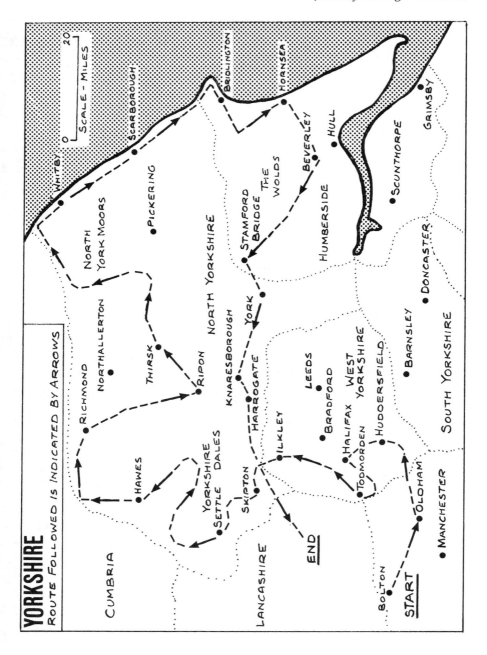

Chapter One

Holmfirth to Todmorden

I climb windswept Saddleworth Moor where I cross the border into West Yorkshire. I explore Holmfirth, follow in the steps of Compo, Foggy and Clegg into Sid's Cafe, then I look at saucy postcards. I admire Huddersfield's magnificent railway station, remember James Mason, then set off for Halifax. I see the pub where our largest Building Society began, explore the Piece Hall and look at the Halifax Gibbet. Then I pass through Coiner's Country to reach Todmorden where I hear of a Victorian murder.

1

May is usually the loveliest month of the year in England, but sadly, this year seemed to be an exception. True, the beech and the sycamore were alive with a magnificent new coat of emerald green, buttercups had sprinkled the meadows with gold, and thrushes, as always, were echoing their songs over the rooftops. But there was something missing – the sun. For weeks a dismal blanket of grey cloud had refused to move, it had enveloped the North with grim stubbornness so that many voices were saying: 'It looks like we're not going to have any summer at all this year.' However, as a well-travelled red Ford Escort left the bustle of Oldham's busy town centre behind the outlook became more optimistic. The sky was looking lighter, the greyness had turned to silver-white, and before long an elusive sunbeam was breaking through.

One of the great surprises which await visitors to northern towns is how quickly 'civilization' gives way to wild rugged countryside and nowhere is this more apparent than here, where Lancashire and Yorkshire meet. One minute I was driving through a sea of lorries, cars and buses, then quite suddenly they disappeared. The suburban houses built of brick gave way to more ancient dwellings of millstone grit. The meandering road which dipped and dived, now allowed me more inviting views of cows grazing on green meadowland, of a church tower on a hilltop, and of half hidden farms in moorland hollows. I passed through the villages of Lees and Lydgate, then saw a reassuring sign which told me 'Snow Warning — A635 Holm-firth Road Open'. This may bring a smile to the face of many a stranger who passes this way in summertime, but some twenty years ago the Peak District did have a heavy snowstorm in June, so the warning is no joke.

After a short hold-up and a brief diversion due to 'Tame Valley Road Works' at Greenfield, I began to ascend the spectacular A635 road which brought with it a splendid feeling of freedom. Soon I was looking out over an open landscape of wild craggy hills, sharply profiled, dark and foreboding, they spread outwards to the distant horizon. Far below me in a deep cut valley on my right, curved the dramatic silver outline of the Dove Stone reservoir which has a Mountain Rescue Post closeby. This is the northern boundary of the Peak District, the Dark Peak as it has become known due to its rugged peaty terrain and dark millstone grit, unlike the southern White Peak which is softer, limestone country.

I passed a young cyclist who was struggling with the steep gradient that rises ever upwards to meet the sweep of Saddleworth Moor; a name forever associated with the evil Moors Murderers, Myra Hindley and Ian Brady. For it was here in 1964 that they buried their innocent child victims; a grotesque crime which shocked not only the nation, but the entire world.

Reaching the high-point of the road, which levels out above the 1600 feet contour, I was rewarded with a marvellous Pennine panorama of moorland that is the roof of England. I parked on the roadside and walked for a short distance into this astonishing peaty wilderness that stretches in all directions. Here, I looked at bootprints which have created a thin line that snakes across the landscape, for this is part of our first long-distance footpath, the Pennine Way. Although at this point the walk has hardly begun, anyone who reaches this road will have already had a baptism of fire on these unforgiving boggy uplands. Starting from the village of Edale their leg-muscles will have been tested to the full on Kinderscout, Bleaklow and notorious Black Hill, whose summit lies less than three miles from this highway. Many will wonder if they will ever complete the walk, but surprisingly most do, for the terrain to the north quickly becomes much more tolerable.

'Kirklees – West Yorkshire', boasted a border sign on the roadside, being highlighted by a welcome surge of yellow sunlight which had at last broken through the thinning cloud. With excited anticipation I felt that my journey had now really begun.

2

Apanorama of isolated moorland farms, drystone walls disappearing into deep-cut valleys and a distant view of the towering Holme Moss TV mast perched on a high hill, was my introduction to Yorkshire. But soon I found myself descending the snaking road, the vast brown moors quickly turning to green meadows where 'Harden Moss Sheepdog Trials' would soon be held. As I approached the outskirts of Holmfirth, 'Compo's Cafe' left me in no doubt that I had reached, what is now known to millions of BBC television viewers as 'The Last of the Summer Wine' country. For it is here that the dynamic trio, Compo, Foggy and Clegg who were created over two decades ago by writer Roy Clarke, have mooched their way into our hearts.

I parked my car on the banks of the little River Holme then strolled along a riverside path towards the centre of the town. Middle aged visitors, lured by the soft morning sunshine, were already sitting on benches listening to the chatter of jackdaws and enjoying the peace. I too was unable to resist sitting on one bench for it was a gift to the people of Holmfirth 'From Bill Owen, your adopted Son, 1991', that great actor who we now all know as Compo. I half expected his cheeky figure, complete with woollen cap, trousers held up with string, black wellies and of course his pet ferret in his jacket pocket, to come racing around the corner. Chased by his true love, Nora Batty, wielding her deadly brush, he would no doubt be uttering his immortal words, 'Hey up!'

Holmfirth I soon discovered is a fascinating, lively town which is a joy to explore. Sitting in the Holme valley surrounded by the rising hills its ancient stone houses tower ever upwards, reached by inviting narrow alleyways and curving steps. Here, hiding on precipitous terraces I discovered rows of marvellous weavers' cottages with mullioned windows, bedecked with flowers. Built like fortresses to

Lovable rogue Compo, played by Bill Owen

stand up to the rigours of the Pennine winter, they remain as testimony to the birth of the textile industry of the former West Riding. Before the invention of the steam engine which led to the building of textile mills in the valley, cloth was produced in these small communities by independent handloom weavers. I suspect it would have been with much reluctance, as technology progressed, that they inevitably had to give up their freedom to 'work for someone else'.

Returning to Towngate, I took time to look at the T'owd Genn Memorial which commemorates the short-lived Amiens peace treaty with France, signed in 1802. This also recalls a local disaster, for it shows the height of water which poured into the town in 1852 when the dam of the local Bilberry Reservoir bursted. It caused widespread devastation, destroying houses and mills, and leaving eighty people drowned. But this was not the first nor was it to be the last flood to swamp the town, for in 1777 a similar deluge had occurred and was followed by another as recently as 1944.

I browsed for half an hour in a second-hand book shop where I bought a thin volume which outlined '24 Places of Interest Around Huddersfield', I wandered into the sparkling interior of the Georgian Parish Church, then inevitably I found myself in Sid's Cafe. Here, in the famous film set where Compo, Foggy and Clegg hatch many of their fiendish schemes, I sat eating a plate of Ivy's delicious scones surrounded by momentos of their escapades. Three women followed me into the cafe, but seeing the 'No Smoking' sign on the green gingham tablecloths they quickly turned around and walked out, unable to face a cup of tea without a puff at the dreaded weed. However, the smoking ban posed no problems to a more healthy group of cyclists who, looking like a parade of Pied Pipers in their multi-coloured racing vests, soon filled the small cafe.

A newspaper cutting on the wall told me that the cafe has a resident ghost, verified by the girl who was serving Ivy's scones.

'No it isn't a joke. I've never seen it, but other people have. Many think that it is Sid's spirit which returns to the cafe.'

With a certificate in my hand, which duly recorded my visit to this site of Yorkshire heritage, I continued my exploration of the town. I gazed over bridges at the fast-flowing river, I admired the timeless atmosphere of quiet backwaters, I looked at Nora Batty's famous steps and the nearby 'Wrinkled Stocking Tea Room', then I went into the small Postcard Museum.

Piers, candy-floss, boarding houses, donkey-rides, sandcastles and funfairs are just some of the features which the mind conjures up when the typical English seaside resort is mentioned. But the list would not be complete without one other item originated here in Holmfirth – the saucy postcard. For a local company, Bamforths, created the fat ladies, delightfully curvaceous girls, bald hen-pecked men, and moustached bounders, whose antics are always explained by a host of double-meanings. For nearly a century these risque messages of mirth have plopped through millions of letter boxes, often accompanied by: 'Having a grand time. Weather lovely. Wish you were here.'

Wandering around this marvellous display of Bamforths history, it seems that like many other original products, it was chance rather than planning that created their success. In 1870 the family was involved locally in a small painting and decorating business, then James Bamforth became interested, like many other men of his time, in the new art of photography. He successfully produced a series of magic-lantern slides, then went on to pioneer some of our earliest moving-pictures using local people in the cast. Bamforths also printed song and hymn sheets, then in 1904 their first postcard was produced. By this time, seaside holidays had become firmly established as part of the English scene, making an ever increasing market for the postcard. But it was when Douglas Tempest, an artist who was then employed by Bamforths, began creating humorous cartoon subjects in 1911, that the era of the saucy postcard really began. His work was later continued by his pupils, including Arnold Taylor, and is still very popular today. It was an american, Major Robert W. Scherer of Florida, who painstakingly collected examples of Bamforths' work from all over the world. In 1975 he passed them on to Kirklees Metropolitan Council who have created this unique museum.

I ended my tour, as every serious visitor should, by watching a display of Parisian Can-Can dancers on a type of What-the-Butler-Saw machine called a Mutoscope. I have a feeling that when Compo is not chasing Nora Batty through the streets of Holmfirth, this is the place where he goes for a mooch!

It is difficult to believe that Bill Owen, that talented actor who has played the lovable character of Compo for so long, is anything but a born and bred Yorkshireman. But William John Owen Rowbotham, his real name, is a Londoner, having been born on the 14 March 1914 in Acton Green. He came from a working class background, his father being a trolley-bus driver and his mother worked in a laundry. But from being a child his natural high spirits and bubbling personality set him apart, making him instinctively choose showbusiness as a career.

Accompanied by his childhood friend, Charlie Burton, he began as a pub entertainer then he joined a local amateur theatrical group. He later found work in a holiday camp which led to him being selected for acting roles at

London's Unity Theatre. His ability now recognised he signed a Rank film contract which was to lead to his highly successful showbusiness career. He has acted, written plays and songs, and directed over a period of almost sixty years.

3

When I arrived in Huddersfield I discovered that like medieval York which is contained by its ancient walls, it is a town also thankfully cocooned from the worst of the roaring traffic. This is achieved not by walls but by an inner Ring Road which quickly carries the lorries we all hate, quickly away. I parked my car outside of this road, close to a sign which indicated 'Sikh Centre and Temple', then began my exploration by walking into this surprisingly gracious town.

Although in Pennine Country, Huddersfield does not give an impression of being hemmed-in like many of its neighbours, for the hills which surround it appear green, wooded and less dramatic. Castle Hill is the most prominent summit crowned with a sturdy Jubilee Tower that dominates the skyline. This was built in those confident days at the end of the last century when the 'the sun never set on the British Empire'. But as the name suggests, this windy hill top has been occupied for a much longer period. The castle which once stood here guarding the isolated Colne Valley, had been built in the 12th century by the Norman de Lacy family on the site of an Iron Age hill fort.

I immediately took a liking to Huddersfield, it seemed to be bathed in an atmosphere of no-nonsense friendliness. People nodded and smiled at me as they strolled leisurely along the streets. There was no hectic rush in their steps, no apparent desire for frenzied activity. This gave a feeling of refreshing security; they seemed to be saying 'Why hurry? We've seen it all before. Don't forget we helped to start the Industrial Revolution and we're the town that bought itself.'

It was in 1920 that Huddersfield Corporation finally bought their own town centre! Until that time it had been owned by Sir John Frecheville Ramsden, the head of an ancient family who had been Lords of the Manor here since the time of Elizabeth I. Each generation of the family had guided the expansion of the town, seeing it grow from a small Pennine community of farmers and hand-loom weavers into a major textile centre.

This began by gaining Royal Assent to hold a market here in the 17th century. A Cloth Hall was built in 1766, then as technology progressed each piece of the jig-saw of progress was slipped into place. Turnpike roads,

canals, and then railways provided the necessary transport links, then a splendid Victorian new-town began to be planned on the drawing board of the famous architect, Sir William Tite. I wandered along the reality of his design; spacious streets of solid two-storey buildings laid out on a sensible grid system, which having been built from local stone blend perfectly into the landscape.

Railway stations are often places to avoid, but I discovered that this is not the case here in

Huddersfield's impressive Victorian railway station

Huddersfield. For as I walked around a busy corner I was astonished to find a magnificent neo-classical facade of towering Corinthian columns looking out over a broad sun drenched square. The town had plunged itself into the railway age with optimistic vigour in 1846, marking the laying of the foundation stone of this station with a public holiday. Four years later the finest provincial station in England was completed; a symbol of progress which told Manchester and Leeds that they better be careful, Huddersfield was on the move.

The excitement that the construction of this station brought to the town seems strange to our age which has become complacent to the march of technology. But to have a special building where travellers could wait for their train, buy tickets, collect luggage and even stay at a sumptuous hotel, was all quite new. Until this time public travel had mainly been by

bone-jarring stage-coaches which stopped outside inns where accommodation could often be sparse.

When passenger railways first began, the picking-up point was just a flat
piece of muddy field from which both young and old had to climb up to
the elevated carriages. But this quickly changed, platforms known as
parades were built, then followed simple wooden sheds to provide shelter
from the weather. Local pride then made it a priority to provide a building
fitting to this wonderful new transport system opening up the country.
Architects began using their creative talents to design these railway palaces
of stone, cast-iron, carved wood and glass.

I stepped beneath the portico into this elegant station where VDUs now
show the times of trains to Hull, Scarborough and Wakefield. Like the poet
and railway enthusiast Sir John Betjeman once did, I explored its hidden
corners, then I returned to the sunshine to look around the surrounding
square. Here, where turbaned Sikh taxi drivers now wait, I looked upon
the other graceful buildings which rose up here in the 1850s. The opulent
George Hotel where those who had risen from muck-to-brass once stayed;
the Lion Buildings where wool merchants made deals which clothed half
the world; and the Brittania Buildings, once warehouses but now thought
fine enough to house the Yorkshire Building Society.

For two hours I leisurely wandered around this modest town which has
much to boast about. I admired its spacious streets, explored its narrow
alleyways and saw posters which reminded me of its rich musical tradition.
For the Huddersfield Choral Society is of course, renowned throughout the
world.

Be strong, be bold, be not frightened or dismayed;
for the Lord your God is with you wherever you go.

This was the reassuring text which I read inside the parish magazine which
I bought inside the gleaming church of St Peter in Kirkgate. The Vicar, who
was about to dash off to a meeting in Holmfirth, told me that it was
reasonably well attended, but had the same problems as all other inner-city
churches which have lost many members of their congregation to the
suburbs.

However this Gothic style building had struggled into existence from the
very start. For when it was built in 1836 to replace an earlier church it could
only attract minimum support from the local people, many of whom had
been attracted to non-conformity. Instead it looked for finance to the
Waterloo Church Fund which had been set up after Napoleon had finally
been defeated. This was created to fight the growing popularity of the

non-conformists who at the time were considered rivals who posed a serious threat to the established church. But happily, in this age of Christian unity such differences of the past have now been largely forgotten. This was borne out by the headlines in a church newsletter which I read for it announced: 'Churches together in Huddersfield'.

I joined the shoppers in the lively Market Place, passing Huddersfield's oldest landmark, the Market Cross, erected in 1671. Then after squeezing into a crowded cafe for a quick cup of Yorkshire tea I explored the Victorian elegance of the Byram Arcade. This was built in 1880, the year Gladstone succeeded Disraeli as Prime Minister, and it has now been restored to its former glory to house gift shops, boutiques and a tempting restaurant.

'Could you tell me please, is James Mason remembered in any way here in his hometown?'

I had wandered into the Tourist Information Centre and confronted the young man who stood behind the counter, with a question that seemed to puzzle him. Had I asked him the way to Castle Hill, where I could catch a bus to Leeds or if perhaps I could have an afternoon game of golf, I feel sure he would have known. But surprisingly, it seemed that no one had ever asked about James Mason before.

'Er, er. Oh yes!', he smiled after a poignant half minute, having at last remembered a half forgotten snippet of information. 'I think there is a local James Mason Appreciation Society. It probably meets in the Huddersfield Hotel – the receptionist will know.'

After a short walk I found the Huddersfield Hotel, but the receptionist sadly, did not know.

'Sorry I can't help you. I've never heard of them'.

Ironically, it seems that one of our greatest-ever film stars who was known throughout the world has now become largely forgotten in his hometown.

4

However, it was here in Edwardian Huddersfield that James Mason was born on the 15 May 1909. He was the youngest of three sons of a prosperous textile merchant, John Mason, and his wife Mabel Hattersley Gaunt. Their home was Croft House, a large residence dating in part from the 17th century, which had a splendid garden and a tennis court. The family was wealthy enough to employ a household staff of four, which included a governess who looked after the children's early education.

James followed his brothers to prep school at Windermere then went on to public school at Marlborough, where both poet John Betjeman and actor James Robertson Justice were among the pupils. At this point in his life he showed no desire to act, was reluctant to participate in sports, but was able to reach an academic standard sufficient for him to obtain a place at Cambridge University in 1928 when he was nineteen years old.

He decided to read Classics at Peterhouse College, with the intention of making his career in the Indian Civil Service, for the family firm was not large enough to employ all three brothers. However he later changed his mind, after discovering a talent for draughtsmanship he transferred his studies to architecture. It was at this time that he took his first fateful steps, if somewhat half-heartedly, into the world of acting. Accompanied by his friend Harry Gulland he appeared in the chorus of Bacchae, a Greek drama being performed by the University Football Club. Although slow to mature, his introduction to the stage had uncovered a latent desire later to become all embracing. Yet he appeared in only two other shows during his time at Cambridge, then in 1931 he successfully gained a first class degree in Architecture.

Now at a cross-roads in his life he was still unsure which path to take, for he was reluctant to pursue more studying which a career in architecture would surely mean. Finally, spurred on by a highly flattering review he had received for one of his performances on the Cambridge stage he decided to try for a job in the theatre. After writing scores of letters he was at last successful in landing a minor role with a touring company, giving his first professional performance in November 1931 at the Theatre Royal in Aldershot. But as the tour continued around the country it hit financial difficulties and eventually it came to a halt with the management making a hasty escape.

In 1932 he obtained another acting part with the Jevan Brandon Thomas touring company for a summer season at the English resorts. Remembered as being handsome but shy, he became friends with the young Patricia Hayes and Leonard Sachs, who were also members of the juvenile cast. After a season with the Hull Repertory Company he then moved to Croydon, gaining a role in Ronald Gow's Gallows Glorious which although not highly successful, moved to the West End. Here came his major break when he was seen by director Tyrone Guthrie, who invited him to an audition at the Old Vic. What was to become known as his 'velvet voice' won the day, he joined the new company led by fellow Yorkshireman Charles Laughton and included such famous names as Marius Goring and Flora Robson. In 1934 he returned to the West End, having another minor part in Queen of Scots, directed by John Gielgud and starred Laurence

Olivier, before joining the highly regarded Gate Theatre Company in Dublin as a leading actor.

Back in London in the summer of 1935 he had a period of 'resting', but was fortunate to meet at a party the American film director Al Parker who worked in England for Twentieth Century Fox. Following a screen test James was signed for his first film contract by Parker, a small part in Late Extra, now almost forgotten. But the film did include an amazing number of highly talented actors, including Michael Wilding, Cyril Cusack, Alistair Sim and Donald Wolfit, with leading-lady Virginia Cherrill who was the first wife of Cary Grant.

Two other equally unmemorable films, Twice Branded and Troubled Waters, followed in quick succession. During the filming James struck up a friendship with cameraman Roy Kellino, who was married to former child-actress Pamela Ostrer. A beautiful, intelligent and strong-minded girl of nineteen, she was the daughter of a rich Gaumont-British executive, and could trace her roots back to a textile family in the northcountry. James was introduced to Pam on the film set and immediately his pulse began to race for she had an air of mystique about her that he found irresistible. Still a reticent bachelor with no home of his own, he eventually became a temporary lodger in the home of Roy and Pam. For several years the three went to many social events as a trio, with Pam and James appearing together in various plays. In 1938 they combined their resources to produce a low budget, full-length film entitled I Met A Murderer. But by 1939 the Kellino's marriage had inevitably broken down, Jame's affair with Pam becoming public knowledge when he was cited in the divorce proceedings. His illicit association had caused great pain to his family from the start, particularly his mother who maintained high moral standards. This rift, which was to last many years, deepened even more when at the start of the war he declared that he was a conscientious objector.

It was at Amersham Registry Office in February 1941, that James and Pam where eventually married. By this time he had appeared in a string of films and stage plays but the elusive 'big-time' had not yet arrived. But this came quite unexpectedly when he played the title role, which he disliked, in a Regency drama for Gainsborough Studios, The Man in Grey (1943). It gained rave reviews, leading to other massive successes such as Fanny by Gaslight (1944), The Wicked Lady (1945), The Seventh Veil (1945) and Odd Man Out (1947). In a few short years he had astonishingly risen to become the biggest box-office draw of the British Film Industry, being later voted the best film actor of the war years, second only to Bing Crosby in international appeal.

During the war he lived with Pam in Beaconfield, an area much favoured by many British film stars, then later he moved to a farmhouse at King's Langley in Hertfordshire. But by 1947 the lure of America had become too great to resist; too many talented actors were competing for too few major roles in British films. They sailed early in the new year on the Queen Elizabeth for New York, accompanied by three members of their staff they had booked in to the opulent Plaza Hotel. It was the intention that they would move quickly on to Hollywood, but they soon found the transition was not as easy as they anticipated. Legal problems with a contract he had signed but was disputing, together with his poor relationship with the press, had cast a shadow on their new life in the land of opportunity. However the couple were able to make a somewhat shaky debut on the Broadway stage, then they wrote a successful book about cats of which they had a mild obsession. The following year brought even more change with the unexpected arrival of their first child, a daughter they named Portland. The family was later to be completed with a son, Morgan.

Much to Pam's elation they eventually made their home in Hollywood, but James was not quite as enthusiastic about the move. A loner and academic by nature he at times felt out of place, seeming to have little in common with his fellow actors. But in spite of this he slowly acquired a wide circle of friends, began attending social gatherings and was soon carving out a new career in the sun. His first Hollywood film was Caught (1949) in which he starred with Robert Ryan, followed over the next two decades by a host of box office successes. These include Pandora and the Flying Dutchman (1951), The Desert Fox (1951), A Star is Born (1954), 20,000 Leagues Under the Sea (1954), North by Northwest (1959), Lolita (1962) and Jesus of Nazareth (1977).

But sadly, over the years, his relationship with Pam began to crumble and in 1964, after twenty-three years of marriage they were divorced. He then made a decision to leave America, dearly wishing to make his home back in England which he missed so much, but the tax laws of the time made this impossible so he settled in Switzerland. While filming Age of Consent in 1969 he was introduced to Australian actress, Clarissa Kaye, who became a close friend. This friendship soon blossomed into love, leading to their marriage two years later.

Although James Mason had been an exile from Yorkshire throughout his career, he always felt his roots were deep in the county of his boyhood. He was never more happy than when walking among the brooding, windswept moors of the Brontë Country, to which he later introduced Portland. This intense feeling that he had for the countryside around Huddersfield was revealed to the public when he made a nostalgic TV documentary, Home James, in 1972.

After the death of his father it was decided that the rambling family home, Croft House, would have to be sold. It was bought by a property developing company who wanted the land for a new housing estate, so it was eventually demolished. But before this happened James commissioned a local artist, Peter Brook, to capture its image on canvas. This painting, together with two stone lions from the house were shipped to his home at Vevey in Switzerland.

James Mason continued to work hard, in both films and television up to the very end of his amazing life. His last, highly acclaimed film, The Shooting Party (1984), included among the cast his old friend of fifty years, John Gielgud. But shortly after it was completed he began to complain of tiredness and severe back pain. He was rushed into a hospital in Lausanne where he died of a heart attack on the 27 July 1984 at the age of seventy-five. The British film industry had sadly lost one of its finest actors.

5

After taking a meandering route which took me through Elland and Brighouse, I arrived in Halifax. My first impression of the town was one of stability; it seemed to emit a refreshing feeling of permanence. This is perhaps because nearly all of its buildings are made robustly from stone, large solid blocks which have been carved with Victorian vigour to last forever. As I wandered along Market Street and into Crown Street I was half in the 1990s and half in the 1850s. Although the shop windows displayed CD players, mobile phones and computers which could be linked to the Internet, a glance upwards revealed another era. For these products of new technology were being sold in premises that had sprung up in the optimism of the British Empire. They were built by workmen who would have chatted about our new territories in India and Africa, heard news of the Battle of Alma in the Crimea and of that heroine Florence Nightingale, and perhaps boasted that it all began when their fathers beat the French at Waterloo.

Surrounded by steep rising hills which soar above the rooftops into windswept isolation the town is washed by the River Calder to the south and the more gentle Hebble Brook to the east. It can trace its origins to before the Conquest when it was held by King Edward-the-Confessor, later appearing in the Domesday Book as Feslei. But the woollen trade, which was to create its modern image during the Industrial Revolution and inspire

Blake to write of its 'dark Satanic Mills', had started much earlier. For it is said that the monks of Cluniac Monastery in Sussex, who had been given this part of the Manor of Wakefield during the 12th century, collected handsome revenue from its wool.

With the clouds scurrying like greyhounds across a blue sky I continued my stroll around the town, ignoring the lure of a bar named Wallace Simpson and the delights of Gatsby's Tea Room. I wandered through splendid Edwardian arcades, saw pensioners buying 'gradely fruit' beneath the spacious roof of the Borough Market, and watched Asian ladies, clothed in saris of gold and blue, choosing earrings. Then I discovered in Southgate an ancient inn named The Old Cock, a hostelry once frequented by that wanton brother of the Brontë sisters, Branwell. But this pub has an even more remarkable tale to tell, for within its walls once gathered a small group of local men who were destined to make the name of Halifax known in every highstreet in Britain.

The beginnings of that uniquely British organisation, the building society, can be traced to the late 18th century, when men were being forced to give up their independent cottage industries to work in the newly erected mills. As people flocked from the countryside into the expanding towns of the north, accommodation became scarce. This led to overcrowding, poor sanitation and later the horror of slum dwellings. However some workers decided to overcome the problem by building their own homes; a costly scheme which could only be achieved by working in groups. They formed what became known as Terminating Building Societies, a club to which each member paid part of their wages. When enough money was available it was used to buy the building material needed for the construction of the first house. The labour was also provided by the members, and a ballot was held to decide who would be given the first dwelling. Other houses were then built in a similar way over a number of years, until each member had a home, after which time the building society was terminated. One of the earliest recorded societies of this type was formed at Longridge in the Ribble Valley.

A similar club, known as the Loyal Georgian Society existed later here in Halifax, but this too was eventually terminated. One local man then had the idea that a permanent building society was needed in the town, so a meeting was called of interested parties. This took place in November 1852 in the Oak Room at the Old Cock, which led to The Halifax Permanent Building Society being ready for business the following year. Jonas Dearnley Taylor was appointed as its first Secretary, a position he was to hold for almost half a century. What was to result is a tale of incredible success, for like Topsy, the society just grew and grew. In 1854 its assets were £12,000, which had grown to about £1m by 1885 when it could boast to have the largest reserves of any society in Yorkshire. Its first branch had been opened in 1862 at Huddersfield, but by the time its second Secretary was appointed in 1903 it had fifty. With assets of £3m in 1913 it then became Britain's largest society, which had reached a staggering £10 billion by 1980! Today the society's gleaming headquarters here in Halifax process the statements of its millions of customers using the latest computers; very different from when they were hand written in an exercise book in the bar of the Old Cock!

'Bloody grand day isn't it?'

I had walked into what is probably Yorkshire's most fascinating building, the Halifax Piece Hall, then I was greeted by an equally fascinating local character. Smiling through a mouth full of broken black teeth, he looked rather like George Formby to which had been added the mannerisms of Compo. Startled, I was about to reply to him when he suddenly turned away, then dashed like a hare down some stone steps.

The Piece Hall, lying in the centre of the town, I found to be just as puzzling. I had entered it through a huge door set in towering walls, which might have been part of a Norman castle except that it had no moat or draw-bridge. Once inside I had half expected to discover an ornate interior,

The interior of the Piece Hall

but was surprised to find myself in a huge open-air courtyard. Enclosing this courtyard on all sides, similar to the Rows in Chester, rise three walkways built one above the other in the Classical style. On the ground level is an Arcade of semi-circular arches, above it square columns support a Rustic Gallery, with the top level being a continuous gallery known as a Colonnade. Craft shops to tempt the visitor have now been housed in the building along the Colonnade level, together with a museum, an art gallery and the Tourist Information Centre. The courtyard was empty during my visit, but I was told that on Fridays and Saturdays it buzzes with activity for an open air market is held here.

The 'Piece' which has given this splendid building its name, could of course refer to nothing else in these parts but cloth. And how long is a piece of cloth? The answer I am told is 30 yards.

Since medieval times the isolated farms and cottages which lay in these sheltered valleys of the South Pennines echoed with the sound of the hand-loom weaver. Once their cloth had been woven a buyer was needed, and it was from this requirement for a central meeting place for manufacturers and wholesalers that the Piece Hall was built. As early as 1572 a cloth hall had existed here in Halifax, but by the mid 18th century it had become overcrowded so a new building was planned. However, like many modern projects, by the time it was opened in January 1779 it was almost too late for new technology was changing the market place. Large mills with new power-driven machines were quickly being built, these employed many former independent weavers so the number of manufacturers diminished. By 1830 a third of the rooms in the Piece Hall remained empty; a deteriorating process which eventually led to many similar buildings being demolished. But Halifax was proud of its heritage so the Piece Hall survived. Surprisingly its greatest threat came in more recent times, for in 1972, now in the ownership of the local council, only a single vote saved it from being bulldozed into the ground.

After exploring the shops and strolling backwards and forwards along the elegant arcade, I thankfully found a small cafe where bread rolls had replaced cloth rolls. After topping up my energy with tea and scones I then went into one of the finest Tourist Information Centres I have yet come across.

'Yes, the replica of the Halifax Gibbet lies on the original site of the executions. It's about half a mile from here. You can also see part of the blade in the museum.'

The assistant then gave me a street map on which she had ringed the ominous words 'The Gibbet' with her pen. I thanked her then I set off in search of the ultimate punishment.

While walking past the Halifax Playhouse Theatre I read a notice which reminded me of those pre-TV days when families used to sit together around the wireless. One programme which was as popular at the time as the present Coronation Street is today, was Have a Go. For over twenty years it was presented by that great entertainer Wilfred Pickles, who the notice told me began his theatrical career here in Halifax. He became one of the most-loved celebrities of his day, brightening up the wartime years with his ready wit and insight into what made us laugh at ourselves.

I found the Halifax Gibbet perched on a grassy slope surrounded by solid stone buildings and the roar of traffic. But again I was surprised to find that it is not really a gibbet at all, for this device was used to decapitate, while a gibbet was a structure from which the bodies of hanged criminals were displayed. However, the gruesome efficiency of what became known as the Halifax Gibbet is remembered by a 16th century Beggars' Prayer: 'From Hull, Hell and Halifax, Good Lord deliver us'. Hull was at this time renowned for being an uncharitable town where the local people despised beggars, while Halifax was even more feared as a place of harsh punishment.

Looking back over the centuries it seems that our ancestors made a pastime of devising cruel, sadistic methods of torture and punishment to inflict on their fellow men. The Iron Maiden, the Scavenger's Daughter, the Skull Crusher and the Gridiron are just a few of the many horrendous instruments of torture which they designed. But it was the Normans who first introduced decapitation as the final solution in Britain, which they regarded as a worthy death fit only for the aristocrat. This was carried out in the early days by the sword, then later the executioner's axe came into general use, being last used in England in 1747 on the Jacobite, Lord Lovat.

Here in Halifax it was again the local product, cloth, which created the need for a strong deterrent against the criminal mind. During the 15th century when cottage manufacturing first began to flourish, the finished cloth was hung outside in a wooden frame to dry. Unattended, it became an easy target for thieves whose activities began to undermine the industry. So to eradicate the problem the Lord of the Manor sanctioned the death penalty for those who stole cloth above the value of thirteen pence halfpenny or more. Then, with Yorkshire ingenuity, an unknown local man invented this efficient head chopping machine, re-invented over two hundred years later in France to become known as the guillotine.

The earliest record of a local decapitation is that of John of Dalton in 1286, but more formal records of executions did not begin until 1541. These state that 52 people were beheaded here during the next 109 years, the last victims being Anthony Mitchell and John Wilkinson of Sowerby who had been caught stealing cloth. The Halifax Gibbet was then dismantled as public opinion was turning against the bloodthirsty public spectacle and the site was reduced to a rubbish tip. But in 1839 when workmen were clearing the ground they uncovered the ancient stone base. Nearby was found the skeletons of two men with severed heads assumed to be those of Mitchell and Wilkinson.

However, while the device was in use an intended victim had one remote chance of escape. If he managed to withdraw his head in the vital seconds before the blade fell, then run the half mile to Hebble Brook, he became a free man providing he never entered the parish again. One such remarkable escape is said to have to been achieved by John Lacy, who gained seven years of freedom but then foolishly came back. He was apprehended again, then duly beheaded.

I climbed the six stone steps that lead up to the base of the gibbet, then I looked up at the terrifying blade which awaited me fifteen feet above. I was about to put my head on the block then I heard the roar of the strong wind. Could a chance gust perhaps loosen the pin, I wondered, bringing a premature end to my journey through Yorkshire? After selfconsciously looking around to make sure no one was watching me I stepped down from the platform and walked quickly away!

6

A s I took the road towards Sowerby Bridge I caught a glimpse of the Wainhouse Tower; a magnificent ornate structure which rises to a height of 253 feet to dominate this part of the Calder Valley. Its origin lies partly in practical necessity and partly in rivalry. It was built during the last century by John Edward Wainhouse as a chimney to carry away the noxious smoke and fumes from his dyeworks. However as things turned out, it was never used for this purpose. But the presence of this towering folly did symbolise to rival industrialists Wainhouse's success. Fashioned from the finest materials at a cost of £15,000, it has an interior staircase which rises to a splendid observation platform not unlike the Campanile in Venice.

I continued up the winding road which hugs the edge of the rising moorland until I reach the village of Mytholmroyd, then I took a byroad into the quietness of Cragg Vale. This corner of the South Pennines through which I was now travelling once had a notorious reputation as being the home of coiners. These were gangs of thieves who made their living during the 18th century by producing counterfeit coins. They operated in two ways; some would stamp out false coins using cheap metal instead of the silver or gold from which coins were made at the time, while a more popular method was to use clippings. This involved reducing the circumference of a genuine coin by removing a small amount of metal, then skilfully reproducing a new serrated rim making it difficult to detect that the coin had been tampered with. When enough metal had been collected from several genuine coins it was melted down and a counterfeit coin produced.

The isolation of Cragg Vale among these wild moorlands made it an ideal place for the coiners to hide out, with the Dusty Miller pub at Mytholmroyd becoming their meeting place. However by 1769 their illegal activities had grown so serious that the government sent top excise-man William Dighton to investigate. Within a short time he had made several arrests and the Cragg Vale coiners feared he was closing in on them. So deciding to take fate in their own hands, two of the gang, Matthew Normanton and Robert Thomas laid in wait for Dighton close to the centre of Halifax. They shot him in the head and he immediately died.

This callous murder sent shock waves around the community and the authorities offered a 100 guinea reward to anyone who could supply vital evidence. This led to a member of the coiners own gang, James Broadbent, coming forward and pointing the finger at the gang leader, David Hartley, who was then arrested. When the reward money was later raised to £200 Broadbent, dispelling any notion of 'honour among thieves', named three other suspects.

The trial of Hartley took place at York in April 1770, where he was found guilty of murder and was duly hanged. His body was then brought back home for burial in the churchyard in the village of Heptonstall. The trial of others also accused followed later, with Normanton eventually meeting the hangman in 1775. The heavy hand of the law had at last caught up with the coiners of Cragg Vale, bringing an end to their reign in this moorland hideaway.

With the barren brown hills sweeping to a blue horizon I drove slowly to the summit of Blackstone Edge where Yorkshire meets Lancashire along a snaking ridge. This is an untamed landscape of sculptured millstone grit; rock fashioned by centuries of wind and rain into weird blackened shapes. Few trees remain among this peaty landscape, many were cleared by man 4,000 years ago then the top soil was washed away by the rain. Today drystone walls litter the land like pieces of spider's web, sheep gnaw ceaselessly in sheltered hollows where packhorses once passed, while curlews send their haunting calls through the clear air.

I arrived in Todmorden on Market Day which gives this little town a lively and colourful atmosphere. Shoppers were crowding among the open stalls then strolling inside the Market Hall, built in 1879. But local folk have been coming to sell their goods here for many centuries before this date. Generations of weavers brought their pieces of cloth here from their isolated cottages, then perhaps got 'merry' on part of the proceeds. This may be why in 1750 the constable was given eightpence 'for cleaning his truncheon' at the fair, but what he needed to clean off we can only guess at!

As I wandered around the town, lying in a narrow green valley surrounded by rising hills, I was at once surprised by the wealth of impressive architecture which I met at every corner. Enhanced by the soft sunlight these solid stone buildings seem to reverberate with the vigour of their Victorian builders. Inns and churches, cottages and halls, stand side by side in splendid harmony. Their design reflects the confidence of the age, making by comparison our modern houses seem flimsy and insignificant.

I stood at the centre of Todmorden admiring the rounded end of the Town Hall which a leaflet told me is built in the Italian-style Renaissance. When it was first opened in 1875 half of the building lay in Yorkshire and half in Lancashire, which is why the sculptured stone figures which stand high on a pediment, represent the achievements of both counties. Since that time the county border has changed, Todmorden now lying firmly in West Yorkshire.

The Town Hall, together with nearly all the fine buildings here, owe their existence to the Fielden family who were great benefactors of the town. The building was originally planned to be funded by a limited company in 1860, but this ran into financial difficulties due to a recession. The Fieldens took over the venture, providing an enormous capital sum of £54,000, and they commissioned the talented London architect John Gibson to complete the work.

Down a quiet street I gazed into the window of one of the few remaining Clogger's Shops in the north. On display were shining examples of this unique form of footwear of which many older readers will have fond memories. This reminded me of a fascinating little book, 'Clattering Clogs', which traces the history of clogs and clog dancing, together with many poems and songs which have been written about the subject. The author, former policeman Bob Dobson, is a clog enthusiast who over many years has collected together what he calls 'Clogiana', believing that clogs have souls as well as soles!

After browsing in an antiquarian book shop and taking a stroll along the towpath of the Rochdale Canal I went to the graveyard of Todmorden's

Gothic style Christ Church to learn about another ghastly murder. Among the moss laden gravestones at the East End, I found the last resting places of the two victims, the Reverend Anthony J. Plow and Jane Smith.

This tragedy which took place in 1868, like so many others, resulted from a love affair. It seems that the Vicar and his wife employed a young girl named Sarah Bell as their cook. Sarah's boyfriend was Miles Weatherill who presumably the Plows disliked, for they forbade the girl from seeing him. However she ignored their warning by having what she thought was a secret rendezvous. But this meeting was discovered by a woman named Jane Smith who informed the Plows, who as a result sacked Bell.

Infuriated by the episode Miles Weatherill armed himself with an axe and four pistols. He then carried out a frenzied attack on the Vicar, his wife, and Jane Smith. The news that both the Vicar and Jane Smith had died from their injuries shocked the people of Todmorden. Weatherill was quickly apprehended, tried for the murders, then sentenced to death. On the 4 April 1868 he had the dubious distinction of becoming the last person to be publicly executed in Manchester.

In the bright sunshine I continued my exploration by walking from the churchyard into the woodland which borders Centre Vale Park. This pleasant open space lies on the edge of Todmorden Moor in the narrowing valley which leads across the county border towards Burnley. Here, in a quiet corner I came upon the imposing statue of John Fielden, the local Member of Parliament who is remembered as one of the great social reformers of the last century. The words on the stone plinth read:

John Fielden, MP.
This statue is raised by public subscription in gratitude to him whose persevering efforts succeeded in obtaining the Ten Hours Act. (Royal Assent 8 June 1847).
Born 17 January 1784. Died 28 May 1849.

The Ten Hours Act was a milestone in the long battle against unscrupulous employers who in the early days of the Industrial Revolution treated their workers little better than slaves. It stated that 'no person under 18 or woman above 18, should work for more than 10 hours in one day or 58 hours in any one week.'

Magpies were prancing along the manicured lawns as I walked back through this pleasant parkland to the centre of the town. On a distant highpoint of the ascending hillside I could see the profile of another stone column which dominates this valley, for the Victorians never tired of erecting such structures. This monument on Stoodley Pike commemorates the surrender of Paris to the Allies following the Napoleonic Wars. It is a landmark which has become familiar to many walkers for it lies on the Pennine Way. Rising to a height of 120 feet the present structure was erected in 1856 to replace the original column which had suddenly collapsed in 1854; an event which many took to be an omen of the impending Crimean War which followed shortly afterwards.

Chapter Two

Todmorden to Ilkley

I explore the Pennine Centre of Hebden Bridge, climb over the moors, then find Japanese tourists on Wuthering Heights. I think of the genius of the Brontë sisters in Haworth Parsonage, and of their tragic brother in the Black Bull pub. I remember John Braine and Yorkshire Terriers in Airedale, see where Yorkshire's National Anthem was composed, then I descend to Wharfedale to see Ilkley where many of the locals have 'a bit of brass'.

1

From Todmorden I took a twisting lowland road that led me to Hebden Bridge. My exploration began with a stroll along the canal towpath where I paused to watch a colourful boat named Gracie Fields slowly glide through the water. A dozen pairs of eyes gazed out at me, visitors who had come here like myself to explore the town that is known as the Pennine Centre. This is a unique community where houses built of millstone grit are perched like castles on the steeply rising hillside. The narrow valley has precious little flat land, so everything that can be is packed into these few curving acres that snake beneath the wild moorland towards Lanca-shire.

The celtic people who once made Hebden Bridge their home preferred the hills, not the valleys. Few Roman remains have been found in the district, so it is likely that these early tribes remained undisturbed by the invasion. Perhaps that is why there is still a striking independence about Hebden folk, for the celtic strain must be purer here than in many other parts of England.

I continued my tow-path stroll, stopping at times to admire the solid, attractive cottages, which like those in Venice have the water lapping up to their very doorsteps. Small sloping gardens, ablaze with flowers, looked down on the passing boats and the squabbling of the ever-hungry mallards. This, the Rochdale Canal, was opened in 1798 to link Sowerby Bridge with Manchester. It played an important role by carrying wool and cotton goods to clothe the world and at the same time made many a millionaire. Famous named families, who now boast homes in Belgravia and whose latest exploits are related in the pages of Tatler or Hello! magazines, can often trace their origins to this 'new money'. For textiles were much more than a dull-sounding industrial product, for they became 18th century white-gold; a passport to the good life.

Returning to the centre of the town I now wandered along the narrow streets whose shops and houses display a fascinating array of architecture. Inviting alleyways lead between towering gritstone walls, steeply rising stone steps disappear up intriguing hillsides and everywhere there is a feeling of strength and vigour. These Victorian builders, like the masons who created our great cathedrals, worked not just with their hands but with their souls.

I leaned over the parapet of the Old Bridge from which the town took its name, watching the silver of Hebden Water. Children skipped and laughed in the warm sunshine, ducks foraged among the weeds, and workmen were busy placing scaffolding on a newer bridge which was being repaired. A wooden structure is said to have spanned this small river as early as 1477, replaced in 1510 by a more substantial bridge made from stone. Around this crossing point the community grew, many making a living serving the needs of travellers. Strings of pack-horses would descend from the moorland, often carrying goods produced by hand-loom weavers who lived in isolated homesteads. But the Industrial Revolution brought this cottage industry to a sad end. Water at first provided the power for small mills which housed new machines, then this was superseded by the might of steam. A new Turnpike Road skirted the Calder Valley in 1772, then in 1840, at the very forefront of new technology, a railway line was built to link Manchester and Leeds.

But of course this is all part of Hebden Bridge's past for today the town has become a magnet for tourists. Antiques, crafts, antiquarian books and expensive furniture now line the shops which once sold soap and bread. It has also become a haven for refugees from the Swinging Sixties, artists who have found sanctuary in this unique valley. Women who once wore 'flowers in their hair' and bared their bosoms at Glastonbury now sell hand-made goods, paintings and health foods.

'That will be one pound eighty, please', said a long haired girl in a floral skirt. She handed me a couple of books which I had bought from the shelves of an Animal Charity Shop.

'All the money goes to the RSPCA in Bradford. But you know we get people who come in here and browse for ages, then leave without even giving a ten-pence donation. Some people!'

2

W as I really in Yorkshire I thought to myself, as I joined a well-worn path fringed with the red of willow herb, that leads high on to the moors above Haworth? For the sky was a clear blue, the breeze was a mere whisper, and although it was only mid-morning the blazing sun had made the temperature soar towards the eighties. Summer had suddenly arrived, proving the pessimists who had predicted a season of sombre greyness to be completely wrong.

As I walked past isolated Drop Farm I had already begun to sweat, an uncomfortable damp patch had formed on my back where my rucksack was touching. Beyond a sign which indicated 'Brontë Waterfalls and Top Withens' I met a middle aged couple who were returning from their walk. The man, who had a healthy tanned face with contrasting silver hair, spoke to me in a Buckinghamshire accent:

'If you're going to the waterfalls I wouldn't bother. Hardly a trickle of water. But the view is really worth seeing, mind.'

I thanked him for his advice then I continued for another mile until I reached a high point on the moorland ridge. Here, among heather that was yet to bloom I sat watching open-winged butterflies sunning themselves and looked upon a magical landscape, surely the very soul of Yorkshire. I was now in an ocean of grassy hills which spread, mile upon mile, to the far horizon. They appeared bronze coloured on the tops where they were caught by the sun, turning mahogany in the shadows, then to a tender green in narrow fertile valleys. Here and there, drystone walls spread like dark outstretched fingers, caressing the summits and disappearing over peaty plateaus. Occasionally the cry of a lamb would break the silence to be answered by the melancholy song of a curlew jealously guarding its Pennine home.

Glancing to my right I saw a narrow valley cut by the dark profile of a meandering stream. Alongside this stream a group of walkers was strolling up a path in a lighthearted mood, their laughter echoing up the hillside. I watched as they continued their ascent under the burning sun, slowly getting nearer and nearer to their goal. At last they reached Top Withens, a ruined farmhouse which shelters at the valley head under the shade of a tree. But this was no ordinary moorland walk, for it was an excursion into a marvellous literary world where fact and fiction imperceptibly merge. For here in 1847 the genius of a 29 year old woman named Emily Brontë immortalised this windswept homestead; it is known today in every corner of the globe as Wuthering Heights.

The rugged spendour of the Brontë moors near Top Withens

Sitting on the heathery vantage point I began to recall the classic story. I remembered how Mr Earnshaw found a waif named Heathcliff on the streets of London, then brought him back to live here on this lonely moor. How later his daughter Catherine fell madly in love with the wild youth, a liaison resented by her brother Hindley. Then followed a complicated tangled web of desire, hatred, double-dealings and vengeance, ending inevitably in tragedy and death. So was born on these Yorkshire uplands the formula which still lies at the heart of scores of best-selling novels; tales which seem only to be successfully written by women.

I sat for almost an hour soaking up the feeling of solitude and freedom that pervades these Brontë moors, my eyes being drawn ever upwards to the dark walls of Top Withens. I learned later that it was last occupied in 1926 by a Haworth man named Ernest Roddy. Having returned from the horror of the trenches of the Great War, he settled for a few years in the isolated farmhouse where he reared poultry. But he later returned to the village to become a postman and yeast-seller, leaving the farm to become an evocative ruin.

Returning along the path I met three Japanese visitors who were smiling, but not enjoying the heat. As they mopped their brow I pointed out the farmhouse which was little more than a speck in the far distance. This brought a sigh of anguish. They told me in broken English, that they lived in Tokyo and loved the Brontë Country. But I knew the hike to Top Withens would be too much for them, and shortly afterwards they returned to their hired BMW. As I waved goodbye I wondered if they had been pupils of Professor Yoshimasa Kiyohara of Kobe University. For this famous Japanese teacher so loved the Brontë novels that he came to stay here to learn the dialect words which appear in the books.

As I descended through the heather memories came flooding back to me of a walk I had over these hills almost thirty years ago. I remembered it had been wintertime, patches of snow lay in the moorland gulleys and low cloud shrouded the summits. Accompanied by two friends who were very experienced walkers, Jack Prescott and Ellis Astle, our route lay close to a remote farmhouse which lay at the heart of the moors. As we approached the building we saw a tall, gaunt man with a black beard and staring eyes, who was busily digging with a spade. Around him were half a dozen small children, the oldest no more than ten years old, who were also busy at work. The weather at this time was quite appalling, with a heavy downpour of sleety rain and a bitter wind.

Normally, strangers who arrive in these remote Pennine areas are greeted with a smile, for it is a rare opportunity to have a chat. However, our visit to the farm proved to be far from welcome. As we approached a shout of 'Hello' was received with a glare of silence. The man then lifted his hand and immediately the children threw down their spades and scurried indoors, but not before we saw that they were all bare footed. He too followed them inside the house, only to reappear when we were a quarter mile down the road.

So it would seem that characters as wild as Heathcliff can still be found in these parts!

3

'It's just the luck of the draw. Many people in their eighties have no trouble walking, then look at me. I'm only in my forties and I need the help of a stick to just hobble around.'

To escape from the blazing sun I had slipped into what was once Branwell Brontë's local pub, the Black Bull in Haworth. Here, the wanton man who brought such distress to his family, drank himself into an early grave. As I sat in a corner sipping a pint of Guinness and soaking up the atmosphere, snippets of conversation drifted my way. A brave woman who was obviously struggling with the crippling effects of arthritis, sat alongside her husband discussing her infirmity with another couple. Dotted around the room, with its high ceilings and framed prints of Edwardian showgirls, were small groups of visitors enjoying their lunch. These were mainly middle aged women with short grey hair and smiling faces, who I suspected had arrived by motor-coach, lured by the romantic tale of Jane Eyre and Mr Rochester.

Out into the sunlight again I joined the crowds on the single cobbled street which, like that in Clovelly, plummets down the steep hillside. Here sturdy shops and stone built cottages are perched precariously on both sides. Occasionally a gap between the buildings allowed me a view of the inviting green of the Worth Valley lying below, leading on to the rooftops of Keighley. As if to bring a glimmer of the present to what is almost completely a Victorian time capsule, my eyes were drawn to a small hilltop on which the gleaming white blades of a wind-turbine were whirling in a turquoise sky.

Opposite to the Black Bull impatient children were queueing to buy ice-cream cones from a mobile stall, whose owner could hardly believe his good fortune. Nearby, on the wall of an apothecary shop, I read a notice which further charts the decline of Branwell Brontë.

When the Brontë family lived in Haworth this was the
druggist's house and shop. Here Branwell purchased
the opium which contributed to his early death on the
24th September 1848 at the age of 31 years.

I wandered into the shop which was brimming with customers, for here
can be bought a marvellous selection of yesterday's products which would
have been familiar to our grandparents. These included mustard baths,
lemon and peppermint foot baths, Sunlight Soap, Zeebo black grate polish,
Doans backache pills, moth-balls, coltsfoot rock, barley sugar sticks .... but
no opium!

Sun-hats, shorts and open-toed sandals had replaced the more usual
thick woollens and waterproof jackets which are often worn by visitors to
Haworth. It was as if for a day part of the Costa del Sol had been transferred
on to the Yorkshire Moors. I wondered what tales the many puzzled foreign
tourists who I saw on the street, would take back to Norway, Australia and
the USA. For having read Wuthering Heights they had arrived here expecting mist, rain and a howling gale, but were amazed to be experiencing a
heat wave.

After looking at a display of leaflets advertising the Brontë Society,
browsing at the ghost and magic books in a shop appropriately named
Spooks, and topping up my flagging energy level with a pot of tea, I went
to the place which more than any other speaks of the great tragedy that was
the destiny of this unique family. Alone, in the cool of the Haworth church,
I copied from a memorial tablet the following names and dates:

Maria (mother), died September 15th 1821, aged 39 years.
Maria (daughter), died May 6th 1825, aged 12 years.
Elizabeth (daughter). died June 15th 1825, aged 11 years.
Patrick Branwell (son), died September 24th 1848, aged 31 years.
Emily Jane (daughter), died December 19th 1848, aged 30 years.
Anne (daughter), died May 28th 1849, aged 29 years.
Charlotte (daughter), died March 31st 1855, aged 39 years.
Rev. Patrick Brontë (father), died June 7th 1861, aged 85 years.

It was on the 29th December 1812, just seven years after Nelson's epic
victory at Trafalgar, that the Reverend Patrick Brontë married Maria Branwell. Patrick, one of ten children, had been born in Ireland, the son of a
Protestant father and a Roman Catholic mother. Although coming from a
poor family, he had shown a scholarly nature and this was noticed by a
local clergyman, the Rev. Harshaw. At this time he was working as a
linen-weaver, but under the influence of the clergyman he began to study

in the evenings, which led to him being offered a position as a teacher in a church school at Drumballerony.

Here his academic talent was further recognised by the Rector, Thomas Tighe, who encouraged him to improve his religious education. Tighe, although a member of the established church had leanings towards the teachings of the Wesleys whom he had known. So, when Patrick Brontë decided that he too would like to become a clergyman, it was the Rev. Tighe who managed to get him financial aid from the Wesleyan Society for his studies at Cambridge University, which began in 1802. He proved to be an industrious scholar who had a great love of literature and an urge to write poetry.

After graduating from Cambridge he first became a curate in Essex and then in Shropshire, before moving to northern England. It was when he was appointed to his own parish at Hartshead, near Dewsbury, that he was introduced to his future wife, Maria Branwell. A native of Cornwall, she had been staying in Yorkshire at the home of her uncle who was a local headmaster.

Their romance quickly flourished, leading to a double wedding in Guiseley Church, at which her cousin Jane Fennell was married at the same time. The couple appeared to be blissfully happy, Patrick carrying out his pastoral duties while writing poetry in his spare moments, and Maria adapting to her busy life as a clergyman's wife. Just a year after they were married their first child, a daughter they named Maria was born. She was joined the next year by a sister, Elizabeth. In 1815, a period of great national rejoicing which saw Napoleon's political aspirations in tatters following his defeat at Waterloo, Patrick Brontë moved to another parish at Thornton just seven miles from Haworth. Here Charlotte was born in 1816, followed in quick succession by Branwell, Emily and Anne.

After spending five years at Thornton, in 1820 Patrick took Maria and his boisterous family of six young children to live here at Haworth Parsonage where he had accepted the position as curate. But their happiness was sadly destined to be short lived, for Maria had become very ill, she was suffering from cancer. Her sister, Elizabeth, came to nurse her during her decline which ended in her death in 1821 at the early age of 39.

Elizabeth Branwell reluctantly stayed on at Haworth to look after the children as Patrick gradually came to terms with his grief. Fortified by his religion he was an enlightened man and not at all a bitter, stuffy person, which is how he is sometimes portrayed. He encouraged his children to draw and write and enjoy music, and he introduced them to the splendour of the Yorkshire moors and to the joy of travel.

As part of their education the four elder girls, Maria, Elizabeth, Charlotte and Emily were sent in 1824 to board at the Clergy Daughter's School lying in the village of Cowan Bridge near Kirkby Lonsdale. It had been established in 1816 by William Carus Wilson, who was the Vicar of Tunstall and editor of England's first penny-papers for children. But the girls were miserable and unhappy at the school, for the food was ghastly and the buildings damp and freezing cold in wintertime. These unhealthy living conditions led to Maria and Elizabeth falling ill with consumption, resulting in their tragic deaths in 1825. This event, just four years after the death of their mother, was to bring lasting grief to the remaining family. Charlotte was later to portray the school, which she blamed for both her and Emily's future health problems, as Lowood in Jane Eyre.

After the death of the two eldest girls the education of the other children was continued at home. Here, in the seclusion of the Parsonage their fertile imaginations were allowed to develop unrestrained, influenced by the many books they read. They began to write simple stories, produce tiny hand written magazines, and create two fantasy kingdoms. Emily and Anne, who were devoted to each other, named their world Gondal, while Charlotte and Branwell invented Angria.

In 1831 Charlotte spent a year as a pupil at Miss Wooler's school at Roe Head, returning later as a teacher, then she became a governess in a number of large houses. Emily also went to Roe Head for a short period, but returned to Haworth because of home-sickness. They went together in 1842 to Brussels to study languages, but had to return home to attend the funeral of their Aunt Elizabeth who had become their adopted mother. Charlotte, who unlike Emily, made friends easily and yearned for a wider experience of the world, returned alone to Belgium. Here she is said to have fallen in love with Monsieur Heger, the husband of the owner of the school. But he did not answer her letters when she later returned to Yorkshire.

Anne, who was the youngest of the Brontë children, is said to have been greatly influenced by her aunt who was a staunch Wesleyan, which led to bouts of religious melancholy. In 1836 she went to join Charlotte at Roe Head, then she too became a governess. Her brother Branwell, who was unsuccessful in his ambitions to become a painter and writer, turned increasingly to drugs and drink for consolation. He drifted from one job to another, becoming first a tutor then an assistant railway clerk from which he was sacked, before joining Anne who had become a governess at Thorp Green Hall near York. Here he had a disastrous affair with the owner's wife, Mrs Robinson.

It was in 1845 that Charlotte is said to have become convinced that their poems, particularly those written by Emily, were worthy of publication. So the following year they published a joint collection, The Poems of Currer, Ellis and Acton Bell, the pen-names chosen by Charlotte, Emily and Anne. The volume received scant attention, but had the effect of crystallising their future literary ambitions. By this time the three sisters had each written a novel which they now sought to have published. Emily's Wuthering Heights and Anne's Agnes Grey were both to their great joy, accepted by publishers Thomas Newby. But Charlotte's Professor was sadly rejected and was destined never to be published during her lifetime. However, in spite of this setback, she went on to write her classic masterpiece, Jane Eyre, published in 1847 and remains to this day one of the world's most cherished books.

The year 1848, which saw the publication of Anne's second and final novel, The Tenant of Wildfell Hall, also marked a rapid decline in the family's health. Weakened by the effects of his alcoholism and opium addiction, Branwell died in September. Less than three months later, Emily, who is now regarded as one of the greatest poets of the last century, died of consumption. Anne, who had also become gravely ill at the same time, made a trip to Scarborough where she too died in May of the following year.

In dramatic and tragic circumstances Charlotte now found herself the sole survivor of the six children. She tried to hide her grief and loneliness by becoming absorbed in her writings, completing Shirley in 1849 and Villette in 1853. Comfort also came from her friendship with novelist, Mrs Gaskell, who was to eventually write her life story. Also, now having become quite famous, she had a number of male admirers including James Taylor who worked at her publishers, Smith and Elder. But it was her father's curate, Arthur Bell Nicholls, who she was eventually, if hesitatingly, to marry on the 29th June 1854. Sadly their life together was to last a mere nine months, for Charlotte who was now pregnant, fell ill and died on the 31st March 1855.

The Rev. Patrick Brontë, who had witnessed so much suffering and was in his later years virtually blind, died in 1861 at the age of 85. He had been looked after since Charlotte's death by his son-in-law who had naturally expected to be given the position as curate at Haworth when Patrick died. However this was not to be, for the living was given to the Rev. John Wade; a decision which so affected Arthur Bell Nicholls that he eventually left the ministry. He became a farmer in his native Ireland, then later married his cousin. Amazingly, he lived with his memories of life in the Brontë household right into our present century, dying in 1906 at the age of 89.

Patrick Brontë's body was laid to rest in the family vault lying beneath the present church floor. But in 1879, in spite of a national outcry, what had become known as the Brontë Church was almost completely demolished. A new church was built on the same site, incorporating the original tower, and the Brontë Chapel, a gift from Sir Tresham Lever, was dedicated in 1964.

I strolled from the church into the sunlit street then I joined the stream of literary pilgrims who are drawn each day to nearby Haworth Parsonage where all of the three sisters' books were written. A marvellous evocative atmosphere prevails, their clothes and letters and scores of their personal items remain. Although it is now almost a century and a half since their pens came to rest, I had the feeling they had just stepped out of the room. Had the sound of their laughter suddenly echoed through the house I would not have been in the least bit surprised.

4

I was still thinking about the astonishing achievements of the Brontë sisters as I slowly drove down the valley from Haworth towards Airedale. But of course they were only the first of an amazing group of highly talented writers who have been born in these parts. It seems that this dramatic landscape of the South Pennines, with its unique mixture of wilderness and industrialization has motivated many to put pen to paper. These include J.B. Priestley, Thomas Armstrong, Phyllis Bentley, Ted Hughes and that world famous lady of fiction, Barbara Taylor Bradford. Then as I saw the sign which told me I had reached Bingley, I remembered one more — that angry young man of the fifties, John Braine.

Brought to national fame by the roaring success of his novel 'Room at the Top' that was published in 1957, John Gerard Braine had been born in Bradford on 13 April 1922. After attending St Bedes Grammar School he took a number of 'dead end' jobs, then having a strong leaning towards literature he became an assistant librarian here in Bingley. Wartime brought a short spell away from home when he joined the Royal Navy as a telegraphist. This he later recalled was 'a singularly uneventful nine months, mostly spent in training'. Then in 1945 he returned to continue his work in the library, where in 1949 he became Chief Assistant Librarian.

But his underlying ambition had always been to become part of the literary world. This led him in 1951 to leave his secure job with its secure salary and pursue a full-time career as a free-lance writer. He began by writing short stories which had a backcloth of the West Riding and a style adopted from Hemingway. But the market prospects were very limited, he had many rejections and was eventually forced to turn to writing features. This brought greater success, his work being published in several up-market magazines and newspapers.

Braine grew to love Bingley where he found tranquillity and inspiration. He loved to explore its green fringes and wander along 'the loveliest stretch of canal in the whole of England.' Here too he found early acceptance of his talent when his verse play The Desert in the Mirror was produced in the local theatre.

But sadly, writing was not paying the rent, to which was added the further worry of his failing health for he had contracted tuberculosis. After less than a year as a writer he was forced to return to his more secure library job, taking a position in Northumberland then later returning here to Yorkshire. In 1955 at the age of 33, he married Helen Patricia Wood, and over the next few years their family grew to four children.

Still dogged by ill-health it was while convalescing in a hospital bed that Braine was to write the first draft of his future best-seller. In a stiff-backed exercise book, he later recalled, the murky, ambitious character of Joe Lampton began to take shape. Out of Braine's intimate knowledge of Bradford and Bingley also rose the towns of Dufton and Warley, for he knew that it was always wise to write from personal experience.

Following on from John Osborne's Look Back in Anger which had started a post-war literary revolution, Braine's Room at the Top spearheaded the kitchen-sink drama. It was published by Eyre and Spottiswoode in March 1957 and immediately headed the best-seller list. From being an unknown author overnight the name of John Braine was on everyone's lips. Reviewers acclaimed him, and due to his left-wing views he even gained fame behind the Iron-Curtain.

Leaving his library job behind him he was now able to once more take up the pen full time. His path now lay inevitably to London where he quickly established himself among the literary and academic set, becoming recognised as one of the great characters of the period. His tale of lust, greed and naked ambition continued to reap success. It was quickly made into a film, gaining an Oscar for Simone Signoret and later becoming the basis for a television series.

But Braine then made the mistake of not building on his success by writing a sequel. Instead he chose a completely different theme for his second book, The Vodi, and this was received with disappointment. It was 1962 before the thread of Joe Lampton's life was picked up in Life at the Top and although it helped to restore Braine's reputation, the age of the kitchen-sink drama was about to end. The anti-establishment and mean-city outlook was giving way to the excitement of the Swinging Sixties, flower-power, the Beatles and James Bond.

By this time the bluff Yorkshireman with the radical outlook had settled to a more comfortable way of life. As well as writing novels he became a literary critic and book reviewer, and his views became much sought after by television presenters. In 1978 he became Writer-in-Residence at Purdue University in the USA, then the following year saw the publication of his life of J.B. Priestley. This he saw not as a formal biography but more as an appreciation of the great man's life, who like Braine himself had been born in Bradford.

When John Braine died in 1986 at the early age of 64, he had written thirteen novels and two works of non-fiction. Most of these had received good reviews and he continued to be very popular with the reading public. But it is for his first book, Room at the Top, written under such adverse conditions, that he will always be remembered.

5

There are pet owners all over the world who have two good reasons to bless this corner of Yorkshire. For this is where those much loved four-legged companions, the Airedale Terrier and the Yorkshire Terrier had

their beginnings. Both are now among the most popular of all dog breeds, who find admirers from all levels of society, whether it be low-income pensioners living in small flats or rich and famous film stars who revel in opulence. However, wealth is thankfully of no significance to these courageous animals, their lifelong devotion is more a just reward for a kind and affectionate owner. But one thing is for sure, when they mischievously scamper into our lives, things are never likely to be the same ever again!

Terriers are said to have taken their name from 'terra', which means earth, for it was by burrowing into the earth that they often pursued their prey. It was usually small animals such as mice, rats and rabbits which they hunted, but on occasions they would attack foxes, badgers and deer. Over the centuries, depending on the type of climate and the terrain in which they lived and the prey available, the dogs developed regional characteristics. They all required very strong jaws and sharp teeth to kill their adversaries; in cold climates their coats would be thick and woolly, while in warm areas lighter and more silky. Small dogs evolved where most of their hunting for food required burrowing below ground, while larger-legged animals developed when a long chase was required. In the third century BC, the Greeks wrote about the existence of dogs that were probably terriers, and by the 16th century these had become accepted in this country as a definite breed. Royalty populised them, particularly King James 1 who mentioned the Scottish Earth-dogges.

Airedale, which has given its name to the King of Terriers, lies at the southern edge of the National Park. The River Aire rises close to Malham, passes through Gargrave, skirts Skipton, then meanders down this green valley, the only lowland corridor through the Pennines. Beyond Bingley, however, much of Airedale has become industrialised, the river curving its path past Shipley and Leeds before pouring its waters into the Ouse four miles from Goole.

The coming of the Industrial Revolution to Yorkshire brought with it an influx of new workers, whose leisuretime activities often included field-sports. Cock-fighting and dog-fighting which later became illegal, still prevailed, as did the pursuit of almost any wild animal unfortunate enough to live in the area. Broken-coated Working Terriers had long been recognised as the ideal dog for the sport and it was from these that the Airedale Terrier probably evolved. It is said that about the middle of the last century they were crossed with Bull Terriers and possibly Border Collies, then with Otter-hounds to produce what became known at first as Waterside Terriers. Rats, present in large numbers at this time due to poor hygienic conditions, became the main adversary of the dogs. Competitions involving large sums of money were held on the riverside between rival terriers, who would swim tirelessly after the fleeing rats, spurred on by the shouts of their owners.

By the 1880s dog-shows were well established in England, and the term 'Airedale Terrier' had become the accepted name for the breed. So it was from this Yorkshire bloodline that the modern Airedale evolved, spreading all over the world it is now used for hunting, herding, trailing, retrieving, as a show-dog, but mainly as a companion and household pet.

In complete contrast to the Airedale Terrier in size and shape, but not in spirit and tenacity, is that affectionate small dog with the delightful personality, the Yorkshire Terrier. Widely known as the Yorkie, it too can trace its origins to the early part of Queen Victoria's reign, when the industrial landscape of southern Yorkshire was being formed. It is believed that mill-workers who came down here from Scotland, brought with them the ancestor of the modern Yorkie, their own breed of small dog known as the Clydesdale Terrier. This, like the Airedale, was then crossed with the popular Broken-coated Terrier, with the aim of producing a dog ideal for poaching which had long been a traditional activity of the now exiled Scotsmen.

The poachers required a tiny dog which could be used in a similar way to a ferret. It would be trained to penetrate deep into rabbit burrows, causing panic among the residents who would bolt out of other exits into awaiting nets. Always intent on perfecting their strain of dog, it is likely that they were later cross-bred with a miniature, silky coated terrier which had originated in Malta. This resulted in a breed which at first became known as a Scotch Terrier, but in 1886 was finally accepted by the Kennel Club as a Yorkshire Terrier. One of the earliest pedigree records which exists is that of Huddersfield Ben, who was born in 1865 and won many major prizes of the day.

By 1898 the breed had grown so popular that a Yorkshire Terrier Club was established. Today this tiny, affectionate dog who thinks it is the size of a bull, has irresistible appeal. With its bouyant, playful temperament no one can ever feel downhearted or depressed in its company, for its tremendous zest for living is contagious. It responds with undying love to its owner, seeing itself as guardian of all her property. One minute attacking from a distance, with aggressive fury, any unwelcome visitor who dares come within a mile of its home. Then like an accomplished actress, it will immediately change its mood and will plant a series of kisses on the face of its friends!

If Yorkshire had merely two things it could boast it had given to the world, the Airedale Terrier and the Yorkie would be more than enough.

6

Every curious visitor to Yorkshire eventually finds himself as I did, drawn to a rugged windswept stretch of Rombalds Moor which separates Airedale from Wharfedale. This is not because this particular hillside is more majestic, more attractive or even higher than its neighbours, for it is none of these. But what urges many people to come here are the words

of a song. After I crossed the River Aire beyond Keighley and began to
ascend a narrow twisting road, these words which many regard as Yorkshire's National Anthem, came flowing back:

> *Wheer wor' ta bahn w'en Ah saw thee,*
> *On Ilkla' Moor baht 'at?*
> *Wheer wor' ta bahn w'en Ah saw thee?*
> *Wheer wor' ta bahn w'en Ah saw thee?*
> *On Ilkla' Moor baht 'at, On Ilkla' Moor baht 'at,*
> *On Ilkla' Moor baht 'at.*

Which for those readers who were born south of Watford who may have a
little difficulty understanding the words, translate badly as:

> *Where had you been when I saw you,*
> *On Ilkley Moor without a hat?*
> *Where had you been when I saw you?*
> *Where had you been when I saw you?*
> *On Ilkley Moor without a hat, On Ilkley Moor without a hat,*
> *On Ilkley Moor without a hat.*

I stopped my car on the edge of the moor to look at the dark profile of an
outcrop of gritstone known as the Cow and Calf Rocks. Apparently there
was once also a Bull Rock, but years before our planning laws prevailed,
this was broken up to build a hotel in Ilkley.

According to a local tradition it was close to these rocks that the words
of the song were composed. Members of a church choir from Halifax were
having a picnic here and the bracing wind sweeping across the moor
motivated them to put pen to paper. With ironic Yorkshire wit the verses
relate how death from cold will surely follow anyone who fails to wear a
hat up here. Then after burial their body will be eaten by worms, ducks
will then eat the worms, we will eat the ducks, so 'then we will all 'ave
etten thee'. However the fell walkers of the north have created their own
versions of this song which are robustly sung in the inns of Yorkshire and
the Lake District. Suffice to say none of these can be repeated here!

When I arrived in the car park in the centre of Ilkley I detected an
atmosphere of demure affluence. For sprinkled among the Fords and the
Vauxhalls parked there, were a large number of BMWs, a black Jaguar, a
Mercedes and two Rolls Royces. This feeling that there is a 'bit of brass'
about around these parts was soon to be borne out by the shops which I
discovered as I wandered around this appealing town. Antiques and
antiquarian bookshops, up-market dress and woollen goods shops, and

The tranquil River Wharfe meanders through Ilkley

select restaurants abound. It seems that the mill-owners of Bradford, Halifax and Leeds, have made their homes where they have space to relax, can breathe in fine country air, and at the same time spend just a little of their money.

I strolled through the streets of what was once the Roman garrison of Olicana to a green parkland which sweeps down to the wooded banks of the Wharfe. Hidden wood pigeons were cooing from the trees, a solitary jackdaw was pecking in the sunshine and a score of mallard ducks lay sleeping in the shade. Here I stopped to admire the glinting water flowing fast from beneath a bridge, then lapping more slowly over moss laden stones. On a large boulder lying in this tranquil grassland I read the words: These grounds were provided by public subscription in memory of the Ilkley residents who made the supreme sacrifice in the Second World War 1939 – 1940.

'I'm not too sure about them myself. I think it's some of the carvings which put me off. Hints of paganism I suppose.'

I had left the river bank and wandered into the interior of All Saints Church where I had discovered a fascinating group of carved Saxon crosses and two Roman altars which have been preserved at the base of the tower. These had been pointed out to me by a helpful middle aged lady, who with her female friend, were here to greet visitors.

When the first Christian missionary, who was probably Paulinus, came to Ilkley during the early seventh century he would have travelled along the grass-laden remnants of a Roman road. Here he would have preached to the Anglo-Saxons who then lived among the tumbled stones of the old garrison, telling them of the wonder of Jesus and how King Edwin had been recently baptised into the living faith.

These sculptured crosses that I looked at bear testimony to the success of the Christian message, for on the site of what is thought to be the temple of Hercules, rose this church of All Saints. Their carvings, which include a grotesque horned beast casting up his hind legs, show how these early Christians saw the battle between good and evil. Their eyes would also have seen the earlier work of the Romans, who two centuries earlier had left Olicana forever. It is believed that the carved female figure who is clothed in a long robe and carries a torch is the earth goddess Demeter.

After admiring the medieval font, seeing the 14th century effigy of Sir Adam Middleton and gazing in wonder at the delicate colours of the William Morris window of the Four Marys, I returned again to the sunny streets of the town. Here I sauntered around the classy shops, listened to the free show being given by a female saxophone player, then decided that I would after all, trek up the side of Ilkley Moor to see the White Wells Spa Cottage.

There was a time when Ilkley was renowned not just for its famous moor but for its Spa water. After hydropathy had been introduced from Germany the craze quickly began to sweep the country, arriving here in Wharfedale in the late 18th century. Several buildings sprung up in the town to cater for the new fad, including the Ben Rhydding Hydro which was built in 1844 and was sadly demolished in recent years. However, the lady in the church informed me that one link with this age of the Spa still exists at a cottage, but this involves a steep climb.

I began the ascent of the peaty hillside, walking towards the white-washed cottage which stood above me high on the moorland edge. After several short halts to gain my breath I eventually arrived at the marvellous vantage point where a handful of hardy visitors was already enjoying the view in the bright sunshine. Walking over to the side of the building I read a plaque that told me that the bath-house had originally been built by Squire Middleton for the people of Ilkley in the 18th century, then after restoration had been re-opened to the public in 1976.

Unfortunately I had arrived at the wrong time for the building was again being repaired and the only view I could get of the bath was through a small window. However, when I walked around to the rear of the building I found a natural spring pouring from the moorland and is probably the source of water for the Spa. A young girl, watched adoringly by her boyfriend, was taking a drink from cupped hands. I too, determined to sample this last vestige of Ilkley's Spa heritage, joined in by gulping the cool moorland water.

The view alone had been worth the effort of the ascent to White Wells, for below me spread a stunning panorama. The rooftops of the town, highlighted by two churches lay below in the green valley, with the meandering path of the Wharfe half hidden by trees. On the far bank was a sweep of rich pastureland that rose ever upwards to meet the moors and then the sky, marking what many people regard as the beginning of the Yorkshire Dales. That is why the 81 mile long pathway known as the Dales Way starts in Ilkley, then continues a marvellous journey through some of England's most beautiful countryside before ending at Bowness-on-Windermere.

For half an hour I sat hypnotised by the view. Then with excited anticipation began the descent down the moorland, knowing that the joys of the Dales now lay before me

Chapter Three

Ilkley to the Yorkshire Dales

*I enter the Dales at Bolton Abbey, explore Skipton where I learn of
Thomas Spencer, then I remember the Water Babies at Malham
Cove. I walk to Gordale Scar, watch the people of Settle from the
Ye Olde Naked Man cafe, then become deafened by the bells of
Giggleswick. I visit the grave of Russell Harty and look at the
Ebbing and Flowing Well, before discovering Clapham where I hear
how a Frenchman descended Gaping Gill. I then reach Ingleton,
where I see a funeral and remember a Scottish snorer from the past.*

1

A s I drove slowly away from Ilkley following the meandering course of
the Wharfe, I suddenly became aware that subtle changes in the
landscape were taking place. The wild, rugged terrain of the South Pennines was giving way to the softer, more gentle countryside of the Yorkshire
Dales. I was entering a land of towering round hills and heather covered
moorland sweeping down from the sky to form a patchwork of curving
valleys. Here, encircled by miles of drystone walls stand ancient villages,
Norman churches, flowery cottages and speeding rivers which sparkle like
silver in the morning sunlight. Each village has at least one bridge, for most
communities have evolved around the rivers and streams that cascade
down the steep hillsides. In these solid inviting homes sheltered by patches
of rising woodland live the hardy Dales folk; tough, independent people
whose Viking ancestors formed this idyllic kingdom a thousand years ago.

But the first embracing impression that a stranger has when he arrives
in the Dales is that of intense greenness; the shimmering green of large
empty fields, the apple green of the higher fells, the tender green of the
riverside foliage and the blue-green of the distant hills as they disappear
into a misty horizon. This was perhaps why, as I parked my car at Bolton
Abbey, I began to feel that in some mystical way I was stepping not into a
new landscape but into the frame of a watercolour.

The sun was shining, the sky was blue and a feeling of intense peace lay over Wharfedale. The Wharfe, which many regard as Yorkshire's grandest river, was twisting like a silver thread past the ruins of the abbey, or to be correct the priory. For Bolton Abbey is the nearby village, while these lovely monastic arches are the remains of Bolton Priory.

It was in 1154 that the Augustine canons, filled with the fervour of their calling which demanded a life of chastity and poverty, began to erect this monument to God. Here it remained for almost four centuries, growing from a simple beginning to become a rich and distinguished community thanks to the generosity of many wealthy patrons. It successfully survived the raids of the Scots, the constant flooding of the river and at times, criticism that some monks were deviating from their original calling by taking to heavy drinking and disorderly conduct. But it did not survive the whim of King Henry VIII who brought about its end in 1539.

After the monks and their Prior had been forced from the building its treasures, its bells and the lead from its roof were removed and it was partly demolished. The remaining nave became the local parish church and the site was granted to the Earl of Cumberland. This large estate, with its wild expanse of grouse moors, was later inherited by the powerful Dukes of Devonshire who have made nearby Bolton Hall one of their residences.

As I sat in the shade beside the sweeping curve of the river memories came flooding back to me of the early sixties when I often came here to walk with the Manchester Ramblers. Although completely unaware at the time, we were witnessing the end of an era, for it was a steam-train not a diesel, which sped us here from Manchester Victoria, Bolton and Burnley. Laughing crowds of walkers would then alight at the station, dividing into smaller parties designated as A, B or C according to the distance they intended to walk. The 'tough' men, eager to get at least twenty miles under their feet, would join the 'A's led by such veteran walkers as Jack Prescott of Horwich or Len Chadwick of Saddleworth. While those of a more sedate nature would leisurely join the C's for an eight mile stroll.

Our path often lay through Bolton Abbey, then following in the steps of Wordsworth and Turner, we would reach the narrow river gorge known as the Strid. Passing through the sombre named Valley of Desolation, our route then took in the imposing grit-stone summit of Simon's Seat which dominates this landscape. Here we would stop for refreshment and, fostered by the wilderness of heather which surrounded us, our talk would often turn to the then Prime Minister, Harold Macmillan. For at the time he was often pictured in the newspapers in his plus-fours and tweed jacket, about to massacre the grouse here at the Bolton Abbey estate. With the dawning of the Swinging Sixties he seemed to be a man strangely out of place; a Victorian at heart he had risen to high office in the wrong century.

Another great character that is still remembered in this corner of the Dales is Dr Arthur Raistrick who died in 1991 at the age of 94. His name came to my mind as I referred to one of his many well-written guidebooks, The Story of Bolton Priory. As an eminent geologist and historian his knowledge of the Dales was unsurpassed. He became one of the founders of the Upper Wharfedale Field Society in 1949 and for many years his authoritative articles written for Dalesman magazine gained a wealth of readers. His name now lives on by an annual memorial lecture that has been established in his honour.

It was mid-afternoon when I reluctantly exchanged the quietness of Bolton Abbey for the busy streets of Skipton, a town that was overflowing with visitors. Coaches from Nottingham, Birmingham and York were being carefully manoeuvred into the packed car-park. Drivers, wiping sweat from their brows, were anxiously hunting for elusive parking places. Sun tanned, smiling ladies, wearing straw hats were hurrying towards the street market, followed a pace behind by reticent husbands. Bemused toddlers at the hand of their mothers, were staring at the ice cream seller with hopeful anticipation. While in a quiet corner a group of indecisive ramblers was studying their Ordnance Survey Map. Should they head for Malham and walk to Gordale Scar, or perhaps climb Pen-y-ghent from Horton, but a riverside walk would be pleasant in this heat? No, it is much too hot and rather late. A shandy in an old inn in the High Street would be better. Let's leave the walk until tomorrow.

Skipton, which boasts that it is the Gateway to the Dales, is an ancient market town with well-hidden hints of industry. Once known as Sheeptown it lies in the district of Craven; a Celtic name which appropriately means Land of the Crags. I strolled up its busy High Street, fighting through the hoards of bargain-hunters who had descended on its colourful market which spills out on both sides of the road. After passing a sign outside a bank that told me that the pillory once stood on the spot, I reached the castle gateway and the church which together dominate the town.

It is believed a Norman named Robert de Romille first built this elevated fortress but it is the famous Clifford family who are remembered most. During the Civil War when Lady Anne Clifford was the owner, the castle managed to hold out against Cromwell's army for an astonishing three years. After the decisive Battle of Marston Moor it remained the last Royalist outpost in the North of England. When it eventually fell the roof was removed by Cromwell's men, but a decade later this was allowed to be replaced on the proviso that it was not made strong enough to withstand cannon balls!

The impressive gateway to Skipton Castle

In the cool of the church, which dates from the 12th century, I gazed upon the many tombs of these illustrious Cliffords. These include that of George Clifford, the 3rd Earl of Cumberland, who as an Admiral at the time of Elizabeth fought off the threat of the Armada. I then stepped out into the sunlight to continue my stroll. For an hour I sauntered along the town's cobbled alleyways, explored its secluded corners, and watched mallard chicks glide beside gaily painted boats on the picturesque canal. Then fortified by more tea and scones I went to see the Craven Museum which a friend told me I should not miss.

He was quite right, for huddled together in this remarkable display I discovered a fascinating array of curiosities that could have kept me occupied for a week. A hand operated lathe lay close to the 'bat' once used for the old game of Knur and Spell. A bone-shaker bicycle and a hippopotamus skull stood facing gas masks, air raid precautions and instructions for putting on respirators; part of Yorkshire's memories of the last war. A horn that once heralded the arrival of the Grassington mail-coach stood forlornly in a case, watched by a painting of the famous Craven Heifer, the subject of many northern pub signs.

But it was the portrait of a full-faced man, who was sporting a large droopy moustache and wearing a flat-cap, which surprised me most. For I was looking at Skipton born Thomas Spencer, the co-founder of what is now considered to be Britain's most efficiently managed company, Marks & Spencer.

The incredible success story of this famous high street store began with the birth of Michael Marks in 1863 at Bialystok, a Jewish village in Russian Poland. This was a time when Jews were being persecuted in Russia, leading Michael, at the age of 19, to emigrate to England. After a short period in London he came north to Leeds to join the large Jewish community. With little money and no knowledge of English he began to earn his living as a pedlar. Carrying small household goods such as pins, needles and cotton in his pack, he would walk the Dales selling to remote farms and cottages.

In 1884 he had progressed by opening a small stall on the open market in Leeds to sell his goods, then shortly afterwards he moved inside the Market Hall. To simplify his business he began to sell all his goods at a penny, creating what was soon to become his famous slogan, 'Don't Ask the Price, It's a Penny'. The five pounds which he had needed to set up his business had been lent to him by Isaac Dewhirst who was a wholesale supplier. Remarkably, this firm, I.J. Dewhirst Ltd, still supplies goods to Marks & Spencer.

The tremendous success of Michael Mark's fixed priced selling together with his new idea of allowing customers to choose their own goods, led to him opening more stalls in several Yorkshire and Lancashire towns. He now called then Penny Bazaars and employed assistants to manage them. But by 1894, with a distribution centre at Wigan, his business had grown so rapidly that he decided he needed a partner to share the responsibility and provide more capital. Isaac Dewhirst was approached by Marks but was unable to accept the proposal as he was committed to his own thriving business. However, Dewhirst suggested that his cashier, Thomas Spencer, might be interested.

Skipton-born Thomas Spencer

Thomas Spencer, the son of a shoemaker, had been born here in Skipton in 1851. In 1870 he had gone to work in Leeds where eventually he had become the trusted book-keeper to Isaac Dewhirst. An intelligent organiser with a flair for economy he was completely opposite to the outgoing, enterprising Marks. But the two men quickly became friends and on the 28 September 1894 they became equal partners in the newly formed company of Marks & Spencer.

Immediately the new venture flourished leading to a spectacular expansion in trade. In just six years the firm, now based in Manchester, had grown to 36 branches and in 1903 it became a limited company. At this time Thomas Spencer, who was in poor health decided to retire to Staffordshire where in 1905 at the early age of 54 he died. Just two years later Michael Marks also died which left a complete vacuum in what had become an exceptional business. For several years it was controlled by non-family members, then in 1917 Simon Marks (later Lord Marks), who was the only son of the co-founder, took the helm. Influenced by the new super-store idea born in America and his perception that orders should be placed directly with manufacturers he sailed his flagship on a course that had dramatic consequences. This is reflected today by the unique position that Marks & Spencer, with their brand name of St Michael, have in Britain. They have gained a world wide reputation for selling high quality, realiable goods at reasonable prices.

I left the Craven Museum then strolled down the High Street to look at Greens Court, a row of cottages where Thomas Spencer was born. These, I discovered, have long since disappeared. On the site, by a strange twist of fate has risen a branch of a rival store — Woolworths!

2

It was a glorious day, the type which photographers and landscape artists often dream about but seldom experience. The slanting morning sun was beaming from a turquoise sky on fields that were glowing golden having just given up their first harvest of the year. These were bordered by hawthorn hedgerows, alive with buzzing insects hovering like miniature helicopters above buttercups and meadowsweet. I was thinking how marvellous it would be if this moment could last forever – then it happened. Apparently from nowhere, the white bobtail of a young rabbit appeared a yard away from my front wheel. I swerved then braked, then swerved again. My heart pounded, then I began to sweat as I waited for what I thought would be an inevitable thud. Miraculously this never happened. A quick glance in my rear-view mirror showed the bungle of fur nonchalantly disappearing beneath a field gate, blissfully unaware of its brush with death.

At Gargrave I turned right to join a quiet country lane which is the entrance to one of Yorkshire's best-loved valleys, Malhamdale. Passing

Eshton Hall, a nursing home that was once the residence of Skipton's first MP, Sir Matthew Wilson, I found myself in a lush green landscape. Moss laden drystone walls fringed the roadside hiding neatly manicured fields which spoke of an estate. Wild-eyed jackdaws watched me with suspicion from the low branches of conifer trees, as I took in the air which was rich with the scent of newly mown grass. Beyond the turn-off to secluded Winterburn I caught a glimpse of Newfield Hall, a fine Victorian building which since 1933 has been a Holiday Fellowship guest house. The winding road then led me alongside the green at lovely Airton village to my first stop of the day at Kirkby Malham.

I parked my car in an idyllic spot which overlooks the rushing waters of Kirk Beck, a tributary of the River Aire that lies a short distance down the valley. 'Welcome, please come in' was the inviting sign outside the church of St Michael the Archangel, a large and beautiful building that has become known as 'The Cathedral of the Dales'. It is said to occupy a pagan site taken over by the Anglo-Saxons who first planted the cross of Christianity here in the early eighth century. They were followed by the Danes who during the next two centuries settled in this green valley. At the end of the 12th century the church belonged to the White Canons of West Dereham in Norfolk, who kept control until the Dissolution of the Monasteries when it was taken by the Crown. Today the church serves a remote parish covering 35 square miles of some of England's most magnificent and isolated countryside. This close-to-nature atmosphere of St Michael's became even more apparent some years ago when a short-horn bull made an entrance down the aisle during Sunday service. Two church wardens, with heroic vigour, managed to persuade the animal to return to the fields, while the vicar remained in deep prayer completely unaware of his unwanted visitor!

Shutting the heavy oak door behind me I entered the ancient building which exudes a feeling of quiet peacefulness. For half an hour I wandered among the sacred stones which unknown Norman hands first shaped. I admired finely carved pillars, wondered if Danish babies had really been baptised in the solid font, ran my fingers over splendid box pews, and looked at the badges of the Royal Flying Corp and the West Yorkshire Regiment.

In the Chapel of Our Lady a recent memorial commemorates General John Lambert, a local man who lived at nearby Calton Hall. He became a powerful leader in the Parliamentary Army and entertained Oliver Cromwell at his home. In the church register for 1655 it is said that Cromwell's signature appeared as a witness to a wedding, but this evidence of his visit has mysteriously disappeared. However it is known that his troops, who were guarding the entrance to the dale, were garrisoned in the church during the turmoil of the Civil War.

The hand of Christian charity stretches out from this church at Kirkby Malham, not so much in its historical links imposing as they surely are, but in a practical way that I have never seen in any other church. For neatly laid out in the vestry are cups, an electric kettle, milk, sugar and tea-bags, with a sign which invites thirsty visitors to make themselves a cup of tea. A simple, but marvellously effective gesture, which sends out a unique message of welcome.

As I walked back to my car the church bells began to ring, which I later learnt was an unsuspected link with my own, and millions of other peoples' childhood. For these same bells were heard by Tom in Charles Kingsley's 'Water Babies', a much loved book that has enthralled generations of children:

> *Once upon a time there was a little chimney-sweep, and his name was Tom. This is a short name, and you have heard it before, so you will not have much trouble in remembering it. He lived in a great town in the North country, where there were plenty of chimneys to sweep and plenty of money for Tom to earn and his master to spend......*

So begins the adventures of the soot-laden boy, who escapes from his cruel master, tumbles into a stream and is then turned into a water-baby by the fairies. A classic tale which has its roots here in the Dales.

Charles Kingsley was born in 1819 in a small village in Devonshire where his father was a curate. He was educated at Helston Grammar School, but as a child he developed a stammer which was to stay with him throughout his life. At the age of nineteen he went to Magdalene College, Cambridge, at first spending most of his time in social and sporting activities, ignoring his studies. However his early doubts about the truth of religion and the difficulties he had reconciling his sexual feelings, quickly left him. He became a devout Christian, devoted himself to his work, and gained a first class degree in the Classical tripos and a Second Class degree in Mathematics.

During this period he fell madly in love with Fanny Grenfell, the daughter of a wealthy family. At first her parents opposed the love-match, but eventually they reluctantly gave in, allowing the couple to become engaged. Kingsley now became ordained into the Church of England and began writing a work on the life of St Elizabeth of Hungary which was to be published in 1848 as 'The Saint's Tragedy'.

In 1844 he and Fanny began what was destined to be an extremely happy married life. He also took up a position as curate in the village of Eversley near Reading where he later became Rector, remaining there throughout his life. Searching to crystallize his religious thoughts, he was influenced by the radical theology of F.D. Maurice and the writings of Carlyle. He liked to think of himself as a Militant Christian, spearheading the fight for social reform. He was drawn to a group of like-minded people, which included Thomas Hughes who wrote Tom Brown's School Days. Together they published the periodical, Politics for the People.

His literary career got underway with his first novel, Yeast (1848), followed by Alton Locke (1850), both of which reflected his concern for the terrible poverty which prevailed in many cities at this time. His writings over the next decade included Hypatia (1853), which attacked the fanaticism of the early church, and his celebrated novel of Elizabethan adventure, Westward Ho! (1855). His outspoken views, together with his ever growing literary reputation quickly made him into a popular establishment figure. He became an influential royal chaplain, then in 1860 he was offered the position of Regius Professor of Modern History at Cambridge, which he accepted.

Like many country clergymen of his time he developed a great love for natural history, being particularly fascinated by the life to be found in streams, rivers and along the sea-shore. This drew him here to the Dales where he stayed with his friend, Walter Morrison, a wealthy landowner who had a home named Middle House at Malham. The unique landscape he discovered as he explored the waterways of the limestone-country, became his inspiration for the 'The Water Babies' (1863). Many of the places to be found in his book are based on actual sites, including 'Vendale' which is Littondale, 'Lowthwaite Crag', Malham Cove and the river which is the Aire.

The Water-Babies, is now firmly established as a children's classic book of timeless appeal. In 1979, over a century since it first appeared in print, it was made into a film made partly on location in Yorkshire. Directed by Lionel Jeffries the cast appropriately included Huddersfield born James Mason as Grimes, Bernard Cribbens as Masterman and twelve year-old Tom Pender as the young chimney sweep.

Kingsley continued to be outspoken on topics dear to his heart to the end of his life. His theological confrontation with the great Victorian intellect, John Henry Newman, in 1864 was one of the taking points of the decade. But he continued to be regarded as a celebrated man of letters his poetry, ballads and sermons, being as popular as his novels. His last major work was Hereward the Wake (1865), then following a tiring trip to America in 1874 he returned home and died the following year at Eversley, at the age of 66.

3

One of Yorkshire's most spectacular features came into view as I reached the brow of a hill outside Kirkby Malham; the towering white cliffs of Malham Cove. Strangers to the Dales are sometimes surprised to meet the name 'cove' so far inland, for it is a term normally associated with a coastal inlet. But instead of the sea they find the clear waters of Malham Beck mysteriously splashing from beneath a huge curved wall of limestone which rises 240 feet above the valley.

A stream from Malham Tarn, lying on the hilltop a mile and a half above the Cove, once sped down what is now a dry valley to produce a waterfall over the cliff edge. It is said that this was apparent up to two centuries ago, then the water began to disappear on a new course underground. The beck that now flows from under the Cove has been proved to originate from near an old smelt mill on Malham Moor.

I was greeted by the laughter of school children when I arrived in the car-park at Malham village.

'I've finished Sir. Now can I go for a drink to the shop?'

A small brown-eyed boy, visibly sweating from his hilltop observations into the structure of the Mid Craven Fault was addressing his geology teacher. A careful check was made of the contents of his clip-board before permission was at last granted.

As I ate some sandwiches in my car I watched a couple of unlikely, overweight ramblers preparing themselves for their walk. Painstakingly slowly they removed their shoes, replaced these with boots, then went through the long ritual of tying their laces, changing their sweaters and checking that each door of their car was locked. 'We'll start at Janet's Foss then head up to Gordale,' the man uttered to his girlfriend, as they ambled like two bears towards the village.

Although it is estimated that up to a million visitors come to Malham each year, as I strolled through the village I saw hardly a dozen people. I admired the delicate watercolour scenes of the Dales in the souvenir shops, I strolled past the Methodist Chapel and then crossed Monk Bridge to reach the small village green. Some walkers were quenching their thirst in the bars of the Lister Arms and the Buck Inn, while others were striding off in determined fashion towards the cove.

I strolled up a narrow lane, fringed by an ascending carpet of wild flowers, the only sound being the occasional cry of a jackdaw from the trees. This led me past the Youth Hostel to a stone footbridge which crosses the beck close to Beck Hall, a lovely whitewashed building where visitors can eat scones and cream in the garden. This stands on the site of an ancient hall which formed part of the estate of Fountains Abbey.

For several minutes I stood on the bridge, listening to the murmur of the water and watching the antics of a pied wagtail as it hopped from one stone to another. It was then that it suddenly happened. I heard a sound coming from the adjacent lane. Turning, I was just able to catch the blurred figure of a middle-aged man on a mountain bike moving at a fast pace towards the ford that lies alongside the bridge. He zoomed straight into the beck, but just failed to make the far bank before his machine came to a complete stop, stuck fast in the pebbles. His feet firmly wedged in his toe-clips both he and his bike then began to slide, as if in slow motion, sideways into the water. Helplessly I looked on as he wrestled to free himself, until at last he emerged soaking wet but thankfully unhurt. He then began to retrace his path, but this time pushing his bike over the footbridge.

'If you don't try you'll never know, is what I always tell my son,' he uttered as he mounted his trusty machine, disappearing in a trail of water towards the village!

Malham has always been a magnet for walkers and now it has a special place in rambling history. For it was here in April 1965 that our first long-distance footpath, the Pennine Way, was opened in an informal ceremony led by government minister, F.T. Willey and that celebrated walker and writer, Tom Stephenson. From this simple beginning in just thirty years, has grown an amazing network of similar trails which provide walking routes into the heart of our countryside.

I am told that the spark of the idea of a long-distance pathway was first ignited in the early thirties. The editor of the Northern Rambler, Edwin Royce, showed a few keen walkers a photograph of the Appalachian Way in North America. He suggested that a similar walking route could be planned across the Pennines and his idea was greeted with enthusiasm. This spurred him on to contact Lancastrian journalist Tom Stephenson who at this time was working in London. The two men began pouring over maps, trying to link a maze of paths into one continuous trail. In 1938 a conference of interested parties was held. There followed an in-depth survey of the proposed route which revealed that over the 250 miles from

The huge limestone cliffs of Gordale Scar

Edale in the Peak District to Kirk Yetholm near the Scottish border, 90 miles
of new footpaths would be required. The war intervened, so it was 1951
before the Pennine Way was at last given official government approval by
Hugh Dalton, and another 14 years before it became a reality.

As I walked along the waterside pathway which leads to Gordale Scar I
was thinking that if there were Seven Natural Wonders of England then
this must surely be on the list. The broad valley, with its scores of shades
of delicate greens, quickly narrowed to bring me closer to the white gash
in the hillside which marks the scar. At last I reached a sharp bend
alongside the stream to be greeted by the huge walls of limestone that soar
spectacularly upwards on both sides of the gorge, almost touching at the
top. Here I stopped in hushed silence to take in the magical scene. The glint
of sunshine on the dripping silver rock, the boulder strewn pathway, the
tinkle of the water and the almost frightening height of the chasm as I
looked upwards towards a narrow band of blue which was the sky.

I continued my walk into the magnificence of this gorge which ends
where the beck leaps down in two waterfalls from the open moorland
above, the upper one pouring through a hole in the rock. Here I stopped to
watch two walkers who were ascending the path, which involves a short
scramble up a rockface. This view of these two figures allowed me to see
the true scale of these craggy heights which ascend over four hundred feet.

With only the rustle of the wind and the occasional echoing caw of a
crow, I stood and watched as the walkers slowly disappeared from my view
up the pathway. Once more I had the splendour of this savage ravine to
myself where I stayed for half an hour before returning to Malham village.

4

On a sunny afternoon I took the road from Malham that winds upwards
between the Cove and Ewe Moor. After two miles it levels out to reveal
a sea of green hills which are interspersed with boulders and pavements
of white limestone. The marvellous contrast of these colours, together with
the summits which are inviting and not in the least bit menacing, lie at the
heart of the appeal of the Dales.

Soon I was looking out on the silver waters of Malham Tarn, partly
shrouded by trees. Here the Pennine Way skirts the far shoreline, overlooked by the rising hillside which hides the highpoint of Parson's Pulpit.
Although by Lakeland standards this is a small patch of water, measuring
only half a mile long, in a land full of rivers and waterfalls which has

precious few lakes, it is jealously guarded. It is now a nature reserve, but was once the property of Fountains Abbey whose monks held the fishing rights. Last century, as well as being the inspiration for Kingley's Water Babies its pathways also resounded with the footsteps of John Ruskin and Charles Darwin who came here as the guests of Walter Morrison.

Curlews were gliding over fields glowing golden with buttercups, sheep were contentedly chewing at the emerald grass and crows were sending their ominous call down the valley. Suddenly, through the windscreen of my car I saw my first view of the sharp blue profile of Ingleborough, then it quickly disappeared. But a few moments later it was replaced by the equally dramatic outline of Pen-y-ghent, looking like a huge whale marooned in a green ocean. This too quickly fell from my sight for I was now descending a steep twisting road, which had I made one wrong move would have buried my car deep in the rooftops of Settle.

Before exploring this ancient market town I followed in the footsteps of generations of travellers to the oddly named Ye Olde Naked Man cafe, to replenish my flagging energy. Sipping a cup of coffee with a plate of sandwiches before me, I sat in splendid contentment looking out as the townsfolk went about their business. The women of Settle were shopping with relaxed enjoyment, perhaps unaware they were carrying on a tradition which stretches back over 800 years ago. The town was granted its market charter in 1248 but this is considered by the local people to be merely yesterday, for 'Setel' was an ancient settlement when it was first recorded in the Domesday Book. Its first residence was Victoria Cave which sits high above the present town. This was occupied by a Neolithic family some 5000 years ago, and still acted as a useful hiding place in the fifth century when the Anglo-Saxons began their invasion.

Reluctantly leaving this popular cafe, once an inn, I strolled out to explore the town. At its centre is the small open Market Place, marked by a 19th century Tuscan Column and overlooked by The Shambles. Bedecked with colourful hanging baskets, this is an impressive two-storey building which has shops below and a row of cottages above. Nearby, on the wall of what is now a branch of the National Westminster Bank I stopped to read a plaque which relates: 'Edward Elgar often stayed here at the home of his friend, Dr. Charles William Buck.' The friendship between one of our greatest composers and this little known country doctor began in 1882. Buck was attending a BMA event near Elgar's native Worcester when he was first introduced to the great man. Their mutual love of music first drew them together in a friendship that was to last half a century until Buck died in 1932. Just around the corner I discovered another historical link, the site of the birthplace of the Rev. Benjamin Waugh (1839 – 1908). Although his name is largely unknown to most people, as the founder of The Society for the Prevention of Cruelty to Children, his social contribution has been immense.

I then wandered for an hour up the narrow, quiet streets which climb steeply upwards, hiding a jumble of old cottages and solid stone houses. These are overlooked by a prominent limestone highpoint, Castleberg, from which flutters a flag. After gazing into a shop, which must surely be one of the few places in England where donkey-stones and mustard-baths can be bought, I strolled down to the lower part of the town. Passing secluded antique shops and the marvellously named Cobweb Cottage, I found myself at a Quaker Meeting House which boasts a date of 1618.

'Do come in. We've just finished setting up the exhibition of old photos. If you recognise any of the places please let me know for we are unsure of some of them.'

I had been greeted by a healthy looking man who was full of enthusiasm. He had mistaken me for a local, for which I was flattered. It seems that in spite of having a camera slung over my shoulder I did not strike him as being an obvious tourist.

The photographs, which dated back over a century, gave a splendid insight into the changing face of the Craven district in which Settle lies. I admired the formal dignity of the Victorians and Edwardians at both work and play; I looked at buildings which were old when the photos had first been taken and which still remain; I gazed at some of the first cars to be seen in Yorkshire and saw an early aviation pioneer who landed in a field near Settle to top his machine up with petrol!

The River Ribble curves its path on the west side of the town, which can be crossed by two bridges to reach the old village of Giggleswick – a name which, had it been found in Lancashire, would surely have become the butt of many a comedian's jokes. However it is said to have been derived from the name of a Norse chieftain named Gigel, but knowing the reputation such men had for ferocious activity it is unlikely that anyone would have ever suggested that his name was funny.

'I've been told that the grave of Russell Harty lies in Giggleswick. Could you please tell me how to get there?'

Leaning out of my car window I had summoned the help of a young woman who was busy hanging out washing in the garden of her cottage.

'Yes he's buried here in the churchyard, but it's the new part at the back. You won't have any trouble finding it for there are only a few new graves, but you may have trouble parking. Just turn right at the junction and the church lies around the corner.'

Giggleswick church

I thanked her for the information then two minutes later I was parking my car in the last space available in the narrow, deserted village street. The hot sun was beaming down and the door of the Black Horse pub looked most inviting, but no I had a mission to complete. I entered the churchyard thinking to myself how lucky these Yorkshire folk really are to live in such a peaceful setting, then it happened – the bells began to ring out. But 'ring out' is the wrong term, for they boomed and boomed and boomed with such intensity that I feared for the structure of the church tower. The jackdaws which had been chattering contentedly in the trees began to scatter and the swifts zoomed off like jet fighters in the direction of Settle. Thankfully, after about three minutes the noise ended as quickly as it had begun, but for the rest of the afternoon I could still hear it in my ears. I then watched at a distance as the church door slowly opened, half expecting a demented Quasimodo to emerge. But instead strolled out an angelic group of blonde haired school children together with their equally respectable teacher who had been giving them lessons in campanology. He smiled, blissfully unaware that his pupils had emptied the area of its bird population and had probably frightened away scores of free-spending tourists!

Giggleswick church is dedicated to the little known Saint Alkelda. She was a Saxon who died for her Christian beliefs by being strangled at the hands of a band of Danish women. Her name is remembered at only one other church in England which is also in Yorkshire, at Middleham. Following the instructions I had been given I walked to the back of the building, then continued along a neat path past the old graves to the marble stone which marks the final resting place of Russell Harty. A simple inscription remembers 'a dearly loved brother and uncle who died 8th June 1988, aged 53 years', together with a bunch of red carnations.

Remembered by millions of TV viewers like myself, who enjoyed his carefree interviews with the famous, Russell Harty was a Lancastrian whose heart was forever here in Yorkshire. He was born in Blackburn in 1934, also the hometown of opera singer Kathleen Ferrier and fell-walker, Alfred Wainwright. He often boasted that his father, who dealt in fruit and vegetables, was the first person to introduce the avocado to the town. Being a bright boy he gained a place at Oxford reading English, then followed a career in teaching. This included a period at the University of New York and also as a master here at Giggleswick's famous school, but his real aim now was to become a broadcaster.

His first steps in this direction came when he joined BBC radio, producing arts programmes and book reviews for the Third Programme. His leap into television came in 1970 when he went to LWT to join Humphrey Burton in the popular Aquarius series. He later became a household name with his highly acclaimed documentaries, then later as the host of his own series of award winning interviews. At the same time he continued to work on the radio, also finding time to write a column in the Sunday Times.

To escape from the blaze of publicity which now inevitably followed him, when possible he would escape to the peace of his cottage here in Giggleswick which he loved. In 1987 in a new televsion series he followed in the footsteps of the 18th century English aristocracy who undertook the famous Grand Tour of the continent. Mr Harty's Grand Tour, which took the armchair traveller on a journey from London to Naples, was brought alive by his searching mind and witty dialogue. This was published in book form by Century Hutchinson the following year. Sadly, around this time his health rapidly began to decline which led to his premature death the following year.

In St Alkelda's churchyard I admired an array of poppies and foxgloves whose perfume filled the air. On an ancient tomb I found a well-used tobacco pouch which I assumed some local man had mislaid; this I later placed inside the church. There I looked at stone coffin lids, effigies of knights, a memorial to George Birkbeck who had 'industry and inflexible perseverance' which led him to found the London Mechanics Institute. Then I read that 'a large group from St Margaret's, Thornbury, Bradford' would soon be visiting Giggleswick 'for a picnic lunch, exploring, walking, playing, etc'. I walked away wondering what the 'etc' would be, a pint in the Black Horse perhaps?

5

With the craggy outline of the Lakeland mountains visible on a misty blue horizon I again joined the roaring traffic on the A65 road heading north towards Ingleton and Kendal. But, risking life and limb from the relentless juggernauts I then made a short stop on this roadside at Buckshaw Brow. For here stands what was once a great curiosity which attracted many visitors, the Ebbing and Flowing Well. Although the well was full of water it did not appear to be either ebbing or flowing, so I had risked my life in vain.

Apparently up to the last war, when extensive quarrying disturbed the surrounding water shed, this unique well functioned with rythmic regularity. To the delight of onlookers it would suddenly completely empty and then, after a few minutes, begin to slowly fill up again. Experts believe that this was caused by the water that fed it being trapped in a double chambered cave. This resulted in a syphoning condition which at regular intervals interrupted the flow to the well.

Having thankfully returned with safety to my car I continued my journey northwards, but soon I was able to escape from the noisy traffic into the peace of Clapham village, sleeping in the drowsy sun. Here I sauntered up the empty street towards the bridge which spans the crystal waters of Clapham Beck. It was then that I saw a horse and buggy which had stopped outside the New Inn.

'Ben's twenty years old,' the woman owner told me, 'but he's still a fit horse. My friend has just gone into the pub to buy him a glass of cider which is his favourite tipple.'

Seeing my surprised look she smiled. 'Well he deserves it. He has carried us over six miles in this blazing sun.'

Deciding that I too deserved some refreshment I then went inside the beamed interior of the Clapham Tea Shop to sample more Yorkshire fare. Here I picked up a leaflet which outlined the astonishing activities of the Cave Rescue Organisation based here in Clapham. Since its creation in 1935 as a self-help organisation run by cavers for cavers, it has been

Ben awaits his glass of cider outside the New Inn at Clapham

remarkably successful. But not only does it come to the aid of those trapped in the pot-holes of Yorkshire, it assists walkers, climbers and anyone who finds themselves in difficulties in this wild terrain. Included among the fifty three incidents its members attended in 1994 were:

Sunset Hole: five cavers reported to be in difficulty .... found fit and well, walking back across the fell in heavy snow.
Lost John's Cave: Caver trapped by moving boulders...died at 01.01 during evacuation.
Catrigg Force: Lamb rescued from ledge behind waterfall.
Ingleborough: Student collapsed near Gaping Gill. Serious asthma attack.
Ingleton Waterfall: Search for woman missing after walking off from her family. Understood to have been depressed.
Pen-y-Ghent: Search for missing walker. Found dead by CRO/SARDA dog.

Of course this invigorating landscape of the Yorkshire Dales, with its limestone pavements and disappearing rivers, is a paradise for those who wish to explore subterranean England. With such marvellous names as White Scar Cave, Death's Head Passage, Jingling Pot, Grey Wife Hole and Black Shiver Pot it is a world which remains forever hidden from all but the stout hearted. However even among this band of tough underground explorers, one cave is regarded with the greatest respect for it is considered to be the finest in Britain. Standing above Clapham on the rising slopes of Ingleborough stands this funnel shaped depression which measures about 20 feet across. Down it tumbles a stream of silver water which falls an astonishing 340 feet into the inky blackness of the chamber known as Gaping Gill.

A century ago this marvellous cavern remained an awe inspiring puzzle for no one had yet managed to conquer it. In the 1840s John Birkbeck, by temporarily diverting the stream, had descended to 200 feet. He became the first man to see the main chamber, but was forced to retreat well short of the bottom.

It was fifty years later that a group of members of the Yorkshire Ramblers led by Edward Calvert decided they would make another attempt, however they had left it too late. For in 1895 French caving fanatic Edward Martel arrived here in Clapham intent on making the first descent. Over a hundred people watched with fascination as he disappeared into the terrifying chasm. Well equipped with a lantern, candles, flares, a life-line and surprisingly a telephone, he slid first down a rope then reached a rope-ladder which had been attached. Just twenty three minutes later he reached the floor of the magnificent chamber, which at 500 feet long and 100 feet wide is almost as big as York Minister!

Since that first great descent of Gaping Gill it has been found that three main passages branch away from the chamber, stretching for several miles and new secrets continue to be revealed. But those who are not experienced pot-holers can still enjoy the thrill of seeing this marvellous natural cavern. Each Spring and August Bank Holiday the Craven Pot-holing Club winch visitors down into the murky depths in a bosun's chair.

Lovely Clapham village, with its mellow stone cottages shrouded by elm and beech and its flowing beck is a delight to explore. It can trace its roots back to Anglo-Saxon England, but it is the Farrer family who once lived in impressive Ingleborough Hall who have helped to shape its present face. They became generous benefactors of the village, and planted a large stretch of woodland and created a lake. Their most famous member was Reginald Farrer who died in 1920 at the early age of forty. He was our greatest expert on alpine flowers at the time, his search for rare plants taking him to the Himalayas and the Far East. A Reginald Farrer Trail has been created as his memorial and his former home is now an education centre used by school children.

In 1954 the Yorkshire Dales National Park was created, embracing 680 square miles it became the third largest in the country. Here at Clapham one of six National Park Centres for the area has been created which provide visitors with all manner of information. Here too stand the offices of Dalesman and Cumbria magazines; two much loved publications that were the brainchild of Harry J. Scott over half a century ago. With their fascinating features and magnificent landscape paintings they continue to attract many thousands of dedicated readers each month.

As I walked back to my car I read one other interesting snippet of information from my guide book. The village blacksmith who died here in 1867, was the father of Michael Faraday, the great electrical engineer.

I took the old road to Ingleton which contours below the limestone slopes of appropriately named Grey Scars. When I reached the village my car was halted by a crowd of mourners who were leaving the Norman church of St Mary's. Clothed in black their faces bore the expression of relief that we all feel when the ordeal of a funeral has ended.

'Sorry we can't stay longer but we have to get back home. Perhaps we will see you soon on a happier occasion.'

The grieving widow put on a brave smile and thanked the departing couple. She turned as they drove away, knowing that she would not see them and that she was now frighteningly alone.

Ingleton, with its magnificent waterfall walk, became a prominent tourist centre in 1849 when the first railway arrived here. I have some happy personal memories of the village, for it was here at the age of eleven that I spent my very first night in a Youth Hostel. I will forever remember the dour celtic voice of a scotsman, who in the Common Room in the evening had us all enthralled by his hilarious traveller's tales.

He told us that he had had several terrible nights the previous year in Glencoe, for in the dormitory was a man who snored so loudly that no one else could get to sleep. Only when we all retired did we realise that he was in fact talking about himself. His unrelenting snores reverberated like a machine gun around Ingleton Hostel throughout that night!

Chapter Four

The Yorkshire Dales to Richmond

*I climb Ingleborough, learn of the tragedies and triumphs of the
Settle to Carlisle Railway line, admire the Ribblehead Viaduct,
then reach Upper Wharfedale where I remember J.B. Priestley. In
Hawes I hear how Wensleydale Cheese was saved, I look at
England's highest waterfall, then I ascend Buttertubs Pass to reach
Swaledale. I have a drink in our highest pub, pass through remote
Arkengarthdale, stop in the James Herriot Country, then learn
about the Green Howards and the Lass of Richmond Hill.*

1

A stranger to the Dales may at first be confused by the term Three Peaks,
which is often the topic of conversation in pubs and cafes in these
parts. For the area is of course blessed with not just three, but scores of
lofty summits. However walkers, runners and even cyclists, who normally
prefer to ride over less rugged terrain, have taken to their hearts these three
Yorkshire mountains, named Whernside, Ingleborough and Penyghent.
After driving around these limestone lanes it soon becomes apparent where
their appeal lies, for like friendly giants their presence seems to dominate
the landscape.

Whernside, whose summit is 2,414 feet (736m) above sea level, is the
highest of the three. Its long ascending ridge divides Kingsdale from
Chapel-le-Dale, overshadowing the dramatic Ribblehead Railway Viaduct
which is the pride of the famous Settle to Carlisle line. Across the valley
rises the marvellous, unmistakable profile of Ingleborough, which at 2,373
feet (723m) is only slightly lower than its neighbour. Shaped by the
elements for tens of thousands of years, it stands god-like over the villages
of Clapham and Ingleton. Penyghent, which completes the trio, lies beyond
Horton-in-Ribblesdale in magnificent isolation. With a shape often com-

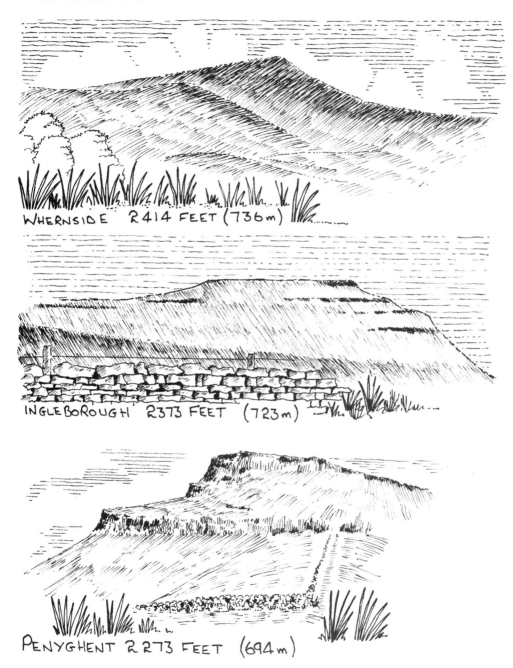

WHERNSIDE 2414 FEET (736m)

INGLEBOROUGH 2373 FEET (723m)

PENYGHENT 2273 FEET (694m)

pared to a crouching animal its rocky outcrops and steep grassy slopes end at a highpoint of 2,273 feet (694m).

The startling beauty of the Three Peaks, lying as they do amidst the largest limestone outcrop in the country, has been recognised by travellers for centuries. When the turmoil of the French Revolution made it too hazardous for the aristocracy to make the Grand Tour, some came here to view the splendour of their homeland for the first time. This coincided with the Romantic Movement, when poets, artists, writers and explorers began to revel in the delights of nature, often grossly exaggerating the 'savage landscape'. Thus started the trickle of visitors to the Dales which today has developed into a major source of local employment.

But it was two teachers from Giggleswick School, D.R. Smith and J.R. Wynne-Edwards, who first created in July 1887, what is now the famous Three Peaks Walk. They began by climbing Ingleborough, then after having tea as it was a fine evening they decided to continue over nearby Whernside. Having conquered two summits the third peak of Penyghent seemed ever inviting, so this they ascended on their way back to the school. The complete circuit of about twenty seven miles had taken them fourteen hours and by chance, a classic walk had been born. Other ramblers, having heard of the teachers' success, followed their lead, quickly making the Three Peaks 'a must' for all strong walkers. The rules which are generally accepted are simply that each summit must be reached during the walk, which must begin and end at the same point. Fell runners have also fallen under the spell of these Yorkshire mountains, beginning what has become one of the most popular races in their calendar in April 1954. Not to be outdone the cyclists also created an annual Three Peaks Cyclo-Cross event in 1961.

Deciding that no journey through Yorkshire would be complete without climbing at least one of these summits, on a dull but warm day I parked my car near the Old Hill Inn at Chapel-le-Dale, intent on climbing Ingleborough. I left the road at a signpost to join a well-worn path across a green meadow. The soaring heights of the mountain lay directly ahead, cloud swirling across its craggy crest. After a few hundred yards I came to a sign that welcomed me to Ingleborough, stating that the 'Ingleborough National Nature Reserve was opened on the 7th June 1993 by H.R.H. The Prince of Wales.'

Healthy looking cows with wide-eyed calves were contentedly eating the grass beneath a limestone pavement. These pale-grey natural outcrops sweep along the dale for five miles, patterning the landscape with a strange moon-like appearance. They are said to have been formed by the scouring action of glaciers which rumbled their way down this valley over 10,000 years ago. The large blocks which are known as clints, are separated from each other by crevices called grikes where many wild flowers have found a fragile hold. At this point I looked back towards the road, then beyond to the long whale-like outline of Whernside lying across the valley. I could clearly see a track winding its way up the side of the mountain with the high-point, unlike Ingleborough, free from cloud.

The path then brought me to a deep conical depression in the hillside which I estimated to be around fifty feet deep. My map revealed it to be named Braithwaite Wife-Hole, one of a series of shake-holes and pot-holes that litter this unique terrain. Its steeply sloping sides were covered in grass, leading to a narrow rocky base in which a small ash tree was growing. This sturdy, graceful tree is one of the few species which flourishes in these narrow limestone crevices. Each year the countryman watches the annual contest between the ash and the oak to see which one bursts into leaf first. This is believed to be an indication of the summer rainfall which will follow, given in the verse:

Oak before ash, we're in for a splash;
Ash before oak, we're in for a soak!

Beyond this point the incline began to get steeper, then I reached what looked like a long brown snake which had lain itself over the peat. Soon I was to discover that this was a monotonous walkway of wood which had been laid out to save the boggy land from erosion which would result from the army of boots that pass this way. This hard surface is far less pleasant to walk upon than the soft turf, but no doubt it is needed. Later I came upon several sacks of small stones in huge canvas hold-alls, which in this isolated spot had probably been dropped by helicopter. I assumed that these would be used to cover over the wood, hopefully making it less slippy and easier to walk upon.

I stopped to rest at the point where the walkway ended and where the side of Ingleborough seems to rise almost perpendicular into the sky. Looking to the north I could now see the curving arches of the Ribblehead Viaduct in the far distance, the narrow road that leads to Hawes, and the ever present bulk of Whernside. Below me, in a long silver line, lay the glistening limestone pavements sweeping down the valley towards Ingleton. Among this fascinating tumble of rocks lies England's biggest cave, White Scar. Formed 200,000 years ago it winds its underground path towards the heart of Ingleborough, revealing a fascinating world of stalactites, stalagmites and hidden waterfalls.

A series of punishing rocky steps now led me up the steepest part of the mountainside till at last I reached the green ridge which links Simon Fell to Ingleborough, allowing my first glimpse of a misty Penyghent. Still ascending, but now at a more civilised incline I finally reached the large summit plateau which covers around 15 acres. Here I met a Jewish man and his young son, whom I identified by their traditional scull caps. I wondered if they were aware how similar Ingleborough is to their famous sacred Massada which stands in Israel, high above the Dead Sea. For both were hilltop fortresses that were used as a refuge from the menace of the Roman legions at opposite sides of the Roman Empire. Ingleborough was the highest fortress in England having been built during the Iron Age. It is believed to have been manned by the native Brigantes during the first century in what turned out to be a futile gesture to fight off the powerful invaders.

The high point of the mountain I discovered, has an array of landmarks around which were dotted small groups of walkers. They greeted me with a cheerful 'How do,' for there is a friendly comradeship to be found on the hills that is sadly lacking in many cities. I feel that this is an acknowledgement that mountains cannot be bought but only conquered by personal effort. Up here a refreshing if temporary, atmosphere of equality pervades, where the millionaire cannot be distinguished from the dustman.

With the sound of a low-flying Tornado Jet filling the air I wandered over to trig-point number S5619 which marks the summit. Several stone cairns lie close by together with a well constructed cross-shelter. This was built in 1953 by the Ingleton Fell Rescue Team to mark the coronation of our present Queen. A pile of stones on the eastern edge testifies to a less successful construction, where in 1830 mill-owner Hornsby Roughsedge built a hut where walkers could rest. However its downfall came with the official opening ceremony when those present celebrated in the traditional way by drinking its good health. The ale must have been of a strong Yorkshire brew, for the celebration got out of control ending only when the newly erected building had been half demolished!

With the mist swirling over the plateau I sat overlooking the wild descending hillside, eating salmon sandwiches and drinking hot coffee from my flask. I was joined by a couple of unusually friendly Swaledale Sheep who demanded a share of my food. Eating out of my hand, it seems they now prefer to feast on tit-bits given by climbers instead of the rough Pennine grass.

Ascending the path from Ingleton came a middle-aged woman, who in spite of the cool breeze often present on the tops, was wearing brief shorts.

She was accompanied by a fit-looking brown spaniel who headed in my direction then began to bark loudly at me.

'Stop it Honey, stop it,' she shouted in vain.

'He won't do you any harm. He seems to love other animals but hates the human race.' She went on to tell me that the previous day Honey had accompanied her on a fifteen mile walk over Whernside and today they were ascending both Ingleborough and Penyghent. Little wonder that he was barking!

After looking over the precipitous rocky cliffs known as Black Shiver and The Arks I began the muscle-tugging descent to Chapel-le-Dale. Then, as many walkers do, I celebrated my One Peak Walk in the bar of the 17th century Old Hill Inn.

2

I took a narrow leafy lane that was resounding with birdsong; this led me to a little church which hides in a corner of Chapel-le-Dale surrounded by the rising fells. In the bright sunlight I walked past leaning tombstones that were half hidden by the gold of buttercups, then I entered the building where I was greeted by a sign which read:

Welcome to St Leonard's Church, Chapel-le-Dale, in the name of our Lord and Saviour Jesus Christ. For hundreds of years there has been a church on this site. It is believed that it was once used as a resting place by monks travelling between monasteries. It serves a vast parish, includes much of Whernside and Ingleborough, and is inhabited by thousands of sheep, but only a few dozen people. Last century the human population grew to thousands for a time to include the men who were building the famous Settle to Carlisle Line. Over 200 of these lost their lives through accident or disease and they were buried in the churchyard. A plaque on the wall commemorates them. There is a service every Sunday afternoon at 3.0 pm and you are warmly invited to join us.

Sitting alone in a quiet corner I began to think of the twist of fate that lured so many men to a premature death in this wild and lovely dale. Living as we do in this Age of Technology which each year brings to us a host of marvellous new inventions that are so readily accepted, it is difficult to comprehend just how profound was the impact of the first passenger railways of the last century. For as the twin lines of steel began to snake their way across our countryside England would never be quite the same ever again. Cities, towns and villages and much of the countryside had for the first time become easily accessible to the many, bringing with it a change that is still felt today.

But another aspect of these first railways was the vast sums of money that businessmen believed there was to be made in the new venture. This led to rival railway companies competing for the more lucrative lines, which included the ones which linked London to Scotland. In the 1860s the London and North Western Railway (LNWR) was ahead of the pack in the North West, for their line went to Carlisle. Their powerful rivals, the Midland Railway Company, could only take passengers as far as Ingleton, who then had to join the trains of the LNWR. This was a situation which Midland boss James Allport found impossible to tolerate; striking out for independence he decided that a new line must be built.

An amazingly ambitious plan was put forward to build a new line from Settle to Carlisle across some of England's most hostile terrain. It would need to span long boggy valleys and cross over craggy limestone mountains, facing hazards which could only be guessed at. At one stage the Midland began to have second thoughts about their scheme, but by this time it was too late. In 1866 Parliament had passed the bill and the company was now committed.

Three years later, in 1869, a massive army of five thousand tough navvies came here from all over Britain to begin what was destined to be the last railway to be built entirely by manual labour. The astonishing 72-mile track took seven years to complete and cost almost double the original £2m estimate. The problems created by the uncompromising plan were immense, for to ensure fast speeds the gradients were not allowed to be greater than 1 in 100. Twenty one huge viaducts spanned the valleys, fourteen separate tunnels were driven through the rocky mountainside and three-hundred and twenty one bridges had to be built.

The blood, sweat and tears that were shed to produce one of the world's greatest feats of engineering ended when it was finally completed in 1876. However a terrible toll in human life had been paid, not only through accidents but also by disease. For at a time when health and safety at work had not been recognised the men had to labour in appalling conditions. For years they had lived in windswept camps that had been erected in the most inhospitable of terrain along the line. To some of these shanty towns they gave names such as Batty Wife and Jericho, but all had only basic facilities and primitive hygiene. This inevitably led to the constant threat of killer diseases such as typhoid and cholera.

In the visitor's book at St Leonard's I read the names of the many people who come here to remember those who died. The previous week they had arrived from Florida, Prague, Cambridge, Cornwall, Oxford, and surprisingly, Her Majesty's Tower of London. By desire or maybe by chance, they had discovered in this hidden backwater this unique tale of endeavour.

From the church I drove four miles up the dale to look at the giant Ribblehead Viaduct; this magnificent structure, perhaps more than any other, highlights the genius of these Victorian railway engineers.

Under a clear blue sky with the sun beaming down I walked along a pathway which led me to a small hill where I had a fine view of this impressive structure. Castle-like, it curves across the valley in a series of twenty four arches, seeming to blend quite naturally into the wild landscape. As I watched a small train suddenly appeared down the track. Looking like a child's model it gave a short toot, then sped over the 165 feet high viaduct to quickly disappear in the direction of Dent. Two sheep who were busily eating the grass closeby never even lifted their heads; they are well accustomed to its sound.

After its completion in 1876 the Settle-Carlisle line became an important section of the romantic London to Scotland service, carrying passengers northwards through the night to Glasgow, Edinburgh and on to the Highlands. But tourists soon recognised that this was also the most scenic track in England. For sitting in armchair luxury they could have a close view of some of our wildest scenery.

The Ribblehead viaduct

However the decline of the railways, which became more apparent after the second world war, slowly began to cast a dark shadow over the future of the line. The high cost of maintaining so many tunnels and viaducts became a crucial factor which eventually led to plans for closure in the early eighties. This caused an outcry from many different organisations who became united in their fight to save the line. The dispute rolled on for many years until at last, under the weight of public opinion, the Government was forced to abandon the plan. Today the Settle-Carlisle line has become a success story, with the Dales Rail service providing a unique gateway to this dramatic countryside.

I strolled back to my car which had been parked close to a T-junction near a roadsign that read: Ingleton 6, Hawes 11 and Horton-in-Ribblesdale 6. I decided that I would head for Horton, but first I would join a small group of other visitors who were cooling down by devouring delicious looking ice cream cones. These had been bought at a mobile stall which stands close to this junction, appropriately named The Fourth Peak!

3

As I drove southwards down Ribblesdale, with the rising greenness of Ingleborough on my right and the infant River Ribble on my left, I suddenly became aware of the marvellous sense of freedom that prevails in these Yorkshire Dales. It is a freedom contagious, for a stranger who might feel depressed and despondent in the greyness of suburbia, having arrived here becomes a different person. The reassuring presence of soft rounded fells, of ancient farmhouses and inviting inns seems to create a feeling of optimism; it is a timeless landscape in which doubts and fears seem to miraculously melt away.

Horton-in-Ribblesdale, which often resounds with the laughter of walkers and cyclists, seemed to be sleeping in the noon day sun. A child looked with interest from a cottage door as I drove past, but an ageing collie defiantly refused to even glance in my direction. Instead he plopped his plump body down on the warm grass, closed his eyes, then began to dream of chasing sheep.

At Stainforth I turned left to join a narrow mountainous road that winds its way between the high summits of Penyghent and Fountains Fell. Crossed by the Pennine Way these spectacular uplands stretch ever onwards, brown and barren to the sky. Once owned by Fountains Abbey which gave the lower of the two fells its name, here coal was once mined but this ended many years ago. Today only the sheep farmer can make a precarious living from this beautiful but inhospitable land of curlews and larks and peregrine falcons.

I continued through lovely Littondale, a remote community of hamlets and villages that remain untouched by the passing of time. Here where Kingsley came to write his Water Babies, I'm told the local families still talk proudly of their ancestors who fought bravely, not at Dunkirk, but at Flodden Field in 1513!

Wharfedale looked magnificent in the bright sunlight, the tender green of its riverside foliage contrasting vividly with the clear blue sky. Fishermen filled with resolute determination were heading for the river near Kettlewell. While less disciplined individuals (whom I was tempted to emulate), were marching in even more determined fashion towards the bars of the Racehorses and the Kings Head.

Hubberholme church

But it was near The George in the hamlet of Hubberholme that I finally parked my car, watched by a group of young American walkers who were suffering from the effects of the hot sun.

'Gee I've just about had enough. How far is it to the bus?' asked a red faced girl of about eighteen who looked as if she might collapse at any second.

'It's only a mile down this lane to Buckden, then we're all finished for today,' answered her male friend with compassion.

The voices of the walkers died away as I strolled over the humped-backed bridge which led me to the tiny church of St Michael that sits on the riverside. With insects buzzing in the churchyard and house martins soaring over the Norman tower it was easy for me to understand why J.B. Priestley chose this idyllic spot as his final resting place. Inside the building I stood in silence reading the words which commemorate this great Yorkshire writer.

John Boynton Priestley, the son of a schoolmaster, was born in Bradford in 1894. He worked first as a junior clerk in a textile office, but at the age of twenty found himself caught up in the turmoil of the First World War, being conscripted into an infantry regiment. When war ended his outstanding academic talent then gained him a degree at Cambridge followed by the start of a promising career in journalism in London.

Here his lifetime of prolific writing began, his breakthrough coming in 1929 when his best selling novel 'The Good Companions' was first published. Plays, novels and numerous other works followed, including his popular north-country farce When We Are Married (1937) and the mystery An Inspector Calls (1947); both of which are still regularly performed in theatres throughout the country.

Having a great love of travel in the autumn of 1933 he undertook his famous 'English Journey' published the following year. Described by him as 'being a rambling but truthful account of what one man saw and heard' he travelled the length of the country. Returning to the Yorkshire he loved he came here to the Dales: 'We stopped, however at Hubberholme, a tiny hamlet that had a fine little church and a cosy inn. There we stayed for lunch.' He went on to tell of his chat with the landlord of the pub and of the fascinating snippets of local gossip that he heard.

During the Second World War J.B. Priestley became a much admired broadcaster on the wireless, his love of England doing much to boost morale at this low period in our history. Full of common sense with uncompromising radical views he did not let age impair his vast writing output. In 1955, with his wife Jacquetta Hawkes, he wrote of his travels in New Mexico in Journey Down a Rainbow, then continued into the late seventies with his volumes of autobiography. An award of the Order of Merit came to him in 1977, seven years before his death in 1984. Although his ashes were buried here in Hubberholme and a statue has been raised to him in his native Bradford, his real epitaph lies in his many volumes that remain for us to enjoy.

4

From a vantage point on a craggy hillside I gazed down on the splendour of a sunlit landscape. Before me stretched this broad valley, lush and green and inviting; in vivid contrast to many of its near neighbours, it had a gentle, soft look about it. Once known as Uredale from its river, in a bout of self improvement it shed this unfortunate name and replaced it with the more pleasing Wensleydale. This was taken from one of the prettiest of the many ancient villages with lie half hidden along is length.

Within minutes I had exchanged the pastoral tranquillity of the uplands for the bustle of Hawes, which due to day after day of unbroken sunshine, had been gripped by a kind of Costa del Sol fever. Visitors had poured into this little town in their hundreds and there was not a tweed skirt or a waxed jacket to be seen. Large brimmed straw hats had replaced deer-stalkers, shorts had replaced corduroys, and many a shirt had been completely discarded to reveal acres of sun-reddened bare flesh. Hawes had not seen temperatures like this for years so it was determined to make the most of it.

I joined these smiling crowds who were parading along the main street. Some were contentedly eating ice-creams, others were admiring flowery cottages which display bed and breakfast signs, but most were looking in the many souvenir shops that cater for tourist needs.

'A nice sheepskin rug would be ideal for Lily. Perhaps a small Wensleydale cheese for Aunt Mary and for goodness sake don't forget that post card for your Fred. No, not that one of the waterfalls, the other with Ribblehead Viaduct would be better. You know he loves trains.'

A sign that announced 'Cream Teas' and 'Spring Lamb with Mint Sauce' was tempting some into the Laburnum Tea Room, while others were heading for the bar of the Bulls Head. I stopped to read the reassuring message carved over the entrance of Crockett's Hotel which states 'Ano Dom 1668, God being with us who can be against,' then I strolled up the ginnel that leads to Kit Calvert's Antiquarian Book Shop. This renowned dalesman was a great book-lover who translated parts of the Bible into the local Yorkshire dialect. His fame however, came not from his book-shop but from another source, for he is forever remembered as the man who saved the ancient Wensleydale Cheese industry.

It is believed that the secret recipe for this tasty product was first brought to these parts from France in AD 1145 by the monks of Jervaulx Abbey. They are said to have used ewe's milk in its preparation, for they were also successful sheep breeders. After the Dissolution it was the farmhouses of the Dales which continued to produce the cheese, now using the milk of cows which grazed on the rich limestone pastures. As demand increased during the last century small cheese factories began to spring up, including one at Hawes owned by Edward Chapman. This became an important source of revenue for the local farmers who supplied it with their creamy milk.

But a decline in fortunes came with the depression of the thirties and it seemed that the dairy would be forced to close. However the clay-pipe smoking Kit Calvert would have none of this; he organised a meeting of local farmers at Hawes Town Hall and positive action was taken. United under his optimistic leadership they formed their own company, then they successfully lobbied the Minister of Agriculture and the unique Wensleydale Cheese was saved from oblivion.

Since that time cheese making has continued in Wensleydale but not without its ups and downs. In 1992 the present owners of Hawes Creamery, Dairy Crest, decided to move the local industry to (horror of horrors) rival Lancashire. Again, filled with the memory of Kit Calvert's fighting spirit, opposition mounted which eventually led to production being rightfully resumed here in Hawes.

After browsing for half an hour in the bookshop and buying two volumes of travel, I continued my stroll down the busy street. Reluctantly ignoring the temptation of a Yorkshire Trencher, described as 'a very large Yorkshire Pudding filled to overflowing with roast beef, with potatoes and veg of the day – for large appetites only.' I then lounged with others on a stone bridge watching the silver water of Gayle Beck sparkle in the bright sunlight. Close to the entrance to the old Station Yard, where the Tourist Information Centre and the Dales Countryside Museum are housed, I saw ropemakers busy at their craft. But I was now too hot and too tired to stay long. However my falling energy was soon restored in the cosy seclusion of a vegetarian restaurant whose lady owner told me about the wonder of herbs. She confided that 'Garlic is my favourite ingredient. I put it in most of my dishes.'

Leaving the crowds at Hawes behind I drove a short distance across the lush valley and over the river to the village of Hardrow. I had been told that often this too can be full of visitors but when I arrived it was happily sleeping in rural solitude. Sauntering up the village street I then strolled into the bar of the Green Dragon, not to buy a pint as you might quite wrongly suspect, but to see a waterfall! Nor is this just any waterfall, for it is the longest single-drop waterfall (above ground) in all of England.

However let me quickly explain that it does not pour through the bar of

Gayle Beck, Hawes

Hardraw Force

the Green Dragon, but this is merely the entrance. After paying 60p I was allowed to continue out of the back door of the pub to join a wide pathway which led me across an emerald meadow towards a small wood. I was then confronted with a sign that warned: 'Danger. Beware of Falling Rocks. Do not walk behind the Waterfall.'

After passing the spot where open-air brass band concerts are sometimes held in a natural auditorium, the path led me into a wooded dell alongside the waters of Fossdale Beck. Birdsong echoed through the trees which rose above towering cliffs on which ferns and banks of wild flowers had gained a precarious hold. Suddenly, as I strode around a bend, I was rewarded with my first view of Hardraw Force cascading in silver splendour from a rocky ledge.

As I sat on a grassy bank watching this dancing water it was difficult to assess its true scale. Only when two walkers who were obstinately ignoring the warning sign, had ventured behind the torrent was I able to make a comparison with their height. Before this I would have guessed that it had a drop of around fifty feet, but now I knew that the guide books were right: it was 100 feet high.

I lounged in hypnotic peacefulness on the beckside bathed in the heat of the summer sun. A small boy wandered along the path, then as small boys do, he began to toss pebbles into the water. Soon bored he quickly returned to his parents who were picnicking around the corner. A yellow wagtail, wide eyed and beautiful, began to hop from stone to stone in its hunt for food unaware that I was watching it. An elderly man then decided he would like to cross the beck to get closer to the waterfall. With uncertainty he ventured on to a series of moss-laden stepping stones, then in mid-stream he stopped, seeming to have become frozen with fear. His wife who had successfully negotiated the hazard then began to shout words of encouragement. This seemed to do the trick for he quickly gained his composure and to the relief of us all, reached his goal.

When I returned to the village visitors were still arriving at the Green Dragon to both drink the beer and see the waterfall. With unusual quietness a party of school children was busy capturing the splendour of Wensleydale in their sketchbooks. And four tired walkers were returning to the blazing heat of their cars, watched by a flock of sheep who had been placed inside the churchyard to nibble away the tall grass.

5

I was gripped by a sense of adventure when I read the road sign indicating 'Muker via Buttertubs', for I knew that before me lay some of England's remotest terrain. I engaged low gear, took a deep breath, then began the slow one-in-six ascent of a narrow twisting lane which within a few minutes led me into the clouds. A strange eerie feeling now prevailed, I was alone in a world confined to no more than twenty yards in all directions. A glance at my map beforehand had told me that the pass would level out above the 1600 feet contour, that on my left would be Great Shunner Fell stretching across to the hills of Cumbria, and on my right a sea of summits that form the barrier between Wensleydale and Swaledale. But these I now had to imagine for I remained a prisoner of the mist. Lost to me also was the feature from which this splendid pass is named, The Buttertubs; a series of savage limestone chasms that plunge sheer for a hundred feet into the heart of the hillside.

But then everything changed. I sped out of the mist into the pale yellow sunlight, the rough fellside quickly gave way to a splendid green valley in which tanned men were busy loading hay. I had arrived in the magic of Swaledale. Here I made a short stop in the hamlet of Thwaite, a cluster of cottages which shelter under Kisdon Hill. Behind the hamlet Straw Beck curves around the corner to meet the waters of the Swale, pushing its path eastwards along the dale to link up the villages of Muker, Gunnerside, Feetham, Healaugh and Reeth.

It was my intention to have a snack in the Kearton Guest House at Thwaite, but unfortunately I had arrived at the wrong time for it was closed. It is here that the world's most famous vet, the late James Herriot, loved to devour a meal of home-made sausages. This was after completing his favourite walk which had begun at Keld, followed the Swale past Crackpot Hall to Muker then climbed to the summit of Kisdon Hill, before descending here to Thwaite.

After admiring the colourful gardens, watching the house martins soar overhead and looking at the little red post-box placed here when Victoria was still on the throne, I continued my journey northwards. A lane brightened with the pink of willow herb and foxglove led me into the seclusion of Keld, which marks the end of Swaledale. Here I read a sign on the Youth Hostel door which announced: Sorry, this Hostel is full tonight.

A stranger to Keld may be puzzled why a large hostel in a rather remote part of Yorkshire would be full. The reason is that Keld lies at the most important cross-roads for long-distance walkers in the country. Here the 270 mile long Pennine Way which runs south to north, and the 190 miles long Coast-to-Coast walk which runs west to east, meet. So here those hardy characters who have endured the boggy uplands of the Peak District and the Yorkshire Dales, can exchange tales with those walkers who have scaled the Lakeland mountains. Following their brief encounter, Keld echoes each morning with the laughter of the walkers as they wave goodbye, with the thoughts of Robin Hood's Bay or Kirk Yetholm now firmly in their thoughts.

Just outside the village, which the Norsemen named 'the place of the spring', I was halted by a flock of sheep that were being driven down the lane by a shepherd and his two collie dogs. The sheep were appropriately of the Swaledale breed, which are renowned for being very alert creatures. They are horned, quick moving and tough, which enables them to survive in these isolated uplands through the most hazardous of winters. As they will not wander beyond their own territory within the high hills they are easy animals to shepherd and their wool is in great demand. I am told that as well as being used in the manufacture of some of our finest carpets, a cottage industry has sprung up here producing attractive Swaledale woollen garments.

'Tan Hill Only' was the sign that led me ever upwards, around a series of steep hair-pin bends, then on to a remote moorland road which looked as if it had been lifted from the Scottish Highlands. Little wider than single-track, it snaked its way through a landscape of windswept peaty moorland which swept majestically to the distant horizon. Over the next five miles I met only one other car before at last seeing the welcome sight of Britain's highest pub, the Tan Hill Inn, looming into view. Standing alone at 1732 feet above sea level, the inn lies at the very end of the Yorkshire Dales National Park, close to the point where Cumbria meets Durham in a rugged unspoilt landscape of brown hills.

One traveller who came here in 1906 described the inn as 'one of the most abject, uncompromisingly ugly buildings that ever builder built,' but perhaps he was just tired from the climb! It stands in an isolated position on the summit of Stainmoor at a point where a series of ancient tracks and moorland roads meet. These were once well-used highways which even boasted a toll-house where carriages had to pay a fee, but when the railways came to the valleys this lucrative business ended. At this time the pub was known as the King's Pit Inn, named from a small coal pit which had been sunk on the moor. Trade quickly declined during the second half of the last century which led to the license to sell ale lapsing. But in 1903 it again re-opened as England's highest pub, and is now firmly established on the tourist map and in the Guinness Book of Records.

Although they were experiencing a heat wave in the rest of England a welcoming open fire still blazed in the inn, with a dozing Jack Russell terrier nearby. The low beamed bar was full of visitors: healthy looking women cyclists with plump legs, a party of five middle-aged Americans who were 'doing the Herriot Country', and a pale-faced young couple who were struggling to make inroads into an enormous cheese salad.

'Half a bitter please, and a bag of plain crisps,' I ordered from the young barman.

As he handed me my change he uttered, 'People who eat plain crisps live right on the edge.'

Undecided whether his comment was Yorkshire wit or confrontational sarcasm, I smiled and walked away. My decision not to force a Clint Eastwood style shoot-out was influenced by his demeanour which suggested he might have been on week-end leave from the SAS.

As I sipped my beer in a corner of the room I looked around at the many photographs and press cuttings that line the wall. These included framed pages from Alfred Wainwright's classic guide books, post cards sent to the inn from all over the world, a feature headed 'Pub at Top T'Moor' and a menu that boasted 'Giant Yorkshire Puddings filled with....' a host of fillings.

Before leaving the building I read a fascinating press release which will interest all romantics who wish to win the heart of their true love. Due to a recent change in the law, civil marriage ceremonies can now be conducted at this windswept spot. What girl I wonder, could ever resist exchanging vows in England's highest Inn?

As I drove slowly away from Tan Hill along a narrow lane which cuts into a corner of Durham, I was again filled with an intense feeling of freedom that seems to exude from these high Pennine hills. Looking northwards I could see not a single building, just layer upon layer of rising moorland that stretches ever onwards to meet the sky. It is said that on a clear day both the North Sea and the Irish Sea can be seen from these lofty summits.

In 1973 documentary film maker Barry Cockcroft, made a programme for Yorkshire Television named 'Too Long a Winter' which uncovered the very soul of these isolated dales. His classic study of the life of Hannah Hauxwell, who in middle age lived alone in a remote farmhouse in Baldersdale, captured the heart of the nation. We saw her fighting against the unforgiving snows of winter, feeding her cows and herself in conditions few knew still existed in this country. But the cheerful, uncomplaining personality and natural charm which she displayed is typical of many Daleswomen who live in these parts. For living in such harsh, remote terrain breeds a special kind of independence which inspires both confidence and common sense.

Under a sky filled with silver cumulus clouds I now slowly descended little known Arkengarthdale, along a road that took me over a series of small bridges. These spanned moorland becks, trickling down the hillside to meet the Swale. The land gradually became more fertile, the brown windswept grass turning in places to green meadowland, bringing with it occasional farmhouses and clusters of cottages. I passed Whaw and Booze, then I paused near Langthwaite to admire an impressive roadside cross. This sad memorial is in memory of the men of Arkengarthdale who eighty years ago had their last view of this lovely valley before facing the horrors of trench-warfare in France. This brought to my mind the last inspirational message of 24-year old Stephen Cummins, a soldier from Portsmouth who, following in this heroic tradition, gave his life in the recent conflict in Ireland. In his pocket was found this annonymous 12-line elegy, based upon American Indian beliefs, and has since brought comfort to many thousands who have lost their loved ones:

Do not stand at my grave and weep.
I am not there. I do not sleep.
I am a thousand winds that blow.
I am the diamond glints on snow.
I am the sunlight on ripened grain.
I am the gentle autumn rain.
When you awaken in the morning's hush,
I am the swift uplifting rush
Of quiet birds in circled flight.
I am the soft stars that shine at night.
Do not stand at my grave and cry;
I am not there. I did not die.

6

Many strangers who arrive in Reeth for the first time, then continue to explore the villages of Swaledale and Wensleydale, often have a puzzled look about them. They seem to be wondering why so many landmarks look familiar; have they been here before and perhaps forgotten? The real explanation is that they have entered the 'James Herriot Country' and they are now looking at the dozens of film locations which they have already seen in 48 episodes of 'All Creatures Great and Small'. Scenes which entered their subconscious mind while they sat relaxed in their favourite armchair watching the fascinating life of a country vet, have now become reality.

What few people know is that the real James Herriot was not a veterinary surgeon at all, but a goalkeeper who played for Birmingham City Football Club! The man who devoted his life to the animals of this corner of Yorkshire, then became a best selling author was James 'Alf' Wight. He chose the pen name of James Herriot for his writings after admiring the first class performance of Birmingham's goalie in a game shown on television.

Alf Wight originally came from Scotland where he grew up, then he settled here in North Yorkshire where he began his career as a vet. He became the assistant to Siegfried Farnon and partner Frank Bingham, whose practices covered a vast area that stretched from the remote head of Swaledale, across the North York Moors to the coast. Before arriving here he was under the impression that no English countryside could ever compare to that of his homeland, but he soon changed his opinion. He quickly fell under the spell of this wild and beautiful landscape where he was to remain for the rest of his life.

But it was only when he reached fifty that he decided the time was right to record his adventures with the animals he had grown to love. If Only They Could Talk was first published in 1970 by Michael Joseph, and was followed in 1972 by It Shouldn't Happen to a Vet. These two volumes were then combined as a single edition for publication in America, under the now familiar title of All Creatures Great and Small.

In spite of his literary success he continued with his veterinary practice based in Thirsk. Writing only part time the next few years brought the publication of Let Sleeping Vets Lie and Vet in Harness. But it was when the BBC decided to dramatise his stories in 1978 that James Herriot became the most famous vet in the world and a reputed millionaire. The hugely successful series, destined to run for 13 years, starred Christopher Timothy as the young Herriot and Robert Hardy as his boss, Siegfried.

It was here in Reeth, a lovely village whose houses and pubs are dotted around a large sloping village green, that Christopher Timothy first met Herriot. The actor later acknowledged the help that the modest writer had given to him and spoke of his role in the series that had changed his life. The actors and crew became a familiar sight in the Dales, with Robert Hardy often staying at the Punch Bowl Inn at Low Row, a few miles from Reeth. Many of the original film locations have now been linked to create a scenic drive around a Herriot Trail which meanders through Wensleydale and Swaledale.

After a courageous fight that lasted for three years, James Herriot died of prostate cancer in February 1995 at the age of 78. He was surrounded by his wife Joan, daughter Rosie and his son James, who is carrying on his father's work as a vet. In spite of his terrible illness he was still writing up to just a few months before his death, his last volumes being a series of children's tales about cats.

I now followed a lane which ran along a lush river valley, overhung with sycamore and beech that formed a welcome umbrella against the hot sun. The high Pennines hills had now suddenly vanished to be replaced by the wide Vale of Mowbray. A plump pheasant walked nonchalantly across the road in front of my car as I caught a glimpse of an ancient milestone under a hedge. It was the type of milestone which Dick Whittington and his cat would have recognised, but instead of indicating London the pointing finger told me that it was '4 miles to Richmond'.

By a miracle I managed to slip into an empty parking spot right in the centre of this ancient town, but then I saw the notice which informed me that I was in a Disc Parking Zone. I soon learned that this meant that I needed a sort of cardboard clock, which must be displayed inside each car windscreen to tell any passing traffic warden how long the car has been parked. This disc was lent to me by the friendly proprietor of a nearby travel agent's shop, who was busy booking a Yorkshire couple on a holiday to Marbella. Surprisingly, I was now charged no parking fee, leaving me a couple of hours for leisurely exploration.

I began by walking up the spacious cobbled hill whose summit is marked by a huge market cross that towers 65 feet into the sky. There has been a cross here since Henry VI reigned over England, but the present one is a mere two centuries old! Here, overcome by continental temperatures, a large crowd of both local people and visitors had gathered. They were gulping cold drinks, licking ice cream cones and displaying, for Yorkshire, an unusual amount of bare flesh. But it was not the young girls, as might be expected, but the older men who had discarded most of their inhibitions. Wearing khaki shorts, sandals and no shirts, they were lying back soaking up the sun. Perhaps inspired by a combination of the heat and a road sign that points the way to nearby Catterick Army Camp, they may have been dreaming of the time they fought Rommel in the Western Desert.

Of course Richmond is a town whose military associations go back many centuries, but few regimental museums can compete with that of the local Green Howards. For it is perched here on this marvellous hillside, housed not in some dreary barracks, but in a converted 12th century church. Uniforms, medals, paintings and scores of simple but evocative items, trace the regiment's history back to its formation.

It was first raised in 1688 by Colonel Francis Luttrel as a company of foot. This was at a period of turmoil when the catholic King James II had been deposed, to be replaced by the protestant William of Orange and his wife Mary. As was the practice at this time each regiment became known by the name of its Colonel, altering its name when a new Colonel was appointed. This system led to much confusion, so it was changed in 1751 when the company became part of the 19th Regiment of Foot. Other titles followed over the years until in 1921 it became known officially as The Green Howards: Alexandra, Princess of Wales' Own Yorkshire Regiment. It had taken 'Howard' from the name of one of its most successful former commanding officers and decided to use 'Green' piping and facings on its uniform to mark the difference from The Buffs, who at this time also had a CO named Howard.

The Green Howards have distinguished themselves on battlefields in many corners of the world. They captured Russian drums at the Battle of Alma in the Crimea, saw action in the Boar War, fought in the mud of Flanders and in Galipoli during the First World War, then saw the despair of Dunkirk in 1940 followed by the triumph of El Alamein and final victory in both Europe and Asia. Eighteen Victoria Crosses and three George Crosses bear testimony to their bravery, together with the blood-stained holsters of the Grand Old Duke of York whose exploits we remember from a childhood nursery rhyme. But it is when a veteran hears the haunting refrain of the regimental march, The Bonnie English Rose, that his frame will stiffen with pride. Remembering perhaps, the words of the motto drummed into him as a raw recruit: Evil be to him who Evil Thinks.

7

As I continued my stroll along the byways of Richmond memories came flooding back to me of my school days in the late forties. With horror I remembered a school teacher who we cruelly but appropriately, nick-named Piggy because of his small eyes and pink complexion, speaking those words I dreaded most,

'We will now have a singing lesson.'

Maths and history I could tolerate, but singing I detested. 'Pitch difficul-ties', Piggy would charitably write on my school report opposite the column marked music, but really he meant that I screeched like an owl.

What had brought back these thoughts of childhood were the words of a song that I can still picture in my mind, being chalked up by Piggy on the blackboard. The Lass of Richmond Hill, I discovered, refers to this Rich-mond, not the one in Surrey which many wrongly assume. The 'Lass' was named Frances I'Anson and it was here in 1787 that she received a love letter from Leonard Mcnally with those splendid romantic words which have been sung in every part of the world ever since:

On Richmond Hill there lives a lass,
More bright than May-day morn,
Whose charms all other maids surpass,
A rose without a thorn.
This lass so neat with smiles so sweet,
Has won my right good will,
I'd crowns resign to call thee mine,
Sweet lass of Richmond Hill.

Quietly humming the song to myself (out of tune), I wandered for half an hour along quiet cobbled streets which wind away from the busy town centre, then plummet down the hillside towards the Swale. I admired stout Georgian doors with shinning brass knockers, saw the spot where John Wesley once preached, then I found myself at the castle, dramatically perched at the top of a crag. Before the Normans made Richmond their own, it was a Saxon settlement ruled over by Earl Edwin. The district was known as Richmondshire, a name which still appears on the signposts. The first castle, quickly built of wood with earth ramparts, had been completed by 1100, then over the next two centuries it was replaced by a more substantial structure made from stone. It provided essential protection from the Scots, who persistently raided this area which they believed was part of their territory. This new found security allowed the town to expand, becoming a place of importance in this large rural area.

At the end of a street with the fascinating name of French Wynd, I came upon one of Richmond's finest buildings, the Georgian Theatre Royal. A poster told me that the drama-lovers of Richmond were this week enjoying You Never Can Tell, a play by 'George Bernard Shaw at his most sparkling'. Future productions included A Tribute to Kathleen Ferrier by Carolyn Savory, Jaleo, which 'explores the passions and colour of Andalucian life', and in complete contrast Mary Shelley's Frankenstein.

The people of Richmond are rightly proud of their unique theatre in which many great performers of the past, including Mrs Siddons, have graced the tiny stage. It was built in 1788 by the actor-manager Samuel Butler, with the audience of up to four hundred seated on rows of ascending benches. Sadly, by the middle of the last century its popularity had diminished which led to its doors being closed for almost a hundred years. The building was put to other uses but the structure fortunately remained largely unchanged. In 1940 it was rediscovered and cleaned up, which resulted in the first play of its new era being performed in 1943. Twenty years later it had been fully restored and it is now the only Georgian theatre in Britain to survive in its original state.

I later spoke with a friend of mine, London based actress Valerie Weyland, who played here in January 1995. She took the lead as the Swallow in an operetta of The Happy Prince by Oscar Wilde. Knowing that she is familiar with many of Britain's best theatres, I asked her how this one compares.

'The Georgian Theatre at Richmond is without doubt the loveliest I've ever worked in,' she told me. 'The space is very intimate and the atmosphere which an actor can create in such a charmingly unusual place is unparalleled. I remember we were sold out most nights. It seems that the

Valerie Weyland: a strong supporter of the Georgian Theatre

people of Yorkshire will travel many miles, not just to see a show, but to enjoy the experience of the theatre itself'.'

Leaving the theatre I walked slowly back through Richmond's ancient cobbled streets until finally I arrived at my car. After returning the cardboard parking disc to the travel-agent, who was still smiling, I reluctantly drove away from this most romantic town.

Chapter Five

Richmond to the North York Moors

On the hottest day for three centuries I discover the magic of Fountains Abbey. I visit Ripon cathedral and learn of the Hornblower, then reach Thirsk where I hear about Lord's. I find a White Horse and a Mouseman at Kilburn, learn about Cromwell's corpse, then arrive at lovely Helmsley where the Cleveland Way begins. I catch a glimpse of hidden Rievaulx, cross the isolation of the North York Moors, learn of the macabre Lyke Wake Walk, then remember a friend who is a Munroist.

1

One of the great pleasures of travelling through Yorkshire results from the fascinating contrast in landscape which occurs within just a few short miles. I was now driving down lanes that might have been in Sussex or Berkshire and not on the edge of the wild Dales. For down the centre of the county, wedged between the high Pennines to the west and the North Yorks Moors to the east, is a large fertile corridor of low-lying rolling countryside. This vale of picturesque villages, ruined abbeys and small market towns is watered by a score of winding rivers and becks which include the Swale, the Ure and the Wiske. Down its centre, linking London to Edinburgh is that highway which in this age of technology is known simply as the A1, but which once had the more colourful title of The Great North Road. During that Golden Age of travel in the late 18th century it would have resounded with the noise of whips cracking, horses snorting, and post-horns screeching. Weary passengers, after enduring forty miles of bone-shaking, pot-holed highway from York, would thankfully alight at ancient inns such as The Golden Lion at Northallerton, The Three Tuns at Thirsk, or The George at Catterick. Here, sitting in the warmth of log-fires with light from oil-lamps or candles, they would feast on boiled fowl, trout, mutton and gooseberry pye, washed down perhaps by a glass of punch or a flagon of ale.

With the hot sun pushing the temperature towards the high eighties I drove slowly along quiet lanes which led me through Leyburn, then south into a landscape of large yellow hay-fields, small patches of woodland and secluded farms. For ten miles I met just a handful of cars, for this was the type of weather to stay at home in the garden sipping lemonade under a leafy shade.

'If you go to the left, it's half a mile to the abbey and there is a guided tour at half-past three.'

I thanked the well-spoken woman who had taken my entrance fee at Fountains Abbey, then I stepped out of the cool Visitors Centre into the hot sunshine that had burnt the grass a golden brown. In the distance, peeping out over the treetops, I could see the top of what has become known as Abbot Huby's Tower. This became my guide as I followed the pathway downhill, passing meadow-brown and cabbage-white butterflies resting on thistles, with sheep munching on a distant meadow. Poppies, willow herb and the bright orange of rowan berries added to the array of colour, until at last I gained my first dramatic view of the largest monastic remains in Britain.

Children, dressed as monks, at Fountains Abbey

Many times I have read of the beauty of Fountains Abbey but nothing had prepared me for the splendour that now lay before me. Lying among green lawns in a narrow river valley bathed in the yellow of noonday sunshine, its sudden appearance made me halt. For several minutes I stared in silence at the towering pattern of ornate stonework whose roofless jagged profile ended triumphantly in the blue Yorkshire sky. For although the monks had been sent away from here four centuries ago with five pounds in their pockets; their stained-glass windows smashed, their oak doors ripped from the hinges and the lead taken from the roof, I sensed that King Henry VIII's ruthless act had not been completely successful. His barbarism had merely destroyed the fabric; the very soul of the abbey remains untarnished. Looking upwards towards the half-tumbled stones I had an intense feeling of peace and spirituality, which I am told is the magic of Fountains.

Slowly I strolled down the pathway which led me into the lush valley. Some sun-tanned visitors were picnicking in small groups on the sloping hillside while others like myself, were gazing in wonder at the medieval edifice. For over an hour I leisurely wandered among its ruined walls; I admired the slender columns of the 13th century Chapel of Nine Altars; I looked in wonder at the finely curved arch of the tower; I walked though the shadowy cloisters, thinking that perhaps I was being watched by ghosts; and then, feeling the effects of the hot sun, I found a cool spot on the bank of the little River Skell to sit and dwell on how it all began.

Like so many great establishments Fountains Abbey owes its existence to chance rather than planning. In 1132 when the Conqueror's son, King Henry 1 reigned over England, there existed at York the Benedictine Abbey of St Mary. But it seems there was unrest among some of the brothers who had become dissatisfied with the way the house was being run; they complained of laxity. This dispute grew more serious leading to thirteen monks breaking away from the parent abbey to create their own monastery.

They found encouragement from the saintly Archbishop Thurstan who gave them this land, in what at the time was an isolated rocky wilderness beside the river, full of wild beasts. It is said that the austere order who later became Cistercians, built their first simple thatched church beneath the branches of a yew tree. Then with a determination fired by religious certainty they began to clear the site. Within fifteen years they had constructed a fine Norman church dedicated to Our Lady of the Springs, which they knew in Latin as Sancta Marie de Fontibus and has now become known as Fountains Abbey.

A fire did great damage to the abbey in 1147 which led to a massive rebuilding programme during the next century. This coincided with the ruthless success of the Forth Crusade whose knights had conquered the rival Byzantine Church in Constantinople, bringing back relics and treasures. Fountains, together with many other abbeys, were given some of these riches to which was added many gifts of land. So ironically, the house which had begun as a simple isolated dwelling, quickly grew to become a massive and beautiful building, both powerful and wealthy.

There were two types of monks at the abbey, the Cistercians who came directly under papal control and a lesser order of lay-brothers. The Cistercians and their Abbot, who were often learned men, lived a self-imposed punishing existence. They wore a coarse white habit woven from rough wool with no undergarments. Living almost in complete silence, communicating by simple gestures and eating a frugal diet, they dedicated themselves to a life of prayer to God. The lay-brothers, who in contrast wore brown habits, were often less-educated men who carried out the large amount of physical work needed to run the vast estate.

On the 30th November in 1539, over four hundred years after the first monks had entered this tranquil river valley, Abbot Marmaduke Bradley surrendered Fountains Abbey to Henry VIII. The monks were forced to leave, the building and land were sold off to rich speculators, with some of the stones being used to build Fountains Hall. In the late 18th century it was purchased by William Aisabie and became an extension to the estate of Sudley Royal. Today the fishponds have become water-gardens and thankfully what is renowned as Britain's most magnificent ruin is safe in the care of the National Trust.

'Hail Mary full of grace .....'

Beyond the empty cloisters where beams of sunlight marked the path once trod by the holy monks, came the sound of prayer. Turning a corner I came upon a crowd of children, who dressed in white habits, their faces hidden by cowls, were erasing the centuries. With touching reverence their voices echoed over the lawns and through the arches, to be answered by the cooing of wood pigeons.

Before leaving I tried to capture Fountains Abbey on film, which of course I knew was an impossible task. For although my camera could easily record the shape of its stonework, the unique feeling of utter tranquillity that pervades this holy place remains ever elusive.

2

Although it was the late afternoon when I reached Ripon the hot sun was still beaming down with tropical ferocity. Young girls, now having the perfect excuse to display their long tanned legs, were walking in pairs towards the suburban tennis courts. Dressed in shimmering white with

Ripon Cathedral

their rackets swinging by their sides they could quite easily have stepped out of a John Betjeman poem.

If you remember when I first began this journey, the weather had been so dismal during the spring that people were beginning to prematurely write off the approaching summer. I was now reminded of the remarkable change which has since taken place by the headlines in the Ripon Gazette and Observer which announced: 'Sunshine Tourist Boom'. Britain was now basking in its hottest and driest summer since records began in 1659 which according to the weathermen, was because high pressure had become almost stationary over the country. This resulted in the sales of beer, ice-cream and cold drinks soaring so much that manufacturers could barely cope with the demand. But these sweltering conditions were not being shared by other countries in Europe. As our temperatures hit the 90s the Algarve could only manage the low 70s, and in Greece rainfall that would normally occur over a month has recently poured down in just 12 hours.

After weeks of such weather there has been a noticeable change in both the look of the English countryside and in the way in which people have started to dress. No one can fail to have noticed that the rolling fields, once emerald green, have now been bronzed by the burning sun giving an uncharacteristic Italian look to the Yorkshire landscape. Cows and sheep, perplexed by such conditions lie drowsily in shady corners, while dogs, positively hating the relentless heat can be seen continually panting at their owners' side. But one of the most surprising aspects of this topsy- turvy weather, as I remarked before, is the effect it is having on many men over the age of sixty. I remember from my youth how this age group used to be the most conservative in matters of fashion, but now this has all changed. Many of them can now be seen wearing the briefest of shorts from dawn to dusk. Some seem to be positively strutting, peacock like, about the streets of the towns, often having completely discarded their shirts to reveal sun-tanned, grey-haired chests! Others, recapturing the flavour of yester-year, have taken to wearing sporty Panama hats for which they are willing to pay upwards of sixty pounds. Many middle-aged women seemed mesmerised by the whole affair having discovered a side to their husbands which they never guessed existed.

Another aspect of this dry summer is the shortage of water which has had 'water chiefs praying for rain'. Yorkshire Water being the first of the water companies to enforce a hosepipe ban, have been in the firing line for criticism from both customers and the newspapers. Managers of the company have been photographed on the beds of dried-up reservoirs, explaining how we are experiencing an unprecedented drought with a massively increased demand. They are being answered by claims that a huge amount of water is lost by leaking pipes, on which money should be spent rather than on high profits and 'fat-cat' salaries to chief executives. As these arguments roll on and are likely to continue well into the winter, the question of weather prediction has also been raised. It has been revealed that an amateur weatherman from Yorkshire, 82 year old Bill Foggitt, was more accurate in his long-range weather forecast than the MET office. Bill, whose family have been keeping daily weather records since 1830, scored 88%. The Met office, which employs 2,300 staff, has a budget of £153 million and uses high-tech satellites and computers scored just 74%. Yes this is proving to be a strange year!

I managed to find a parking place in the Market Square lying at the very heart of this busy town, which in common with Skipton, likes to be regarded as one of the 'Gateways to the Dales'. In fact, as I was soon to discover, it has many 'gates' of its own which include Stonebridgegate, Kirkgate and Allhallowgate. However, the term 'gate' merely means 'street', a word probably brought here by the Vikings for it is Scandinavian in origin.

After barely escaping with my life, for Ripon is cursed by nose-to-tail traffic at rush hour, I at last crossed the road and found a shady doorway from which I could observe my surroundings. Opposite lay a high obelisk that dates from the 18th century, having been erected as a replacement for the ancient market cross. On its top stands two symbols of the town's past, a horn and a rowel spur. The latter commemorates the time when the town gained a national reputation for producing spurs which were the accelerators of their day. This local industry which started in Elizabethan times, gave us the now little-known proverb 'as true steel as a Ripon rowel'. A rowel being the small spiked wheel at the end of a spur.

But to find out about the horn, so I have been told, you need to come here to the Market Square at nine o'clock in the evening when the infernal traffic has disappeared and a medieval quietness has returned to the city. You will then see a man emerge from the shadows dressed in a long grey coat with brass buttons, red cuffs and collar, and wearing a three cornered hat. Hanging from his shoulders by stout leather straps you will see a huge animal's horn, which has been embellished with hoops of silver. The man will then proceed to each corner of the square in turn, where he will blow the horn allowing its haunting sound to echo over the ancient rooftops. Strangers look on in amazement while the citizens of Ripon just take it all for granted. After all, the Hornblower has been performing this ritual every night since the Conquest, so the town has had time to become accustomed to him!

The Hornblower now carries out the duties once performed by the Wakeman. He was Ripon's most powerful citizen from the time when the city was first incorporated in 886, up to 1604 when the first Mayor was appointed. The Wakeman was responsible for protecting the houses of the town:

It is ordered that the Wakeman for the time being, according to ancient custom, shall cause a horn to be blown every night during the time he is in office, at nine o'clock in the evening, at four corners of the cross in the market-stead, and immediately after to begin his watch, and to keep and continue the same until three or four o'clock in the morning, and if it happens any house or houses be broken on the gate side within the town of Ripon, and any goods taken away, then the Wakeman shall make good unto the party so wronged such value as the said 12 of his brethren shall adjudge if it can be shown that the Wakeman and his servants did not do their duty at the time.

Looking out over the bustle of the Market Place I could see the 14th century home of Ripon's last Wakeman, Hugh Ripley, who became the first Mayor. It has now been made in to what must be one of England's oldest shops where hand-crafted goods and greeting cards are sold. Nearby stands the impressive Town Hall which dates from 1800, with a message from the Psalms printed on a frieze in large gold letters.

Dodging the traffic again, I walked past the Unicorn Inn where the London coach once changed horses, and continued along Kirkgate which led me into the quiet of the cathedral. This magnificent building was empty except for three agile ladies, all well over seventy, who where discussing the merits of the building.

'I never get tired of coming here Joan, it's really beautiful. You get such a feeling of peace. It's also a pleasure to get out of that heat.'

After buying a guide book I too began to soak up a little of the tranquillity of this holy place. I gazed up at its towering arches, admired the blaze of colour beaming through its stained glass windows, ran my fingers over medieval woodcarvings, and thought of the Norman babies that were baptised eight centuries ago in its ancient font. Then after finding a comfortable seat I began to read a little of its history.

It was Saint Wilfred who was born here in Ripon in AD 634, then went on to become a powerful Christian force in Northumbria, who built the first great church. The Venerable Bede, a contemporary of Saint Wilfred, tells how 'a little monastery was planted in the heathen village of Rhypum about AD 655.' Wilfred, who then became its second Abbot, had one of Europe's finest buildings constructed here in AD 672 which he dedicated to St Peter.

Many scholars believe it was the first stone church to be built in the north. However disaster struck two centuries later when the pagan Danes carried out a devastating raid. Apart from the Saxon crypt which still remains, the entire building was destroyed.

A second church was later built on the site but this too was destined to be destroyed by invaders. This occurred because the men of Northumbria were reluctant to accept the rule of William-the-Conquerer after the Battle of Hastings. When the rebellion was cruelly crushed the new King then laid waste to much of the North including Ripon where the church was destroyed. But a century later this was just a memory, the Normans had by this time become established and had built the third church on the site. However the magnificent cathedral, built in the Norman Transitional style which we see today, was begun in 1154 by Archbishop Roger Pont l'Eveque.

After ending my stroll around this unique building I found myself at the door where the three women were also about to leave.

'No point in you trying to pass through Wilfred's Needle, Joan. It's fifty years too late'

Her comments were followed by loud laughter.

I later learned that in the Saxon Crypt can be seen a narrow hole that is known as Saint Wilfred's Needle. Anyone who can pass through it into the passageway is leading a chaste life!

3

'Yes, this is the house which is now a museum, where he was born. You can see the plaque over the door.'

On another very hot, humid day I had arrived in Thirsk, then I had found my way to the small tourist information centre that stands in Kirkgate. Here a cheery middle-aged man had taken me outside into the ancient street to point out the modest home in which Thomas Lord was born in 1756.

Who was Thomas Lord, you might wonder, for few people outside Thirsk are immediately familiar with his achievement. However, a look of recognition will soon prevail if Lord's Cricket Ground is mentioned. For even those people who are not in the least bit interested in cricket, (if this is you, don't mention the fact while in Yorkshire!), have heard of the most famous ground in the world. Perhaps, like myself, you wrongly assumed that the name Lord's was derived from an aristocratic origin. But I had now discovered that this is not the case, for it is named after its founder who began life here in this small but bustling Yorkshire market town.

Thomas Lord came from a catholic family who moved from Thirsk to

The clock tower at Thirsk

Norfolk where they were farmers. While still a young man he was lured to London, but with true Yorkshire blood in his veins, he was drawn to the game of cricket which was still in its infancy. He became a bowler with the Gentleman's White Conduit Club, but soon saw the potential for making 'a bit of brass.' With the help of a number of patrons he built his first private cricket ground in 1787 at Dorset Square, lying close to Sherlock Holme's fictional home in Bakers Street. By fencing off the ground he was able to charge spectators an entrance fee which led to the venture becoming profitable.

But eventually the cost of leasing the land became too high so he moved on to another pitch near St John's Wood, taking his turf with him, where he stayed for just two years. The building of the new Regent's Canal forced him to move yet again, to what this time was to become the site of the present world famous ground now known simply as Lord's. The first match on the new ground was played in 1814 when the resident Marylebone Cricket Club, the MCC, beat Hertfordshire. This time Lord knew he had created a winner, for in spite of being regarded as rough and dangerous his ground had quickly become accepted as the national home of the game. In 1825 he decided to sell it to William Ward, a wealthy banker and keen cricket player, who paid an amazing £5000. Lord invested his money in property, then later retired to the tranquillity of Hampshire where he died in 1832.

Lord's, with its playing area of 5.5 acres and a crowd capacity of 27,000, has grown to become a shrine to a sport watched with almost religious devotion. Its patron saint is of course W.G. Grace, who took 654 wickets at the ground and is remembered by its sturdy entrance gates which have been named in his honour. But the sound of 'leather on willow' heard by thousands of avid fans each season is merely the end product for a massive on-going management exercise. For every year on this site are held hundreds of official meetings by the MCC, the Test and County Cricket Board and the National Cricket Association, which together control all aspects of cricket in Britain. Looking down on their proceedings from a place of honour in the Long Room is a portrait of Thomas Lord; his sharp profile and intelligent eyes seeming to be taking in every word. Some even feel his face takes on a look of inward satisfaction when the words 'of Yorkshire and England' are written by the selectors, as they so often are.

'That tall house down the street is the vet's surgery which belonged to James Herriot, who was really named Alf Wight of course. He was married in St Mary's church here in Thirsk and his son now carries on the practice. His daughter is a local doctor.'

I thanked the enthusiastic man for his snippets of local information then I continued my stroll, first gazing up at the home of All Creatures Great and Small, then exploring the quiet alleyways that eventually led me back to the centre of the town. Here I wandered across the large cobbled market place similar to those I had recently seen in both Ripon and Richmond. Lying at the heart of Thirsk it is guarded by the town's best known landmark, an ornate clock tower.

Known in the Domesday book as Tresche, the town began as a Celtic settlement built on a bend on the Cod Beck, a meandering tributary of the River Swale. During the last century excavations of an artificial mound known as Pudding Pie Hill, unearthed the skeleton of a man from this period. He was probably a chief of the tribe, for with arms and legs crossed he had been ceremonially buried with his sword and shield. After the Conquest most of the land in this green vale came into the possession of Robert de Mowbray whose descendants built a castle here. However, during the 12th century they took part in an unsuccessful rebellion against the first Plantagenet king, Henry II, after which the castle was demolished.

I would have liked to have had more time to explore the Thirsk of today, for it is a bright lively place full of inviting inns and old shops. But I had chosen one of the hottest days for two centuries, my energy was waning and hopefully, the cool of the North Yorks Moors lay before me. So I reluctantly returned to my car whose interior was like a raging furnace.

4

As I drove slowly through Sutton-under-Whitestonecliffe I saw tiny yellow stoned cottages sleeping in idyllic splendour. It was one of a handful of marvellous villages which I discovered nestling among golden fields filled with huge cylinders of hay. At this point the eastern edge of the fertile Vale of Mowbray gives way to the rising Hambleton Hills and the more gentle Howardian Hills, which then descend into the Vale of Pickering. However these are not the wild and menacing Pennines normally associated with Yorkshire, but soft green ridges half covered by woodland in which hide the rural communities of Kilburn, Coxwold and Ampleforth.

Strangers from southern England often rub their eyes in dismay when they pass this way, for suddenly they get the feeling they are back home in Berkshire. The reason for this is that they have seen the Kilburn White Horse staring down from the hillside, a huge image inspired by the famous White Horse of Uffington. It was a local man, Thomas Taylor, who during the latter part of the 18th century was filled with the desire to give Kilburn its own White Horse. However, it took another fifty years before his plans became reality when village school master John Hodgson instructed his pupils to first peg out the shape of the animal. The outline, which measures 228 feet high by 314 feet long, was created by the men from the village in 1857 who cut away the turf to reveal the limestone. Locals will tell you that it takes 20 people to cover the horse's eye, but their much cherished landmark, unlike the chalk horses, which are more durable, is made from porous limestone. This means it suffers from weathering so it requires constant maintenance, with the occasional coat of whitewash to liven it up.

I soon found that around every corner in this part of Yorkshire there are fascinating tales and historical associations to uncover. Kilburn, as well as having its White Horse can also boast its Mouseman. But he was not a noted rodent-exterminator as his title may suggest, but one of the greatest wood-carvers which England has ever produced.

Robert Thompson, who was born here in 1876, was the son of the local carpenter. He was sent to the West Riding as a young man to learn another trade but his inborn talent for intricate carving in oak brought him back to Kilburn. Inspired by the work of the 15th century craftsman William Bromflet, his breakthrough came when the headmaster of nearby Ampleforth College gave him a commission. This led to his outstanding talent quickly gaining national recognition and a demand for his work from churches, schools and individuals throughout the country. But he was determined to remain a village craftsman of the highest quality, completely avoiding any commercialism. He chose as his trademark a mouse, symbolising 'industry in quiet places', and this he carved in hidden corners of his work. As well as the many pieces he carved for Ampleforth samples of his art can be found in over 500 locations, including most of our great cathedrals. He died in 1955 at the age of seventy-nine but his legacy is carried on at Kilburn by the local craftsmen whom he trained.

The delightful village of Coxwold, down a winding lane beyond Kilburn, once boasted the novelist Laurence Sterne as its vicar. A man who loved bawdy humour and who ate huge meals, he served here from 1760 to 1768. In gabled Shandy Hall which he named, he penned Tristram Shandy and The Sentimental Journey Through France and Italy; two works that led to him becoming recognised as the greatest humorist of his day.

It is said that nearby Newburgh Priory hides a more gory secret, for in an enclosed vault on an upper floor rests the headless corpse of Oliver Cromwell. The man who rose to become Lord Protector following the execution of King Charles I, died in September 1658. His son Richard, who inherited his father's position proved to be an ineffective leader, which led to unrest in the country by those who were also growing tired of the strict Puritan rule. This swiftly led to Richard Cromwell being forced to abdicate in 1659, followed by the Restoration of the Monarchy the next year.

When King Charles II entered London in May 1660 there was great rejoicing in the streets, but there was also an inevitable reaction against the former leaders. This resulted in the dead bodies of Oliver Cromwell, and his two colleagues, Bradshaw and Ireton, being dragged from Westminster Abbey and hanged at Tyburn. They were then taken down and the public executioner cut off their heads, which were placed on spikes on the roof of Westminster Hall. The bodies were said to have been buried at Tyburn, but there is a tradition that Oliver's daughter Mary, had her father's body secretly removed. This is believed to have been brought here to Newburgh Priory which was the home of her husband, Lord Fauconberg, and quickly bricked up in a vault where it remains today. Earlier this century when the Wombwell family were entertaining the Prince of Wales at the house, their guest is said to have implored them to open the vault while he watched. But this request, even from the man destined to become King Edward VII, was tactfully refused.

With the drowsy sun beaming down I passed through the quiet green countryside which surrounds Ampleforth College. This reminded me of the time in 1976 when an astonished public first learned that the new leader

102

Journey through Yorkshire

of the Roman Catholic community in England, the ninth Archbishop of Westminster, would be the Rt Rev George Basil Hume. For this highly intelligent and spiritual man, a Benedictine monk and the Abbot of Ampleforth, was hardly known outside this corner of Yorkshire. Snatched from relative obscurity he had been chosen from a list of ninety to carry on the work of his predecessor, the much loved Cardinal Heenan. Since that time Cardinal Hume has built up an international reputation for being a skilful, diplomatic holy man. He has forged special links with other religions and has guided his church through a period of great change. But at times he must reflect on that carefree day in 1933 when as a ten-year-old boy he began Prep School here, happily oblivious to the fact that the burden of high office was awaiting him.

Ampleforth Abbey is now home to one hundred monks, making it the largest Benedictine community in Europe. It can trace its origins back to Westminster Abbey which was founded by King Edward-the-Confessor in AD 1065. Following the turmoil of the Reformation it moved to France in the 17th century, but returned to England in 1802. Ampleforth College was founded the following year and has grown to become one of the finest Roman Catholic schools in the world, having 700 pupils. Carrying on a tradition that began in Northumbria with St Wilfred and the Venerable Bede it combines academic study with the teachings of Christ.

After glancing at a sign near Sutton Bank which told me that I was now entering the North York Moors National Park, I was confronted by a steep hill that took me by surprise. With a perspiring brow and gears grinding I took a series of hairpin bends up a 1-in-4 gradient that climbed ever upwards. At last it flattened out onto a splendid ridge, rewarding me with a stunning aerial view of Ryedale. Now I found myself looking at wave upon wave of cornfields whose rythmic undulations swept tirelessly on to meet a misty horizon. It was a landscape unlike any other I had so far met in Yorkshire. Lit by a bright sun it could easily have been a corner of Provence; an illusion further added to by the orange pantile roofs of secluded farms shimmering like beacons among the yellow fields.

Helmsley has a fairy tale look about it, the type of place where gallant knights might quite easily be expected to rescue fair maidens from wicked barons. Perhaps I was led to this conclusion by the presence of the castle, whose jagged profile seems to dominate this delightful market town. So I was not the least bit surprised to learn that the 16th century vicarage is haunted by the ghost of a beautiful nun. Indeed, if there had not been hints of the supernatural here I would have been disappointed.

Elmslac, as it was named in the Domesday Book was bustling with

Helmsley market cross, start of the Cleveland Way

visitors. They were strolling in the sun by the river, sipping glasses of cold shandy in ancient inns, or choosing postcards of Rievaulx Abbey or Kilburn White Horse to send home. But other people of a more adventurous nature, had departed from this picturesque town many hours ago. At the crack of dawn when the streets were still empty, they had walked in silence up the steps that lead to the Market Cross. Slowly they had touched its stone column, then after taking a backward glance they had strode away with resolute determination. Some medieval ritual you may think? No, you would be wrong. They were merely starting out on one of our most popular long-distance walks, The Cleveland Way, which begins here at Helmsley Market Cross.

It was at Helmsley Youth Hostel on 24th May 1969 that the Cleveland Way was officially opened. It was Britain's second long-distance footpath, following the Pennine Way which had been opened at Malham in 1965. The 108 mile long horse-shoe route first meanders west to Sutton Bank, then veers northwards over the exhilarating summits of the Hambleton Hills to reach Osmotherley. Moorland pathways then lead past Kildale and over the pyramid-like peak of Rosebury Topping to reach the East Coast at Saltburn. The views now change from moorland to seascapes as the coast is followed south through Whitby, Robin Hood's Bay and Scarborough to reach the finishing point at Filey.

The sharp profile of Rosebury Topping

For those walkers who prefer to complete a circular route, a Missing Link section was pioneered by Malcolm Boyes in 1975. This 50 mile long unofficial extension is joined at Scarborough, then continues inland over rights-of-way, ending here at Helmsley.

But the thought of such activity in this heat was too much; the bar of the Black Swan was beckoning me!

5

I decided that I would like to breathe in the solitude of the North York Moors so I took a minor road northwards from Helmsley. This followed a curving valley that has been shaped by the little River Rye and its tributary, the Seph. Half hidden by trees just two miles from the town, I stopped to look down on Fountains biggest rival; for many believe Rievaulx Abbey to be the most beautiful in England. This roofless Cistercian ruin is just one of scores of religious houses in Yorkshire which surrendered to King Henry VIII, standing as a forlorn legacy to the ambition of this cruel tyrant. The spring of 1540 must rank as one of the saddest in our history, for in just four short years over eight hundred monasteries and nunneries had been destroyed and 10,000 holy men and women had been forced from their vocation. Despite some claims that the Dissolution of the Monasteries was needed to subdue moral laxity or that they were a political threat to the crown, scholars now generally agree that finance was the real motive; the great wealth of the abbeys was simply stolen by the King.

Although there were many independent monastic rules in Saxon England most of the monks eventually began to embrace the teachings of St Benedict who lived in Italy during the Sixth century. The principles of his order were silence, solitude, prayer, humility and obedience. Living as a community with an abbot as their head they took a vow of celibacy, wore a rough habit with a fur-trimmed cowl, and had no personal wealth. Their main function was to pray to God for the sake of the world; this they did eight times through both the day and night, being summoned by the sound of a bell. These prayers and the daily Mass took place in the Abbey Church which lay at the centre of the monastery.

These first abbeys in Yorkshire, which at this time was part of Northumbria, suffered greatly during the Danish invasions of the ninth century and were virtually wiped out. But once the area had been settled by the Danes they proved not to be as violently anti-Christian as was at first feared. Many began to forsake paganism for Christianity, including Guthfrith, who was the first Danish King of the region. However the inevitable decline in monastic life which followed this Danish occupation continued into the mid-tenth century. Then following a spectacular revival in France a similar upsurge began in southern England spearheaded by St Dunstan. But it was not until after the Conquest that Yorkshire's great abbeys began to spring up in its remote river valleys. New orders of monks now included Cistercians, Carthusians, Premonstratensians and Cluniacs. Friars too, who unlike monks carried the message of God around the countryside, now became a common sight in the villages and towns.

The Cistercian order began as a revolt against the 'too easy' way of life which had developed in many monasteries in France. When Stephen Harding, an Englishman, became the abbot of a French monastery in AD 1098 he began to draw up a set of rules which laid the foundation of this new order. Austerity was to be its theme; abbeys were built in hostile wild places, the monks must do their own chores, eat just one meal a day, wear coarse undyed habits and live a simple life devoted to prayer. Bernard of Clairvaux became an enthusiastic member of the order in AD 1112, which led to over three hundred Cistercian monasteries being built during the next forty years, twenty five of them in England. Rievaulx was founded in AD 1131 by his secretary, William, on land given by Walter l'Espec. Due to the narrowness of the valley it was erected on a north-south line instead of the normal east to west, in 'a place of horror and vast solitude'. But in spite of its remote location it quickly grew to become the most important Cistercian house in the country. The number of monks and lay brothers rose to three hundred in just twelve years with several daughter houses later being founded. When its third Abbot, the famous St Ailred, died in AD 1165 a community had then been established which would dominate this corner of Yorkshire for four centuries.

Leaving the abbey behind me I drove up the curving road which led northwards into the isolation of the hills. Freckled fields, sloping and fertile, lined the valley, with remote farms nestling in sheltered hollows. This greenness gave way on the rising uplands to the dark of heather, ending in a wide horizon of high moorland and blue sky. Not a vehicle did I meet for a dozen miles, the drowsy heat having attracted most visitors to the coast; I seemed to have these six hundred square miles of magnificent wilderness to myself.

A glance at my map revealed that this lonely road is crossed by both the Cleveland Way and that other popular walking challenge, the Lyke Wake Walk. The latter begins at the Lyke Wake Walk Stone near Osmotherley Reservoir, then continues across forty miles of windswept moorland with 5,000 feet of climbing, before ending at Beacon Howe near Ravenscar. There is of course, a condition attached to walkers who wish to become members of the Lyke Walk Club; they must complete the entire route within 24 hours!

So what do Lyke and Wake really mean, and why are they associated with a moorland walk? Well it seems that it all began in 1955 with a feature in The Dalesman magazine concerning the possibility of a west to east crossing of these North York Moors. Taking up the challenge after weeks of indecision about the best route, a group of strong walkers set out on October 1st 1955. Following in the steps of Roman soldiers, invading Danes and 18th century smugglers, they made their first successful crossing of this rugged terrain in just thirteen hours of walking. However, while bivouacking as darkness approached they had become affected by the wild, ghostly atmosphere of the moorland that seemed to stretch unending towards the horizon. For they knew that on these lonely uplands lie buried the cremated bones of the Bronze Age people who lived here over three thousand years ago. This brought to mind the words of a medieval dirge sung in these parts which relates that when we die, paradise is only reached after a hazardous journey across a moorland such as this. So, from this macabre association with death evolved the name of this unique walk; Lyke meaning corpse, and Wake being the watch made by mourners over the corpse.

The monument to Captain Cook

'This is one for the record books,' said a softly spoken Scotsman who served me with a can of ice-cold orange.

I had arrived at a small picnic-site at Cringle Moor, at the northern edge of the Cleveland Hills. The Scotsman, who must have saved the life of many a weary traveller with his mobile refreshment van, was referring to the hot weather which seemed to be unending. I smiled in reply then walked to the far end of the carpark to enjoy a breathtaking view. Here where the moorland ends the hillside plunges almost sheer to meet the rolling fields of the Cleveland Plain. Through the blurr of heat haze I could see a mosaic of farms and cottages, woodland and lanes, spreading outwards towards Middlesborough and the coast. In the distance lay Easby Moor, a prominent high point on which stands a sixty feet high monument to the celebrated explorer and navigator Captain Cook. Beyond, completely separated from the other hills, rises the impressive grassy pyramid of Rosebury Topping. Although rising to only 322m (1,057ft) above sea level it has the presence of a mountain, which is perhaps why in the 18th century it was said to be a mile and a half high!

It is here at Great Ayton, in the shadow of these brooding moorlands that Neil Heaton, a Lancastrian friend of mine has made his home. In 1991 Neil achieved a lifetime's ambition, for after climbing to the mountain summit of Buachaille Etive Beag located near Glencoe in Scotland, he had qualified to join a small elite band who have conquered every Munro. But what is a Munro, you may ask, for it is a term little known outside the walking and climbing fraternity?

Neil Heaton – a long-distance walker who has climbed all the Munros

The tale behind the Munro's began in 1856 with the birth in London of Sir Hugh Thomas Munro who came from a wealthy Scottish family. While a teenager he was sent to live in Germany so that he could learn the language. At this time mountain climbing, which was in its infancy, had begun to attract many adventurous upper-class men. Sir Hugh began to follow the trend by climbing in the Alps which quickly led to what was to become his lifelong devotion to the sport. His career led him to South Africa for a period as the private secretary to the Governor of Natal, then he returned home to manage the family estate in Scotland. This gave him the opportunity to pursue his first love of climbing in the Scottish mountains, which led to him becoming a prominent member of the newly formed Scottish Mountaineering Club (SMC), later being elected as its president. In 1891 he published in the SMC journal a list of all the Scottish mountains which rise over 3,000 feet above sea level. They had a title of Munro's Tables, so since that time these summits have become affectionately known as the Munro's.

The race then began for the title of the 'first man to have climbed all the Munroes'. This was won in September 1901 by the Reverend A.E. Robertson who in a flurry of emotion ticked off his last summit of Meall Dearg. Ironically Sir Hugh was never to achieve the distinction of ascending all the mountains which bear his name. He died of pneumonia during the First World War in France leaving just two of the summits unclimbed.

I remember over thirty years ago accompanying Neil Heaton to the top of a few of these magnificent mountains which were later to become his lifetime's challenge. Always a keen long-distance walker, forever exploring the wilds of the Dales and the North York Moors, it was only in later years that the pull of the Munro's became irresistible to him. His wife Margaret was by his side on a hundred of the ascents and their two young children also managed to bag a handful of the peaks while on family holidays. On one occasion he reached seven Munro's in a single day, but many lie in splendid isolation requiring a long day's trek across boggy terrain. In 1986 after completing the arduous Scottish coast-to-coast walk known as 'The Ultimate Challenge' his total had risen to two hundred. He averaged about 15 peaks each year until at last he qualified as a Munroist; the exclusive title which only about 800 people have attained. However there are always more Scottish mountains for Neil to climb, such as the Corbetts which rise over 2,000 feet and the Dochartys which are between 2,000 and 2,500 feet!

Chapter Six

North York Moors to Whitby

I reach the East Coast, see where Captain Cook once worked, then I sleep in Lewis Carroll's bedroom in Whitby. I learn about whaling and the adventurous Scoresbys, admire the photographs of Frank Meadow Sutcliffe, then hear how St Hilda slew all the snakes. I explore the abbey which the Nazis once shelled, see a memorial to our very first poet, I buy a jet ring then I look where Dracula landed. I am reminded of Whitby's ship wrecks and the legendary Harry Freeman, then I hear about the Penny Hedge Ceremony.

1

It was with excited anticipation that I headed down from the high peaty moorlands towards the distant blue line that highlights the Yorkshire coast. As I descended through a wide green valley a salty breeze suddenly began to flow through the open car window, bringing with it a welcome coolness. Perhaps because I knew that this was Captain Cook Country, my head became filled with romantic thoughts of the sea. Half remembered stories from my childhood came flowing back, images from the works of Joseph Conrad, tales of the Spanish Main, of typhoons in the China sea, the horror of going round the Horn or being locked in the ice of Antarctica. For there was a time not long ago, when British children listened wide eyed to such adventures, often being reminded that we are 'an island race'.

Staithes is a tantalising place from which to view the North Sea for the first time, for as an oyster hides a pearl it at first hides its glory. I parked my car at the top of a hill then walked down a steep, narrow lane which slowly began to reveal the true beauty of this quiet fishing village. Framed by the gold of gorse which covered the roadside I looked down on the orange rooftops of tiny cottages that could easily have been part of toytown. The curving lane narrowed even further till at last, beyond a bend, I reached the edge of the murmuring shingle. Only a handful of visitors stood on the shoreline; two children paddling, a couple in the distance picking up pebbles, a solitary man walking his dog, while gulls shrieked nervously overhead. Strolling down to the sandy shoreline I then knelt, as many strangers feel the urge to do, and baptised my hands in the lapping sea.

On the edge of the village I stood on a footbridge which crosses a small creek looking down on a score of blue rowing boats which lay marooned in the mud. My eyes were then drawn to the towering yellow cliffs which curve outwards to form the little bay in which Staithes shelters. Shaped by centuries of gales into rounded profiles, they end in a contrasting green where the grass maintains a fragile hold. Around the corner at Boulby these cliffs reach a dramatic height of 666 feet, the highest point along this entire coastline, which perhaps appropriately is also regarded as the Devil's Number. For there is something untamed, almost supernatural about this rugged East Coast; like a caged animal it needs to be watched.

As I stood looking out at the cluster of white washed cottages that hug this secluded cove, I began to think of the many people who regard Staithes as a place of pilgrimage. Each year dozens of visitors from Vancouver, Australia, New Zealand, Hawaii and many other islands that dot the Pacific Ocean, arrive here. They walk up a narrow cobbled lane, then with a look of excitement on their faces they stop outside a small house. Over the tiny blue door they read the words, Captain Cook's Cottage, which brings a smile of inward satisfaction. For they have arrived at another landmark in the life of one of the world's greatest explorers; and importantly, he is the man who first put their homeland on the world map.

It was on the 27th October 1728 in a small thatched cottage in the village of Marton, near Middlesborough, that James Cook was born. His mother was a Yorkshire woman whose husband, a farm labourer, originated from Scotland. Their child was baptised in the local Parish Church, then gained his early rudimentary education at the caring hands of a farmer's wife named Mary Walker. But when he was eight years old the family moved a few miles to Great Ayton on the River Leven, where his father had got a new job at Airyholme Farm. The owner of the farm was Thomas Scottowe, who recognised that James Cook was a gifted child so generously paid for his education at the village school. Later, when James had entered his teens and begun working on the farm, it was Scottowe who found him a better position here at Staithes. This was in a shop owned by merchant William Sanderson, where James became a mere errand boy, but importantly obtained his first real taste of the sea.

Enthralled by the tales he heard from the many sailors who lived in what was during the 18th century, a lively fishing port, James Cook had an irresistible urge to join them. His ambitions soon became apparent to his employer who paved the way for his new career by introducing him to a ship owner in Whitby named John Walker. This led to him in 1746, becoming an apprentice seaman, working in the small sturdy ships known as colliers. These were used to transport coal along the coast and across the North sea to the Baltic ports.

On his first vessel, Freelove, Cook soon became curious about the mathematics of navigation, which he began to study with intense interest. Over the next nine years he rose from an ordinary seaman to become mate, then in 1755 was about to be given the command of his first ship, the Friendship, when he decided to join the Royal Navy. This was an unusual decision at the time for a man from a poor background as seamen were mainly 'pressed' into service and officers chosen from the gentry.

However his knowledge of seamanship and navigation soon became apparent to the Navy and in less than two months he was promoted to Master's Mate. At this time war was raging between Britain and France for the conquest of the rich lands of Canada and Australia which had only been partly explored. Cook soon saw action in the Eagle which captured the French merchant ship, Duc d'Aquitaine. His outstanding ability then brought him more promotion to Master of one of the ships which formed part of a large fleet sent by the Admiralty to take Canada from the French in 1759.

The small French settlements which lay on the St Lawrence were soon captured, but the large prize of Quebec proved more difficult. Cook was chosen by General Wolfe to chart the approach to Quebec up the river, full of islands and dangerous shallows. Then later, in the darkness, he success-fully guided a convoy of small rowing boats that carried the British soldiers. General Wolfe and his men then scaled the towering cliffs known as the Heights of Abraham, took the French by surprise, which led to the well-documented victory that resulted in Canada becoming a British possession. Wolfe, of course died 'gloriously' and James Cook had gained a reputation as being the finest navigator in the Royal Navy. In the period of peace which followed he began a precise survey of the St Lawrence then went on to chart the complete coast of Newfoundland. So accurate were his charts that they were still being used in recent years.

During his time in Canada there occurred, on the 5th August 1766, an eclipse of the sun. Cook, with immense patience, made accurate drawings of the event which were sent to the Royal Society to be published. In the atmosphere of scientific enlightenment which prevailed in Britain at the time, these caught the imagination of the establishment. This resulted in him being chosen to undertake a voyage of scientific exploration to the South Pacific Ocean to observe the Transit of Venus from the island of Tahiti.

In his famous Whitby built collier Endeavour, which he regarded as 'unexcelled for exploring and charting', he set out in 1768 on the first of his three famous voyages which were destined to change the map of the world. It was to be three years before he saw the shores of his homeland again. During this time he became the first white man to sail completely around New Zealand, proving it to be two large islands. He then achieved another 'first' when he sailed up the eastern coast of Australia, discovering the Great Barrier Reef, which almost wrecked his ship. Landing on the shore to carry out essential repairs the Union Flag was hoisted, claiming yet another massive British possession.

In 1772, only a year after his return to England he again set sail. This time his ship was the Resolution, and he had orders to find out if a great Southern Continent extending into the Pacific and Atlantic Oceans really existed. He proved that this was not the case when he took Resolution to within a hundred miles of the southern ice pack which was the farthest south that man had ever been. Thanks to Cook's careful control of his crew's diet only one man died of sickness during the entire voyage. On his return the Royal Society presented him with a gold medal, the Admiralty promoted him to the Fourth Captain of Greenwich Hospital, and he was received by King George III.

His final voyage began in July 1776 when he sailed from Plymouth in search of the legendary North West Passage reputed to link the Atlantic and Pacific Oceans to the north of Canada. His ship Resolution met up with its sister ship, Discovery, and the two vessels picked up supplies in Cape Town. They then discovered the Prince Edward group of islands which they claimed for Britain before continuing to Van Dieman's Land, now known as Tasmania. After sailing on to New Zealand where they anchored for a fortnight, they continued into the Pacific where they discovered uninhabited Christmas Island. Their next major discovery was a mountainous archipelago which Cook named the Sandwich Islands, but now known as the Hawaiian Islands and is one of the states of the USA. The officers and crew of the vessels established a good relationship with the islanders, but were eager to proceed towards their goal.

After sailing for a month north easterly they reached the coast of North America at Oregon where they met severe gales which lashed their ships. These damaged the masts which then required repairing before they could continue northwards. Later they dropped anchor at the inlet at Nootka, discovering what is now the Canadian Province of British Columbia. Here they were greeted by a large number of natives who swarmed out to meet them in dugout canoes. George Vancouver, who was a twenty-one year old officer on board Cook's ship, in later years came back here to carefully explore the region. This is of course recalled by his name which was given to the now thriving city and seaport.

Charting, surveying and naming landmarks they journeyed on past Alaska, his own name being given to the great inlet which leads to present day Anchorage. Their epic voyage then led them through the Bering Straits into the Arctic Circle. By this time the temperatures had plummeted well below zero and the ships met a 12 feet high wall of ice which stretched unbroken to the North Pole, making it impossible to continue. Cook had no alternative but to turn his vessels around and return to the Sandwich Isles; his intention was to pick up provisions then resume his exploration in the springtime.

The vessels eventually reached one of the islands named Maui, where William Bligh, who later became the infamous Captain of the Bounty, went ashore to ensure it was a suitable anchorage. Another officer, James King who came from Clitheroe in Lancashire, later recorded in his log book that at least nine thousand natives in hundreds of canoes came out to greet the two ships. These were the first white men that they had ever seen and they became convinced that James Cook was their tribal god, Orono.

At first the sailors were greeted with friendliness but as the weeks passed this relationship began to deteriorate. The cost of feeding the visitors, jealousy of Cook's status as a god, and the alleged theft of the ship's cutter contributed to a tense atmosphere which led to heated arguments. On the 14th February 1779 James Cook went ashore to try to resolve the situation but he was met by an inflamed mob who had within minutes savagely cut him to pieces. The remains of the world's greatest explorer were later recovered by James King from a now penitent band of Hawaiians. His head, leg bones and hands had been completely severed from his body. Identification was only possible from powder-burn scars which he had suffered while in Canada. There then followed a poignant ceremony before his burial at sea.

One of the finest descriptions of what James Cook was really like has been left to us by the surgeon on board Discovery, David Samwell:

'His constitution was strong, his mode of living temperate. He had no repugnance to good living and always kept a good table, though he could bear the reverse without murmuring. He was a modest man and rather bashful; of an agreeable lively conversation, sensible and intelligent. In his temper he was somewhat hasty, but of a disposition the most friendly, benevolent and humane. His person was above six feet high, and though a good looking man he was plain in address and appearance. His head was

Captain Cook's statue at Whitby

small, his hair, which was a dark brown, he wore tied behind. His face was full of expression, his nose was exceedingly well-shaped; his eyes, which were small and of a brown cast, were quick and piercing; his eyebrows prominent, which gave his countenance altogether an air of austerity.'

Samwell then goes on to describe what made Cook the greatest explorer of the 18th century, revered by both his officers and crew:

'Nature had endowed him with a mind vigorous and comprehensive, which in his riper years he had cultivated with care and industry. His general knowledge was extensive and various; in that of his own profession he was unequalled. With a clear judgement, strong masculine sense, and the most determined resolution; with a genius peculiarly turned for enterprise, he pursued his object with unshaken perseverance, vigilant and active in an eminent degree; cool and intrepid among dangers; patient and firm under difficulties and distress; fertile in expedients; great and original in all his designs; active and resolved in carrying them into execution. In every situation, he stood unrivalled alone; on him all eyes were turned; he was our leading star, which at its setting left us involved in darkness and despair.'

The people of this part of Yorkshire are rightly proud of the local lad who once ran errands from this shop in Staithes, then went on to astound the world. Many landmarks can be seen which highlight his early life, including a Captain Cook Birthplace Museum at Marton and an impressive statue on West Cliff at Whitby. But if you want to see the little cottage where the Cook family once lived in Great Ayton you will need to travel half way around the world. For in 1934 it was exported to Australia where it now stands in Fitzroy Gardens in Melbourne!

2

I am writing these notes in what is probably the last available hotel room in Whitby. After arriving in the town about an hour and a half ago, feeling hot and tired after my journey, I discovered with horror that every hotel appeared to be completely full. Slowly I drove around street after street, being confronted by 'No Vacancies' signs wherever I went. On half a dozen occasions I parked my car and walked into a hotel reception with a smile of hope, instantly dashed.

'I'm very sorry, there's not one vacant room. It's because of Folk Week you see and of course this glorious weather.'

What made the matter appear even worse were the crowds of people who were happily strolling through the town, laughing and joking. For I knew that they all had somewhere to lay down their heads, but I did not!

It was with this feeling of self pity that I 'gave it my last shot' at a hotel that stood in a splendid position on the East Terrace which overlooks the harbour. Only half heartedly did I ring the bell on the reception desk, for I had almost given up hope. But my frowns instantly disappeared when a middle aged woman told me in a deep theatrical voice, 'Yes, you are lucky, I've just one empty room and it's the best one in the hotel. A friend of mine was staying in it but she had to leave unexpectedly. It's £22 per night for bed and breakfast. We hate asking people, but would you mind paying in advance? We have been let down so many times, you see.' As she handed me the key I asked her if the building was old. 'It's early Georgian I think,' to which she casually added, 'Lewis Carroll once lived here.'

Later, as I lay on my bed looking through tired eyes at the ceiling, I began to imagine Lewis Carroll lying in this same room. Perhaps it was while

Whitby harbour

staring at this ornate plasterwork that he dreamed up Alice's wild tea-party with the Mad Hatter, the Dormouse and the March Hare; for Whitby has gained a reputation for stimulating the imagination of writers.

This room, once stately, now emits a marvellous feeling of departed grandeur; but like a favourite jacket or a ten year-old pair of slippers it feels instantly comfortable. The walls which are covered in pink flowery wall-paper, soar at least ten feet high ending in a solid cornice of plaster and a huge chandelier. To the left of the bed hangs a large gold-framed mirror with a solid table and a wardrobe nearby, while on the opposite wall are two framed prints which show 18th century English country scenes, with children, a thatched cottage and farm animals. Facing me are two huge windows, separated into small glass panels they stretch almost from floor to ceiling. When fully opened they act also as doors which lead out on to a small wrought-iron balcony, providing an absolutely stunning view over the whole town. At the moment these windows are wide open allowing the sounds of Whitby to filter in; the loud shriek of gulls, the chatter of passing visitors, the whirl of cars and the roar of the sea.

If I were a Whitby sea-captain facing my declining years, this is the bed I would choose, for without moving a muscle it allows me to view the full sweeping panorama of the town. Looking out I can see the green of carefully manicured lawns which plunge steeply downwards passing a road named Kyber Pass, then towards the harbour shimmering far below. Beyond the water, following the curve of the valley then rising precariously up the ascending cliff stands the higgledy-piggledy fisherman's houses of the old town; orange roofed with wooden frontages and balconies they look mag-nificent in the warm glow of the evening sun. To my left I can see the twin breakwaters which guard the harbour entrance on which are perched lighthouses, overlooked by the sharp profile of an eroded cliff face. Stand-ing sentinel on the summit, which the guide book says is reached by a climb up 199 steps, lies the landmark which I have seen printed in scores of calendars; the majestic outline of Whitby's ruined Abbey with the ancient church of St Mary nearby.

The layout of Whitby can be confusing to a stranger, so before I begin my exploration I have decided to consult a map laid out on my bed. It reveals that the harbour lies at the estuary of the River Esk, which winds its path to the sea along a deep cut valley dividing the town into two parts. These are linked by two bridges, a low swing bridge close to the old town and the New Bridge, about half a mile away, spanning a high gorge. And although Whitby is of course an East Coast town, its portion of coastline actually faces northwards. This results in the sun both rising and setting

Whitby Abbey

over the sea; an event which I am told only occurs at one other place, Cromer in Norfolk.

Walking out from the hotel into the warm evening air I stopped to admire a fine statue of Captain Cook which stands with pride on the edge of West Cliff. I then passed beneath one of the towns best known landmarks, a unique archway created from the jawbone of a whale as a constant reminder of Whitby's seafaring history. Ravenous by this time, I then found a cosy restaurant which overlooks the harbour entrance. While feasting on a delicious piece of haddock, I watched the sky turn from blue to gold, and the twinkling lights of the ancient cottages bring a touch of magic to the scene.

Tired but contented, I slowly ascended the steep pathway back to my hotel, anticipating the joy of sleep in Lewis Carroll's bedroom.

3

I gulped down a marvellous Yorkshire breakfast while listening to the lyrics of The Phantom of the Opera which boomed out across the dining room, confirming my belief that the lady who owned the hotel was indeed theatrical. Then after excitedly stepping out into the sunshine I suddenly became possessed by indecision, should I turn left or should I turn right? The many inviting facets of Whitby which I wanted to discover were drawing me in both directions. It would be the harbour I finally decided, so like Jonah I stepped through the jawbone of a whale, but happily this brought me not into its stomach but down a steep pathway to the quayside.

A man could quite easily spend a contented retirement on the waterfront at Whitby and never feel bored, for in this atmosphere of shrieking gulls and salty air there is a feeling of perpetual activity. Joining a score of staring visitors I watched in admiration as the driver of a huge articulated lorry manoeuvred his vehicle down a narrow road which hardly seemed wide enough to take a bicycle. Swinging it around he than backed it within six inches of the quayside, and when his brakelights finally flickered we all breathed a sigh of relief. His was a refrigerated lorry which had of course come here to load up with fish from a waiting trawler; a task which kept us indolent watchers riveted. With vigour and stamina the fishermen began hoisting box after box of ice laden fillets from the hold, swinging them with precision upwards and into the lorry. To a stranger the amount of fish which the little boat seem to hold was quite astonishing, while the gulls remained disappointed for not a single one could they snatch. Finally the doors of the vehicle were snapped tightly shut and it was driven expertly away in the direction of the motorway; tomorrow its contents would no doubt be tempting the housewives of a dozen cities.

God's Spot is how the local people describe Whitby, said not with misplaced pride but with sincere conviction for they adore their town. Its life-blood is of course the sea, a liaison which had begun long before the Vikings brought their longboats up the Esk to sack the Saxon settlement over a thousand years ago. Since that time the lives of generations of men and women have become dominated by the rise and fall of the tide, the ever-present dangers of the weather and a haunting superstition that is common to all seafaring communities. A town was created where fishing and trading were the spurs which drove young men, like James Cook, into a life of adventure in faraway places. Even today the Shetlands, Iceland, Greenland and the Baltic are spoken of here in casual conversation as say Halifax, Wakefield or Doncaster may be discussed in the households of Leeds.

Bustling as the harbour appears today, there was a period during the 18th century when hardly a yard of water could be seen for it was completely covered in a forest of sails and masts. This was the time when Whitby became the centre of the whaling industry, the blubber being rendered down to produce lamp-oil and the bones used in the production of ladies corsets. The industry flourished here for over a century, resulting in the slaughter of 1761 of the huge creatures. But by the 1830s a rapid decline began; coal-gas was replacing oil, whalebone corsets became less fashionable, and whales had become rarer due to this intense hunting.

Two of the great seafaring adventurers who lived in Whitby at this time, but whose exploits have becoming overshadowed by those of James Cook, were the Scoresbys. William Scoresby Senior was the captain of a whaler who hunted for over thirty years around Greenland and the perilous Arctic Ocean. He is reputed to have been the inventor of the crow's nest from which the whales would be spotted, and he also sailed further north than any other vessel had ever ventured at the time. His son, William Scoresby Junior, followed his father by first becoming a whaling captain then a great navigator and scientist. He charted the sea around Greenland, observing the action and composition of the ice in the remote arctic waters. Landing on isolated islands he also recorded the plant life which he found, then later he collaborated with Sir Joseph Banks in his search for the North West Passage. Being an intensely religious man in 1825 he exchanged the rigours of the sea for the church, becoming the Vicar of Bradford and a prolific author.

In 1991 Whitby skipper Jack Lammiman decided that the achievements of the two adventuring Scoresbys deserved more recognition. So he set sail in his wooden two-masted schooner, Helga Maria, for arctic waters. Initially his intention was to erect a commemorative plaque near Scoresby Sound; a large inlet on the east coast of Greenland named after William Scoresby Senior. However this site proved inaccessible due to a build up of solid ice, so he chose Jan Mayen Island as an alternative, this being the place were William Scoresby Junior did much of his scientific work. He and his crew eventually reached the remote island, but as the hard volcanic rock proved too hard to cut he was forced to leave the unmounted plaque in the care of the weather station. On his return to Yorkshire Jack Lammiman faced more problems, for the Helga Maria had failed to comply with new maritime safety regulations; this led to him being fined £600. However in 1994 on a second voyage his vision at last became reality; the Scoresby Memorial was proudly mounted in a cairn built of Whitby stone near a hill named Scoresby Berget.

Anyone who wishes to stepback in time to see other amazing characters who lived around Whitby during the last century, can visit as I did, the fascinating Sutcliffe Gallery. Looking down at me from scores of sepia tinted photographs were the weatherbeaten faces of seamen, their wives and families, their simple cottages, and the tall-masted ships and small fishing cobles from which they made their living. These superb images were captured by Frank Meadow Sutcliffe, a Leeds born photographer who came to live here in 1870. His work displays an unequalled artistry which won him world acclaim with the award of over sixty medals at international exhibitions. After his retirement in 1922 his love of Whitby and its people led him to become the curator of the local museum where he remained until his death in 1941 at the age of 88. His original negatives, produced on glass plates, were given in 1966 to the Whitby Literary and Philosophical Society by Bill Shaw who had taken over the photographic business. But the Sutcliffe Gallery retains the sole right of commercial production of the photographs, which range from low cost postcards to large framed prints.

Clasping copies of Retired from the Sea, Fetching in the Lines, The Opal of Whitby and Fisher Folk, I dashed into a harbourside inn for a pint of bitter and a crab sandwich; strolling round Whitby can be a hungry business.

4

There is a handful of highpoints in England that are forever clothed in a veil of mystery, you get the feeling that they hide secrets which may never be revealed. Glastonbury Tor and Pendle Hill immediately spring to mind as two well-known examples, but now I have found a third; the East Cliff here in Whitby. As I wandered through the abbey ruins, which stand majestically on this green summit with the North Sea pounding the shoreline far below, I could detect a strange supernatural atmosphere. If I had seen the saintly Hilda in her long flowing robes sweep across the lawns, or come upon the young Caedmon poised with pen in hand, then I would not have been in the least surprised. For you quickly come to expect the unexpected here in Whitby; it is a place where Celtic magic lives on.

Saint Hilda, who became the first Abbess of Whitby Abbey, was born in AD 614. She was of royal blood, being the daughter of Hereric who was a nephew of King Edwin of Northumbria. Both Hilda and Edwin were baptised into the Christian church in AD 627 by Saint Paulinus at York, who had been sent by the Pope as a missionary from Rome. This was an important landmark in the history of Northumbria as many thousands then followed the path from paganism to Christianity. However, when Edwin was slain just six years later at the Battle of Hatfield Chase, paganism quickly returned to much of the region.

Hilda remained a Christian but continued to live the secular life of a noblewoman until she was thirty three years old. She then went to Chelles

Monastery in France to join her sister Hereswitha as a nun. She was later asked by St Aidan, the Bishop of Lindisfarne, to return to Northumbria where she became the Abbess of a monastery at Hartlepool. She then moved on to become the first Abbess of this abbey, then known as Streanaeshalch which means 'the harbour of the watch tower'. It had been founded by King Oswy in AD 657 to commemorate his victory over the pagan King Penda of Mercia. Under her leadership it quickly became renowned as a centre of spirituality and learning, attracting both nuns and monks. These included the young Princess Elfled who was the daughter of King Oswy.

One legend tells us that St Hilda slew all the snakes around Whitby, took off their heads, then turned them into stone! You do not believe this tale? Perhaps you will change your mind after a walk below the shale cliffs, for St Hilda's Snakes are abundant around here. Known to geologists as ammonites these 170 million year old fossils have a generic name of Hildoceras bifrons which has been derived from the name of St Hilda. They have become so intrinsic to the local scene that the Burghers of Whitby have even incorporated three of them into their emblem.

A most important event took place in the first simple wooden abbey in the autumn of AD 663, the well-documented Synod of Whitby. On this windswept cliff Abbess Hilda called together the holy men of her own Celtic Church and those from the Church of Rome; two Christian traditions who needed to settle their differences. The Celtic Church which had spread from a base in Iona, had become isolated from Rome due to its remote location and many of its customs had become outdated. These included its observance of the most important festival in the Christian calendar, Easter, which they calculated using an antiquated method based upon the writings of St John. The widely accepted date was based upon the authority of St Peter and King Oswy decreed that this would now be adopted by the Celtic Church in spite of St Hilda's reluctance to change. With diplomacy he joked 'lest, when I come to the gates of the Kingdom of Heaven, there should be none to open them, he being my adversary who is known to possess the keys.'

But much more than this was settled at this famous synod, for it involved a fundamental change in the whole Celtic Church organisation which led to the establishment of a single English Church. The abbey flourished for another two centuries until AD 867 when it was attacked by the invading Danes. They destroyed the simple building, then took over the small community which had grown around the river estuary, renaming it Whitby which means the 'White Village'. After the Conquest the land came into the possession of William de Percy, he allowed a new Benedictine abbey to be built on the site in 1220, its first prior being Reinfred. Despite more Viking raids during these early years and several re-buildings, the abbey survived until the Dissolution in 1539. Its last Abbot, Henry Davell, together with twenty monks, were forced to surrender both the building and its possessions. The land was later leased to Richard Cholmley who in 1580 built a residence nearby using stone from the abbey. The present ruined structure, which dates from the 14th century, remained unprotected from the storms which sweep this turbulent coast and much of it tumbled down at the end of the 18th century. In December 1914 the West Front was further damaged by shells fired from the German battlecruiser Von der Tann and the light cruiser Derflinger, these having been aimed at the nearby coastguard station. However, in spite of the greed of Henry VIII, the storms of four centuries and the might of Nazi Germany, the abbey still remains as one of the most beautiful ruins in Britain that is now proudly preserved by English Heritage.

I followed a pathway along the cliff edge which gave me a stunning view of the harbour far below. Here I looked down on tiny ant-like figures who lay sunbathing on the curved beach while others were more actively ascending the stepped hillside. Turning to the right away from the town, I now faced the shimmering open sea, which led placidly from the cliff to end in a misty turquoise horizon. Gulls were gliding and shrieking over homeward-bound trawlers, small rowing boats bobbed slowly up and down as weekend fishermen cast their lines, while in the distance huge cargo vessels slid silently past like grey ghosts. The path led me into the graveyard of St Mary's church which for a thousand years has guarded this green clifftop. Gravestones, black and eroded by the centuries, lined the path which led me into this splendid building. In the coolness I sat alone, admiring the most impressive array of box pews that I have seen in any church; some built perhaps, by the same skilled hands which fashioned Endeavour and Resolution.

Do you love the poetry of Wordsworth or Tennyson or Betjeman, or perhaps you are one of those people who recently voted Kipling's If to be the nation's favourite poem? Then this is reason enough for you to make a pilgrimage here to Whitby. When you arrive you must dash up to the top of the 199 steps, then for a moment ignoring the church and the abbey, you must stop beside a large towering cross. Here you must pay silent homage to Caedmon, even if you have never heard his name before or read a word of his verse. For this Anglo Saxon cow-herd was our very first poet, his pen began the flow of great literature which still makes us the envy of the world.

The names of only three poets have survived from Anglo Saxon England;

St Aldhelm, Cynewulf and Caedmon. Aldhelm left us only his reputation but no writings, Cynewulf just four poems and nothing of his life, but thanks to Bede who wrote our first literary biography we know a great deal about Caedmon and his works. 'In the monastery of this abbess (St Hilda) there was a certain brother specially distinguished by divine grace because he was accustomed to making poems fitting to religion and piety.' Bede tells us. He reveals that Caedmon was a shy, uneducated cowherd who was employed by the Abbess, but following a dream in which he heard a Heavenly voice he miraculously changed into a gifted singer and poet. He pioneered the art of composing sacred songs from the scriptures, his Song Of Creation being our first English poem. His talent had a revolutionary effect on other writers of his day, leading to a golden age of Anglo Saxon poetry and starting our great literary tradition. Caedmon died in the same year as St Hilda, AD 680, but was not remembered on this windy clifftop until 1928 when this impressive memorial cross was unveiled.

'As black as jet' is a saying that has entered into our language, but if you want to know what jet is really like then Whitby is the place to see it. As I wandered along the narrow streets and alleyways, gazing into small cosy shops which were once fishermen's cottages, I became absorbed by the array of jet jewellery on display. Rings, brooches, earrings and necklaces glistened with the highly polished black stones set in contrasting silver.

Geologists tell us that jet is a lustrous black mineral found among the shale cliffs, and that it is really fossilised driftwood that has been formed over many millions of years by the intense pressure of the earth. As early as the Bronze Age man was using it for ornaments and it became very popular with the Romans, unworked blocks of the rock having been excavated in York. But it was during the last century that the jet industry here in Whitby began to flourish in a big way. This followed a fashion started by Queen Victoria who first saw examples of jet jewellery at the Crystal Palace Exhibition held in London in 1851. Ten years later when her husband Prince Albert, died of typhoid she began wearing the black stone as a sign of mourning and others quickly followed. By 1870 over 200 small workshops had sprung up here in Whitby to cope with the demand and over 1,500 people found employment. The widespread popularity of jet continued into the early years of this century, then it began to decline into what is today a small, but highly skilled local industry.

Unable to any longer resist the lure of this shining mineral which gazed out at me from a shop window, I went inside and bought a ring as a present for my wife, Wynne. Then clutching the package in my hand I went to see the place where Dracula landed!

The warm air was rich with the salty smell of the sea mingled with the appetizing aroma of smoking kippers when I walked along the East Pier which guards the harbour entrance. It was a far more tranquil day than the one described by Bram Stoker in his classic novel: 'Then without warning the tempest broke. With a rapidity which, at times, seemed incredible. and even afterwards is impossible to realize, the whole aspect of nature at once became convulsed. The waves rose in growing fury, each over topping its fellow, till in a very few minutes the lately glassy sea was a roaring and devouring monster.'

Thus the scene was set here in Whitby for the arrival of the vampire Count Dracula, a chilling tale of horror which has continued to enthrall each generation of readers since it was first published in 1897. Dracula arrived here in the guise of a large dog which rushed ashore from a shipwreck, climbed the 199 steps to the church, then hid in the grave of a man who had committed suicide. The book, which cleverly discloses its dark secret through a series of letters and journals, became an immediate best seller and is the only volume for which the Irish born writer is now remembered. Bram Stoker died in 1912 at the age of sixty five leaving a legacy that has continued in a host of films, first starring Bela Lugosi and later Christopher Lee. The local connection is further explored in a museum named the Dracula Experience sited on Marine Parade.

Of course this hazardous East Coast, with its hidden rocks, stormy seas and enveloping mists is a perfect place to fire the imagination of any novelist. It has inevitably become the graveyard for thousands of ships and behind each wreck there are fascinating tales of both heroism and tragedy to be told. The first mission carried out by the Whitby lifeboat was in 1802 when the sloop Edinburgh grounded near the harbour, but happily the crew were rescued.

Sadly, thirty nine years later in a year of unprecedented storms it was a different story. Nearly eight hundred vessels were lost along this East Coast during 1861, with 355 sinking in February alone. After weeks of coping with endless emergencies the fatigued Whitby lifeboat crew must have been near exhaustion when on the 9th February they were called out five times. They successfully rescued the five crews but when the collier schooner Merchant ran aground in huge seas near the West Pier, disaster struck. Many of Whitby's townspeople watched helplessly as the lifeboat capsized and sank with the loss of twelve men. Only one survived, the legendary Henry Freeman, who was saved by his new cork lifejacket. In later years he became the Coxwain of the Whitby Lifeboat which during the next four decades resulted in the saving of over 300 lives. The portrait

The legendary Henry Freeman (photo by Frank M. Sutcliffe, copyright: the Sutcliffe Gallery)

of this amazing giant of a man was taken by Frank Sutcliffe and remains as one of the most popular in the collection.

On Ascension Eve a strange custom known as the Penny Hedge Ceremony is acted out here on the shoreline in Whitby, which may be a link with pagan times. A local legend relates that on the 16th October 1159 three aristocratic huntsmen had wounded a wild boar, which they then chased into a hermit's chapel in Eskdale. The hermit tried to protect the animal, the angry huntsmen retaliated by beating him and sadly he died from his injuries. When the powerful Abbot Sedmon of Whitby Abbey heard of the terrible murder, he made the three men carry out a curious penance for their sin which they had to pass on to their successors. On each Ascension Eve they were to use a penny knife to cut down timber from the woods, with which they were to build a hedge at the estuary which must stand three tides without collapsing. If the sea stopped the estuary being reached by the builders then the penance would end!

Over eight hundred years later this custom is still carried out in spite of many heated discussions about its real origins. 'Penny' is believed to relate to 'Penance', but some believe the ceremony may be a pagan superstition concerned with the power of the sea, while others feel it might simply have been derived from the beginning of the salmon season when the fish were netted at the estuary. However in 1981 disaster struck for a freak tide stopped the hedge being built. But the local people decided to quietly ignore this; so the tradition continues!

I walked back from the estuary to the centre of the town still bustling with crowds of sun-tanned visitors. In Grape Lane I escaped into the coolness of the Captain Cook Memorial Museum, appropriately housed in the 17th century home of the Quaker Mariner, John Walker. This fine collection which superbly captures the era of Cook, is the base from which he got his first taste of seamanship from 1746 to 1749. I saw the attic where he slept as a young apprentice and I looked out from the same window from which he too would have gazed. Across the river were the shipyards of Fishburn and Langborn, who would later build the Whitby Cats in which Cook was destined to change the map of the world.

In later years Cook returned here to this house in Grape Lane, no longer a humble seaman he was now a finely dressed Captain in the Royal Navy with a glowing reputation. The housekeeper, Mary Prowd, who had looked after him when he was a young apprentice had been told she must now greet him with great respect, referring to him as Captain. Of course she completely ignored this advice, for like a mother, she still saw him as a child. 'Oh honey James how glad I is to see thee,' was her sincere greeting to him.

Later in the evening I walked out from my hotel into the twinkling lights of the town. The sky was clear and starlit, while across on the East Cliff the romantic ruins of St Hilda's Abbey were highlighted like a stage set with floodlights. In the timber church of St Ninian, built by the same hands which fashioned Cook's vessels, I joined a group of other visitors. Here I saw nostalgic images of Old Whitby vividly captured on photographic slides; it was a fitting end to my visit to this unique town.

Chapter Seven

Whitby to Flamborough Head

*I hear of smuggling in Robin Hood's Bay, of the golf-balls of
Fylingdales Moor and how the life of a country policeman captured
our hearts. I explore bracing Scarborough, see Anne Brontë's grave,
learn about a Viking named Harelip and watch the holiday crowds.
I remember Charles Laughton, Stephen Joseph and our leading
comic playwright, Alan Ayckbourn. I arrive at Flamborough Head
where I admire a stunning view, hear about the Egg-men, Dane's
Dyke and the audacity of John Paul Jones.*

1

Down, down, down. That is the feeling which I had when I approached
the stepped hillside which leads into Yorkshire's most romantically
named coastal village, Robin Hood's Bay. However this steepness seems to
deter few visitors. Aged ladies with grey hair, walking sticks and smiling
faces; red cheeked men whose bulging stomachs suggested they had
'propped-up' many a pub bar; and young couples with toddlers by their
sides, all ignored the gradient to reach this unique hideaway.

Part way down I stopped to admire an absolutely stunning view. My eyes
followed the line of the narrow lane which plummets ever downwards
where I could see the orange rooftops of fisherman's cottages perched
precariously on the cliff edge far below. Crowded together on any small
piece of flat land which could be secured from the hillside, their white-
washed walls contrasted marvellously with the surrounding green foliage.
However, picturesque as this village surely is, it is the magnificent sweep
of the bay beyond which really makes visitors stop and stare. For in the
glow of summer sunshine it could easily have been mistaken for Capri. A
magnificent half circle of sea lay before me, the deep blue water broken
only by the occasional white wash from a small boat. It was framed in the
distance by the towering grey cliffs which end at the dramatic 600 feet high
point of Old Peak at Ravenscar.

This snaking street, full of souvenir shops and cafes, and often compared

Picturesque Robin Hood's Bay

to Clovelly, has a special significance for long-distance walkers for it marks the eastern end of the Coast-to-Coast Walk. Last year when I was writing *A Journey Through Lakeland*, I visited St Bees in Cumbria which is the starting point chosen by its creator Alfred Wainwright. Since 1972 when his book was first published many thousands of enthusiasts, wind-blown and travel weary, have walked these last few poignant yards to dip their feet into the sea. Having achieved a personal Everest which they will remember for the rest of their lives.

I sat in a small cafe eating a mouth-watering plate of home-made vegetable pie and chips, while looking out at the crowds of visitors who were heading down to the shoreline. A notice on the wall told me that the building had once been the local bakehouse. In the old days residents of the village would bring their Sunday joint of beef to be cooked here, for few had cookers of their own. The cottages, which are tiny, have very steep, narrow staircases and a special landing window. This is said to have been designed so that if a man dies in his bed a coffin could be taken into the bedroom through the window, which would be impossible up the staircase.

Fishing, alum working in the nearby quarries and of course smuggling, were once the main occupations of the men of Robin Hood's Bay. It was said that during the 18th century contraband would be landed by boat and taken into the cottages which lay nearest to the sea. It was then quickly passed from house to house through adjoining doors, reaching the top of the village without ever seeing the light of day! Much of what went on during this period is highlighted in an exhibition called the Smuggling Experience.

During the 16th century when both Whitby and Scarborough were small villages, a flourishing fishing fleet was based here and this continued into this century. Herring was a popular catch which was smoked or salted before being sold throughout the north. But as all these East Coast communities have learned, there is always a price to pay when making a living from the sea. Many tragedies have occurred locally but the one still talked about in the local pub happened in 1914 when the hospital ship Rohilla ran aground just north of the village. Five lifeboats bravely fought the storm to rescue over eighty seamen, while another sixty managed to swim ashore.

In the early years of this century Shipley born Leo Walmsley grew up here where he became enthralled by the fascinating stories he heard from the local fisherfolk. After serving in the Royal Flying Corp during the Great War he returned to the village to write; his first novel Three Fevers was published in 1932. This book whose plot revolves around the rivalry of two local families, became a best seller with Robin Hood's Bay becoming the fictional Bramblewick. It was later made into a film, Turn of the Tide, filmed along this splendid coastline.

As I stood looking out over the sparkling water from a vantage point on the sloping cliff top a loud screech suddenly filled the air.

'Help me Dad. I've been stung by a wasp!'

A young boy ran panic stricken towards his parents who lay sunbathing in a hollow. But the commotion did not in the least disturb two young lovers who continued their embrace, cocooned beneath two large straw hats.

I spent the rest of the afternoon exploring the tempting narrow lanes which twist and turn upwards from the beach between picture postcard cottages. After browsing for an hour in a second-hand book shop teeming with volumes, I asked the owner if he had a copy of a rare travel book which has so far eluded me.

'Sorry I just could not tell you. We have three shops and sell around 6000 volumes a week so it is impossible to keep track of individual books. It's just a case of taking pot-luck and searching through the travel section.'

Unfortunately I was unable to find the book and I was running out of time. After a lung bursting ascent up the hillside in the full blaze of the sun, I at last reached my car which was as hot as a greenhouse. With the open windows bringing a welcome breeze I then started out in the direction of Scarborough.

The A171 road which links Whitby to Scarborough skirts the eastern edge of Fylingdales Moor, mile upon mile of heathery wilderness that sweeps to the sky. Few walls or fences break the vastness, with only an occasional sheep to show signs of life. It was here in 1964, amidst a wave of local objections, that the controversial golfballs of RAF Fylingdales began to dominate the landscape. These huge spherical radomes measuring 84 feet in diameter and weighing 112 tons, were used to scan the skies to give us an early warning of any ballistic missiles attack on Britain. The station, whose equipment at the time was at the very forefront of technology, was a joint British-American venture with the USA providing the funding. In the sixties our potential enemy was Russia, but of course the end of the Cold War and the signing of peace treaties changed the situation. The mechanical radar system became obsolete so the giant golfballs were doomed, being replaced by what the experts tell us is 'a phased array system' with can track up to 800 satellites at any one time, known affectionately as 'the Toaster'.

Television viewers are more likely to be familiar with the splendour of these brooding moors from watching the highly successful ITV drama series of Heartbeat which is filmed here. The adventures of the country policeman Nick Rowan and his wife Kate who is a doctor, have made actors Nick Berry and Niamh Cusack into overnight superstars. Set in the nostalgic sixties the village of Goathland is transformed into fictional Aidensfield, with the magnificent countryside and coastline around Whitby forming a natural background.

The original idea for Heartbeat came from the Constable series of books written by police officer Peter Walker who uses the pen name Nicholas Rhea. Yorkshire TV, who first bought the rights for the series over fifteen years ago, at first had problems getting the programmes underway. But in 1990, after making several changes from the original books, including transforming Kate from a normal housewife into a doctor, the series really took off. The title has cleverly been created by combining the two main elements of the stories, Heart from the medical part and Beat from the policeman's beat, and using sixties musical soundtracks. However, in recent weeks a major change has taken place with over 15 million viewers avidly watching the tragic death of Kate, for Niamh Cusack wanted to leave the series. We now sit glued every Sunday evening to our TV sets, wondering if romance will come again into the life of PC Nick Rowan!

Of course Yorkshire has over the years become a major location for many popular TV series which include Last of the Summer Wine, All Creatures Great and Small, and Emmerdale Farm, together with such award winning documentary films as Too Long a Winter which introduced us to Hannah Hauxwell.

But TV directors have only been following the lead given by the British film industry who from the early days of cinema recognised the contrasting appeal of the county. In the thirties Yorkshire became the natural location for a number of J.B. Priestley's works including An Inspector Calls and The Good Companions and Winifred Holtby's South Riding, filmed around Beverley and Hull. Since that time many more have followed which include: The Way to the Stars (1945) filmed at Catterick Camp, Billy Liar and Room at the Top (1958) both located in Bradford, Agatha (1978) filmed at Harrogate and York, The Water Babies at Malham and The Railway Children (1970) located along the Worth Valley Railway.

2

The great appeal of exploring the towns and villages of Britain lies in their uniqueness; each one is different from its neighbour, possessing its own individual characteristics. But how they appear to the casual visitor today is largely a matter of chance because their present face has been shaped by so many different factors. The landscape which surrounds them is of course important, hills or rivers or a coastline can be an obvious advantage, for these provide either a fine backcloth or a natural focal point around which the town can grow. Famous historical buildings sometimes dominate, towns like Winchester, Salisbury or Durham centre around their cathedrals, while Edinburgh, Pembroke and Lancaster always have one eye upon their castle. But Scarborough seems to have a little of everything; a sweeping coastline with two unspoilt bays, a headland on which is perched a Norman castle, a fine harbour full of gaily painted fishing boats and a history which stretches back to the Bronze Age. As I was later to discover it also has its rowdy side, but after all it is a holiday town where people come once a year to let their hair down. And if eventually you find the noise just too much as I did, a few minutes walk will bring you into the tranquillity of acres of fine spacious gardens with spectacular views of wide skies, towering cliffs and the ever present sea.

After parking my car in the busy shopping centre I stood on a street corner, being instantly recognisable as a visitor by the town-map I was consulting. At last convinced that I had pinpointed my location, I set off in the direction of my first objective, St Mary's Church. This 12th century building stands in an elevated position surrounded by small hotels with a fine view of the curving bay far below, its grey tower echoing with the cry of gulls.

Before going inside the building I stopped to read the words on a plaque that has been erected on the churchyard wall. Giving an outline of its history it mentions that 'the central tower and the chancel were destroyed by artillery during the Civil War when the Parliamentarians used the church for their batteries to attack the Royalist held castle.'

'Can you tell me how to get to Anne Brontë's grave please?'

I had entered the church to be pleasantly surprised by the sight of two smiling ladies who were selling cups of tea and scones close to the entrance. They were members of the fundraising Friends of St Mary's Church who urgently require donations to buy window guards to protect against vandalism, so a leaflet informed me.

Anne Brontë's grave

'Yes, of course. Go back to the main road then turn right towards the other entrance. You will find the grave behind the wall. It is easy to spot because it is always covered in flowers which are placed there by members of the Brontë Society.'

After drinking my tea, with the taped chants of monks appropriately providing background music, I made a quick tour of the church then went in search of the grave. Following the instructions I had been given I was soon gazing at the last resting place of

Anne Brontë which was indeed a feast of coloured flowers. The words on the moss laden grave stone with its carved urn and books, were highlighted by the bright sunlight: Here lie the remains of Anne Brontë, daughter of the Reverend P. Brontë, Incumbent of Haworth, Yorkshire. She died aged 28 on May 28th 1849.

This grave epitomises the most tragic episode in the life of these talented sisters which began in September 1848 with the death of their brother Branwell. Still grieving from their loss another great shock followed just three months later when in December 1848 Emily also died. Charlotte, devastated by this second tragedy, now saw that the health of her remaining sister Anne was also deteriorating for she had been particularly close to Emily. Clinging to the hope that the sea air of Scarborough would restore her vitality, the pair left Haworth on the 24th May. After breaking their journey in York they arrived here the next day, staying in a house on St Nicholas Cliff. But sadly Anne's condition continued to cause concern. A doctor was called to her on the 28th May but she was now beyond all medical help, she died the same day. Leaving this world her last words to Charlotte were 'take courage'.

It was here on this breezy hillside on which stands both this church and a nearby castle erected by William de Gros in the 12th century, that Scarborough really began. About 700 BC an Iron Age tribe chose this commanding headland for their fortified village, then 800 years later the Romans followed their lead by building a signal station. But it was a Dane nicknamed Scardi, meaning Harelip, who is regarded as the founder of the town. A Norse document, Kormakssaga, tells how two brothers named Kormak and Thorgils ventured down this east coast and settled here in AD 966. Their village became known as Scardiburgh meaning Harelip's Hill, from which the name Scarborough evolved. Since that time it has suffered from a succession of raiders, starting with the Norwegian Harold Haardaade during the 11th century and continuing into recent times.

The sturdy walls of the Norman castle have witnessed many famous visitors; King John stayed here four times, Edward I twice held his court here, and Richard III had many links with the town, the Queen's Tower being named in honour of his wife, Anne Neville. And in 1665 George Fox, founder of the Quaker Movement, who had become familiar with the inside of many English prisons tasted the unwanted hospitality of the dungeons.

It has also seen a great deal of military action over the last 800 years. In 1312 Piers Gaveston, who was the influential friend of Edward II took refuge in the castle. A siege followed which eventually ended with his capture by the Earl of Pembroke and after being interned at Warwick, his execution. During the turmoil created by the Dissolution in 1539 there followed the northern rebellion known as the Pilgrimage of Grace when adherents of the old faith tried unsuccessfully to take the castle.

But in 1563 the rebel leader Sir Thomas Wyatt was more successful, for he and his followers managed to enter the town one busy market day while dressed as peasants. He was then able to take the castle by surprise, but his victory was short lived and his life ended with the fall of an axe on Tower Hill. However his spectacular surprise attack did add a new colourful saying to the English language, a Scarborough warning.

The end of the castle as a formidable fortress, like so many others, followed the Civil War. It was held in 1643 by Sir Hugh Cholmley for the King, but after a siege which lasted for over a year its occupants were forced to surrender. Surprisingly the Royalists were again in possession in 1646, but this time after their defeat the building was reduced to a ruin. A prominent hill to the south of the town, on which now stands the war memorial, is named Oliver's Mount after the Parliamentary leader.

During the Great War the same German cruisers which shelled Whitby also raided Scarborough, but here they had more tragic results for many children were killed. Winston Churchill labelled them as 'the baby-killers of Scarborough', a term that shocked the world.

A steep narrow lane which wound its way down the hillside brought me to the red-roofed buildings that surround the bustle of the colourful harbour, and to the heart of this Queen of the East Coast. Crowds of visitors of every conceivable age, size, colour, creed and accent jostled happily side by side.

Here where Viking longboats once moored, sauntering middle aged men stared with curiosity at gaily painted pleasure crafts and wave-battered fishing boats. Fishing was of course Scarborough's first industry; this was recognised by Henry III who allowed the first real harbour to be constructed here in 1225. Three centuries later, in the reign of Elizabeth 1 when it needed to be rebuilt, the industry was still flourishing and continued to do so up to recent times. In 1974 it boasted a record herring catch valued at £5M, but the fish wars and treaties since then have led to an inevitable decline. Today the fishermen rely mainly on shellfish and whitefish trawled off the sea-bed to make a precarious living.

Holiday makers were gazing down from open topped buses at the crowds who were spilling off the pavement. Children whose mouths were whitened by melting ice cream looked in wonder at their magical surroundings, tugging hands towards bouncy castles. Excited screams came from fairground rides, while the hypnotic drone of electronic music which echoed from the amusement arcades drowned out the monotonous voice of the Bingo caller, 'Three and one, Thirty One.'

Ignoring the tempting notices which advertised 'Scarborough Cod and chips' and 'Double egg and ham', I continued my stroll along the waterfront. Here I passed a historic landmark which seems strangely out of place in this atmosphere of wild make believe, the King Richard III House. It dates from 1350 but gained its name in 1484 when the King is reputed to have stayed here. For many years it was a popular cafe but now it has a new role as a House of Mystery Museum.

The present holiday face of Scarborough owes much of its origin to Elizabeth Farrow who in 1620 discovered an unpleasant tasting spring near the South Shore. When the water, rich in iron and magnesium sulphate, became widely known for its medicinal properties it began to attract the visitors to the town. In 1700 the first Spaw House was built where the water could be taken in relative comfort, but thirty seven years later it tumbled into the sea. However by this time the magnificent coastal scenery which surrounded Scarborough together with the new fashion of sea-bathing made it inevitable that the town would expand. It had become England's first real holiday resort.

The appeal of the Spa water continued well into this century, with an impressive Spa building set in sweeping gardens having been constructed in 1858. Sadly this was burned down in 1876 but was quickly replaced by an even grander complex. Now much more than a place merely to take the waters it contained a Grand Hall where some of our greatest actors and musicians have since performed.

Paying a fee of just twenty five pence I was able to escape from the noise and bustle of the lower part of the South Bay. Riding in England's first cliff railway which started in 1875, I sedately ascended to the more genteel world of the Belvedere Gardens. Here, with the hot sun beaming down and the curving sea below I discovered the real charm of Scarborough – perfect peace!

3

Dodging Scarborough's busy holiday traffic I at last reached the remarkable Stephen Joseph Theatre in the Round, whose exterior was covered in builder's scaffolding following its latest move. I had arrived at a milestone in its history for it is exactly forty years since that great eccentric theatre director Stephen Joseph, together with his equally eccentric group of travelling players first arrived here. Once described as 'half genius, half madman' Stephen Joseph towered six-feet-two high, wore leather trousers, boots, a loud check shirt and a donkey jacket. He was a man of immense character and foresight, which no doubt he had inherited from his parents, for his father was the famous publisher Michael Joseph and his mother was the highly talented actress, Hermione Gingold. He became one of the great driving forces of post-war drama in Britain, being an advocate of the theatre in the round; a new concept which he successfully introduced in several provincial towns.

Two years later a young stage manager named Alan Ayckbourn came here to Scarborough to work for Joseph, and a friendship blossomed which became the catalyst from which Ayckbourn's amazing writing talent was to flourish. In 1959 his first two popular plays, The Square Cat and Love After All, were both written and performed here and his great gift for making people laugh became immediately apparent.

The death from cancer in 1965 of Stephen Joseph brought great sadness to the theatre, but in 1970 Alan Ayckbourn was persuaded to leave the BBC to become Director of Production here, where he remains. Over the last two decades he has continued his amazing output of classic plays; in 1975 he made theatrical history when five different plays which he had written were being performed in the West End at the same time.

Inside the foyer of the theatre I learned that yet another world premier was taking place, an event to which the people of Scarborough have grown happily accustomed. A Word from our Sponsor is a new musical which the adopted Yorkshireman has both written and directed, with music by John Pattison. It will then transfer to the Minerva Theatre in Chichester, then if past events are anything to judge by, will face rave reviews in the West End. For what Scarborough does today, London does next year but one!

This bustling resort is a marvellous playground where sea-gulls screech overhead, the laughter of holidaymakers fills the air and the grey cold waves of the North-sea pound the cliffs. This could be nowhere else but England's east coast which seems a world away from the sophistication and opulence of America's showbusiness capital of Hollywood. Yet a link does exist between the two, for here on the 1st July 1899 was born a man now regarded by many critics as being Hollywood's greatest ever screen actor, Charles Laughton.

He was the first son of Eliza and Robert Laughton who were the owners of the small but popular Victoria Hotel which did a thriving trade as the new Edwardian era dawned. This hotel lies close to the railway station, and is still in existence today. Soon after his two brothers, Tom and Frank

Charles Laughton

had arrived the successful family moved to the more splendid Pavilion Hotel where, as tenants, they could afford a large staff including a nanny for the children. Their mother who came from an Irish farming family, was a devoted Roman Catholic and the driving force behind the business. She ensured that the boys had a well disciplined, happy childhood, but spent little time with them.

Charles was cursed from childhood with a weight problem that was destined to be with him throughout his life. This Billy Bunter image led to much private anxiety, alienating him from friendship with other children as he often became the butt of their jokes. After being initially taught by nuns at a convent school at Filey, at the age of thirteen he became a pupil at the renowned Roman Catholic public school of Stonyhurst College in the heart of the Ribble Valley in Lancashire. Following in the footsteps of such famous pupils as Sir Arthur Conan Doyle, this sadly proved to be an unhappy period in his life. Due to his weight problem he was hopeless at games, regarded by the school as being very important. He also had an inborn hatred of all manner of authority, so the discipline which the Jesuits administered at Stonyhurst made his life even more miserable. His only joy lay in his love of art which was later to becoming a consuming passion, and the countryside, where he enjoyed identifying rare wild-flowers. This love of nature had been influenced by his mother's sister, Aunt Mary, who had been his close companion at Scarborough. However it was at Stonyhurst that he made his first stage appearance in the school play, Charles Hawtrey's The Private Secretary.

In 1915, after passing his School Certificate, he was expected to take up training in Hotel Management for the position which awaited him in the family business. This began at Claridge's Hotel in London where he enjoyed two years working in a lavish atmosphere of luxury created for the many rich and famous guests. It also gave him the opportunity to savour the delights of the West End theatre for the first time; a magical new world which by now seemed to be reaching out to him. But any thoughts of a stage career were quickly forgotten when like so many others of his generation, he became caught up in the horrors of the First World War. After joining the Royal Huntingdonshire Regiment as a private, refusing an offer of a commission, he was transported to the trenches of France where he faced the nightmare of bayonets and mustard-gas. Luckily his ordeal was short-lived; the war thankfully ended in 1918 so he was now free to return to Yorkshire. But the terrible suffering that he had seen was to remain with him for ever.

Back home he began working at the Pavilion Hotel where he was more interested in the interior design than in the business side. As a pastime he then joined an amateur dramatic group, the Scarborough Players, which at last gave him an opportunity to test out his talent. Any thoughts he had had of a career in the hotel business now quickly vanished; he knew his destiny lay elsewhere.

Disappointed that their eldest son felt he was unable to fulfil their hopes for him, yet sympathetic to his single-mindedness, his parents agreed that he could begin studying for the theatre at the prestigious Royal Academy of Dramatic Art (RADA). Being fat and plain he hardly seemed to be the matinee-idol type, yet from day one his outstanding natural acting ability became apparent. At the end of his course he took the gold medal award for the best actor of his year, then after leaving RADA made his debut on the London stage in 1926 as Osip in Gogol's The Government Inspector.

With astonishing energy by the time he was 28 years old he had already established himself as one of the leading actors in the West End. Then while starring in a play by Arnold Bennett he met Elsa Lanchester, a young lively actress who was regarded as an outrageous Bohemian. They became devoted to each other and in 1929 they were married. After two happy years together, a hectic period when they both acted on the stage and in silent films, a dramatic incident happened that was to have far-reaching effects. A male prostitute came to their home causing a great disturbance, claiming that Charles had used his services then refused to pay. The police arrived on the scene which resulted in both Laughton and the boy being summoned to court. Fortunately through the generosity of the magistrate the case was dismissed, for a guilty charge would have undoubtedly made any future move to Hollywood impossible. But he now confessed privately to an unsuspecting Elsa that he was indeed a homosexual who had had many affairs with young men. She was extremely shocked, but having been raised in a free-thinking family she was able to cope with the revelation. She still loved him, so decided she would remain by his side but that they must never have children as he would be a completely unsuitable father; their life together was slowly to change into a platonic relationship.

Still revelling in his many London triumphs which were constantly being acclaimed by the critics, in 1931 he and Elsa crossed the Atlantic to Broadway where Payment Deferred had a short but successful run. He then signed a three-year contract with Paramount Studios to star in two films a year, with the opportunity to choose his own roles. These included The Old Dark House (1932), based on Benighted, written by fellow Yorkshire-man J.B. Priestley. But it was when he took the major role in Alexander Korda's masterpiece, The Private Life of Henry VIII (1934) that Charles Laughton really became recognised as a great screen actor. This success also gave the British film industry a much needed boost, setting a pattern for the next three decades.

He starred in many all-time greats during the thirties, including The Barretts of Wimpole Street (1934), Mutiny on the Bounty (1935), Jamaica Inn (1939) and The Hunchback of Notre Dame (1939). But by this time he seemed to have reached a peak and the forties brought with them his slow decline. During this period he began giving public readings, mainly to troops as part of the war-effort and he also started giving acting classes to many potential stars. Much of the money he had earned from his many successes was spent on works of art, for his love of paintings never diminished.

In 1950 he began a partnership with impresario Paul Gregory, who introduced him to the lucrative recital tour in which he would give readings from great works. Then followed a welcomed change in his fortunes when his film career once more began to thrive. This revival resulted in more great performances in such films as Hobson's Choice (1954), Witness for the Prosecution (1957) and Spartacus (1960).

To the end of his life Charles Laughton remained a powerful, unique and complex man, who had been blessed with the greatest of acting talents. Forever tormented by the guilt of his inescapable homosexuality he could be both brutally cruel and marvellously endearing, but could never be ignored. His last film, Advise and Consent (1962) was made as his health quickly began to fail. After much suffering he died of bone cancer on the 15th December 1962, at the early age of sixty three.

4

As I drove through the neat suburbs of Filey I had the distinct feeling that I had arrived on the South Coast. Elderly women in flowery dresses were quietly chatting on the street corners while their husbands, shielded from the hot sun by trendy hats and dark glasses, stood by in silence. This could easily have been Eastbourne or Folkstone or Dover, but surely not the bracing Yorkshire Coast. However there was a simple explanation for this deception, the uncharacteristic sweltering heat continuing to astonish everyone..

I took a byroad near the attractively named Honey Pot Inn close to a sign which reminded me that I was in the 'Historic East Riding of Yorkshire'. This led me through Speeton and Buckton and Bempton, quiet secluded villages that have thankfully remained untouched by motorways or supermarkets. A poster proclaimed that a Flower Festival would soon be held and a hand written notice invited me to have 'a cup of tea'. But tempted as I was to stop the lure of what lay ahead proved too much. Even the 13th century church of St Oswald could not halt my progress; like a lemming I was heading straight for the cliff edge. But this was no ordinary cliff edge, it was Flamborough Head which I had been told (by a Yorkshireman) is the most magnificent peninsula in the whole of England.

I had now entered 'chalk country', a mineral we normally associate with the White Cliffs of Dover and the southern countryside which sweeps inland from the English Channel. However, a glance at a geological map reveals that a narrow chalk-bed curves eastwards through Norfolk towards the Wash. It then appears again near Skegness to reach its northern extremity close to Filey. Formed over 70 million years ago from the remains of minute sea organisms, chalk gives a distinctive soft look to the landscape. This is apparent in the Yorkshire Wolds which begin near this stretch of coastline; fold upon fold of green rolling fields separated by ancient hedgerows and gentle low hills in which hide half forgotten villages. It is a land whose light soils are easily cultivated and whose sweet chalk pastures make ideal grazing. So it is no surprise that early man made his home here, leaving behind a rich legacy of burial mounds and earthworks.

On a windswept cliff top in the shadow of a splendid white lighthouse I parked my car alongside a dozen others. I was about to walk away when a voice called out to me.

'Please can you tell me how much it is for the parking fee? I only learned to drive last year and I keep forgetting that I need to pay. I've already been fined £20 once this year!'

Flamborough Lighthouse

I looked across to the next car where there stood a healthy looking woman in her late sixties. In the bright sunshine her silver grey hair contrasted vividly with the deep tan of her face, from which sparkled the bluest eyes I have ever seen. At her side were two King Charles Spaniels that were friskily tugging at their leads, eager to begin their walk.

After explaining to her about the parking fee we had a short conversation. She told me that she came from Doncaster and that her husband had died three years ago immediately after he had retired. 'It was a terrible shock to me, his death seemed so unfair. So many men like him work all their lives then have no real retirement. The retirement age should be fifty five not sixty five.' She then confided how she had taken driving lessons after his death and had at last passed the driving test. This notable achievement now allowed her the freedom to come here to Flamborough where she had bought a caravan. 'It was one of our favourite places so I feel very close to him here. Those we love never really die, do they?'

With a cheery wave she walked away and I then began my exploration of this famous headland by strolling along a pathway with took me close to the lighthouse. This prominent landmark, 92 feet high, was built in 1806 by a Bridlington builder named John Matson. He is reputed to have taken a mere nine months to complete his work and he used not a single piece of scaffolding. The light, visible up to a distance of twenty one miles, originally gave a signal of one red and two white flashes but this was changed in 1925 to four white flashes every fifteen seconds. In 1859 a signal cannon was added for use in foggy weather, later superseded by rockets and a bullhorn, and in 1985 by a series of radio bleeps.

But this is not Flamborough's first lighthouse, for on my approach to this headland I had stopped to look at the oldest surviving one in the country. This was understandably being repaired, for the Chalk Tower dates from 1674. Its beacon was provided by a coal fire housed in a basket called a creset and the flame is believed to have given the name to this headland.

From a vantage point on the cliff edge I stood looking nearly two hundred feet down to the pounding waves breaking on the white rocks far below. Here and there were clusters of visitors; some were carefully descending narrow paths, others picnicking in sheltered hollows or looking as I was, at the magnificent sweep of the coastline. The sea, disappearing to a misty horizon, had a handful of fishing boats bobbing on its surface while the cry of seabirds echoed through the air.

Nesting seabirds make these cliffs different from those on the Channel Coast, for the busyness of the southern shipping lanes together with pollution has driven many of them away from Kent and Sussex. Here happily it is a different story, for Kittiwakes and Fulmers, Gannets and Guillemots thrive in relative safety. Much of this has been brought about by legislation which began in 1869 and continued with the Protection of Birds Act of 1954 which made egg collecting illegal. Until that time as many as 130,000 birds' eggs were harvested each year in a local industry which had been going on for centuries. Most of these were not used for food, but sold to the tanners of Leeds who used the whites as a leather softener.

In 1928 the great travel writer H.V. Morton paid a visit to Flamborough which he recorded in his best selling book, The Call Of England. Here he witnessed the Egg-Men who wore tin hats and blue dungarees, being lowered on ropes down the sheer cliffs to collect the eggs in canvas bags. He too was lowered over the frightening white wall, but quickly gave the pull-up signal for the 'steel-grey sea hissing over spikes and needles of rocks' below him was just too much!

For two hours I wandered along this fascinating cliff-top where fields of corn, coloured bronze by the sun, sweep down to the sea. Here I read a commemorative plaque which records one of the more curious events ever to happen in these parts, concerning the man whom many regard as the Father of the US Navy, privateer John Paul Jones. This Scottish born sailor

The chalk cliffs of Flamborough Head

who had become widely recognised for his audacity, was commissioned in 1775 as a Senior Lieutenant in the Continental Navy. This was at the time when that young upstart, the USA, had recently decided to break away from British rule.

Jones brought the fight into British waters with his ship Ranger, which attacked many English vessels in the Irish Sea and even landed at White-haven in Cumbria. He ended his mission of 1778 on a high note by capturing HMS Drake, which he triumphantly sailed into Brest harbour.

Spurred on by his victory he became even more ambitious, returning the following year in his new ship Bonhomme Richard, with the US frigate Alliance and three French vessels. He continued his raids on the shipping lanes around Ireland and Scotland then in September 1779 he learned that a merchant convoy, escorted by two British war ships was anchored here in Bridlington Bay. Confident that he could out-shoot them he opened fire on the ships as they rounded Flamborough Head and a fierce sea battle followed. It continued well into the night watched by onlookers from these cliffs, who eventually saw the surrender of HMS Serapis. But a high price had been paid, the British had seen 49 men killed and 68 wounded, while Jones had an even greater loss with half of his crew of 300 dying. At the moment of victory the Bonhomme Richard sustained a direct hit and sank shortly afterwards, so Jones transferred his command to the Serapis.

This battle off Flamborough Head proved to be a great morale booster for the rebels in the USA who regarded John Paul Jones as a hero. Louis XVI awarded him the Order du Merite Militaire and in the USA he was given a special gold medal. But he was a man more interested in action than accolades. He later sold his services to the Russians, and took part in several battles against the Turks in the Black Sea. He then went to France during the Revolution but could find little to occupy him and he died a bitter man in Paris in 1792.

A much older historical association with these parts is Dane's Dyke, a ditch which runs for over two miles across the peninsula. Experts tell us the name is misleading for it really dates from the Iron Age and was probably part of the settlement's defences at that time. However the Danes are known to have lived in these parts, many villages having distinctly Scandinavian names. One local legend even relates how an ancient local family paid rent for their land to the King of Denmark. They did this by fixing a gold coin to an arrow, then shooting it from the clifftop into the sea!

Before leaving Flamborough I went for a stroll around the North Landing, a secluded sandy cove where the lifeboat stands guard over a row of beached fishing cobles. Hemmed in by towering cliffs where the sound of lapping waves and screeching kittiwakes fill the air it is the kind of place where Long John Silver would feel completely at home.

Chapter Eight

Flamborough Head to York

*At Rudston I discover Britain's tallest standing stone then I go to
Hornsea for a last look at the Yorkshire Coast. I arrive in Beverley,
home of the White Rabbit, where I hear a curious tale about the
bones of St John. I learn of England's oldest horse race, see where
King Harold had his last victory, then exhausted, reach York. Here
I explore the Minster, hear of Dick Turpin and Guy Fawkes, take a
trip back to Jorvik, remember St Margaret Clitherow, then after
eating in York's oldest house, end by walking along the city walls.*

1

Any sensible person would have spent the afternoon lounging in a
deckchair on the beach at Bridlington, for the soft sand and the
cloudless sky made it look almost irresistible. But I had seen something
even more tempting indicated on my map. It said that if I went to the nearby
village of Rudston I would find the tallest standing stone in the whole of
Britain; this I could not resist.

I reached the village at the hottest time of the day, the sun was blazing
down with mediterranean ferocity. Not a single person out of the population of 320 could be seen, not even the sound of a car or tractor disturbed
the air. Quietly I closed my car door, trying my hardest not to break the
spell, then I walked up the road once trod by Roman sandals, towards the
church of All Saints. The churchyard was alive with the drone of insects
and house martins were zooming around the tower as I strolled towards
the north-east corner of the building. Suddenly I stopped with
astonishment; before me lay a huge towering block of gritstone, much larger
and much grander than I had ever imagined, it dominated the whole
churchyard. Standing just twelve feet from the church wall it was as if
Christianity and Paganism were almost holding hands.

Protected by a small fence at its base and crowned with a protective cap
of lead, this monolith is 25 feet 9 inches (7.9 metres) in height and is said
to weigh around 46 tons. It is believed that it was originally even higher,

once having a sharp point at the top, but at some time in its history, this two-feet long portion was broken off. In the late 18th century Sir William Strickland, intrigued by the huge stone, began excavating alongside it. He came to the conclusion that its depth below ground was equal to its height above, which if this is true would make its complete length almost 52 feet (16 metres).

Inevitably the origin of this unique monument has been a source of speculation in the Wolds for centuries. One local legend relates how the devil became angry with the people of Rudston because they were so good. One sabbath as they flocked into church, he hurled a stone spear at them but this was deflected by God, so it ended up in the ground close to the church. This could well be a very ancient tale which recalls when the community first began to worship the new god, Jesus Christ.

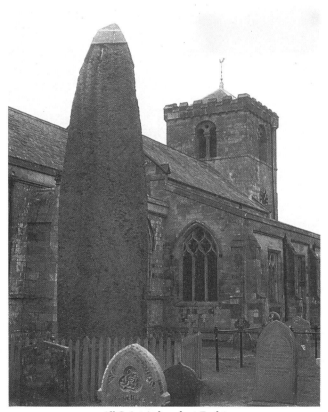

Gritstone, not found around Rudston, has its nearest local source at Cayton Bay, ten miles away. This means that the huge stone was either dragged here by prehistoric man, a tremendous task, or was carried here by the movement of a glacier. But even if the latter was the case, just to erect the stone into its present vertical position would have taken amazing effort and ingenuity.

A single freestanding stone is often referred to as a Menhir; a Celtic term which means 'long stone'. Often these were arranged

All Saints' church at Rudston

into groups to form part or full circles, or long rows known as alignments. The Neolithic people who first started erecting these monuments in Britain about 3000 BC were immigrants from the Middle East. It is believed that they were built for religious purposes of which we know little. The worship of dead ancestors, the belief in a goddess of fertility or in a sun god, are among a host of theories which have been put forward.

What is not often realised is that these Neolithic and Bronze Age people, our ancestors, were little different in intelligence to ourselves. They merely lacked the knowledge of science and discovery which time alone has brought to us. Many of their religious beliefs were founded on an astute comprehension of the world as they knew it, a world that appeared to be much smaller and more mysterious than our own. However although science may have robbed us of much of the sense of wonder which these people had many of their basic fears and doubts remain with us today.

The sadness and grief brought by death is a dark thread which runs unending through all our lives. Few of us are fortunate enough to reach even into our thirties before the loss of a close member of our family occurs. Grandparents, parents, brothers and sisters, then our wife or husband are inevitably taken from us as we grow older, until, if we survive beyond eighty few of our contempories remain. Each death brings with it, even if we choose to ignore the fact, a constant reminder of our own mortality. And for early man, whose life cycle was much shorter than ours, this was even more apparent. So instinctively he looked beyond the boundaries of his own world to the place where the spirits of his dead ancestors resided, and in some cases they became the object of his worship.

At the other end of the life cycle is birth, the miracle by which the human race is allowed to continue and which we now take so much for granted. Maternity wards, scans, and fertility clinics have made our entrance into this world predictable and controlled, overcoming the many problems which our forbears wrestled with for tens of thousands of years. So it is not surprising that they looked to the power beyond birth, a Goddess of Fertility, for favours that were so important to the destiny of their people.

Other major factors essential to their survival also became the object of their worship. The Sun god, who brought light, warmth and food; the spirits which resided in water; and in some cases the power of the moon. However when the Christian missionaries first came here to Rudston to convert the local people to the 'new faith', they would have found that this stone was at the centre of their pagan beliefs. As Bede relates, it was the practice to keep existing holy places, so the stone would probably have been crowned with the Christian symbol of the cross. This is borne out by the name of the village, Rud being derived from Rood, meaning Cross, and Stun from Stan which means Stone. As Christianity slowly became accepted a simple church would have been built here, the circular churchyard which still exists suggests this may have been of Saxon origin. It would later have been superseded by the present Norman church erected in 1100 AD by the new Lord of the Manor, William Peverel.

In a secluded corner of this holy ground I came upon the grave of the novelist Winifred Holtby, who after writing the best-seller South Riding, died at the early age of 37. She was born in a farmhouse close to the village in 1898, then spent much of her girlhood living in Rudston House. Her appropriate memorial is an open book on which is inscribed:

God give me work till my life shall end
And life till work is done.

Stepping into the cool of this beautiful church I read of another event which confirmed Rudston's position on the archaeological map. In April 1933 a local farmer, while ploughing his fields, turned up some fragments of tiles. They were later found to be part of three Roman mosaic pavements which had lain undiscovered eighteen inches beneath the soil for 1800 years and were in excellent condition. Made from small pieces of coloured stone taken from various parts of Yorkshire they had been part of a Roman Villa. These were later removed to the safety of Hull Museum where they now form part of a permanent exhibition.

For half an hour I explored the gleaming interior, I read fascinating memorials, admired stained glass windows and enjoyed the marvellous serenity of the place. From these odd snippets of information I learned that the Macdonald family, who are Clan Chiefs in the Western Isles, have had a residence in these parts since 1818 and that the church was nearly destroyed by a land mine during the last war.

Returning to Bridlington I then followed the coastal road southwards, passing through the ancient villages of Skipsea and Atwick which lie in a landscape of wide skies and fertile fields. This region, known as Holderness, sweeps to a shifting coastline mercilessly battered in wintertime by the stormy North Sea. Since the Romans first passed this way over two miles of land has been lost to the waves, together with several villages whose church bells are reputed to still ring out from beneath the water.

My journey down this magnificent Yorkshire coast came to a reluctant end when I reached the small holiday town of Hornsea. After taking a stroll along its lively narrow streets, looking at samples of the famous Hornsea Pottery and gazing out over the largest freshwater lake in these parts, I turned inland. A short drive in the afternoon sun took me westwards over the River Hull into the splendour of Beverley where the twin towers of the Minster beckoned to me across flat green pastures.

Among the stream of traffic rushing around the perimeter of the town were a number of military vehicles which reminded me that this is a region which has long been associated with defence. There remains an RAF airfield at nearby Leconfield where pilots and navigators are trained and the town boasts the Museum of Army Transport. Among its prized exhibits is the Rolls Royce car once used by Field Marshal Lord Montgomery and appropriately, a huge Beverley transport plane which was an important troop carrier.

I have many personal memories of the Beverley aircraft, or at least the huge four bladed propellers and their pitch change mechanisms, for these were manufactured by the Dehavilland Aircraft Company at their factory at Lostock near Bolton. Here I began my engineering training and one of my first tasks as an apprentice was to prepare a number of Beverley props for assembly. Every bolt, every nut and every washer had to be neatly lined up by me on immaculately clean benches, awaiting the scrutiny of the aircraft inspector. God-like and unsmiling he would at last appear with his clip board. Carefully he would check each part as I watched from a distance, for should even the slightest flaw be detected I would be the subject of his torrent of abuse. So I am well aware of the meticulous workmanship that went into every aspect of the manufacture of the much-loved Beverley.

Sir John Betjeman, whose poetry so many admire, said that 'there is a great surprise in store' for anyone who visits Beverley and of course he was quite right. This ancient market town is a feast of delight for those who love good architecture, enjoy historical connections or just merely like to browse in an atmosphere of unpretentious elegance. But of course there is always one snag; I only allowed four hours to explore the town, but to really do it justice I needed four days.

I began by walking from North Bar Without into North Bar Within, the only remaining gate from the old wall that once completely circled the town. It was built in 1409 from local hand made brick and remains one of the most impressive town entrances in England. Within minutes I was admiring a group of fine magpie houses which looked as if they had been built in the time of Elizabeth I but really date from the 1850s. Here lived James Edward Elwell, a distinguished wood carver who worked for Sir Gilbert Scott. When his business flourished his political allegiance also began to switch from the Liberals to the Tories. This led him to carve a series of political cartoons which can be seen on the wall of his home.

Before I reached the centre of the town I made a diversion into the glorious interior of St Mary's Church by North Bar which is a treasure house of medieval carvings. It was built in 1120 as a chapel-of-ease attached to Beverley Minster and contains a wealth of interest. Among these is a series of panels on the chancel ceiling, depicting the Kings of England. They begin with the little known Sigebert II who reigned in the 7th century, and end with Henry VI who was on the throne when the panels were originally painted. However one recent monarch, George VI, was included during a restoration which took place in 1939; his effigy replaced that of King Lochrine whom, it was discovered, had never existed!

If like me, you are one of those people who in the secrecy of their homes furtively read such children's books as Wind in the Willows, the Water Babies or Alice in Wonderland, then you should come to this church. For if you seek out the Sacristy doorway you will find the statuette of a rabbit carved in 1325. But this is no ordinary rabbit for many believe it was the inspiration for the famous White Rabbit created by Lewis Carroll. As a child the author was brought here by his grandfather who lived at nearby Hull and it is believed that he incorporated his childhood memory into his classic book.

Crowds of shoppers and visitors were bringing a lively, colourful atmosphere to the bustling streets that radiate from the cobbled market place. Some were standing in the sunlight admiring the impressive Market Cross, others were sauntering down narrow alleyways in search of old inns, while two young women I saw were wrestling with their consciences. Gazing adoringly into the window of a baker's shop they were discussing whether to ignore their diet and have a binge on the tempting Yorkshire fare on display.

Slowly I strolled through the town, passing a pub named the Monk's Walk and the splendid Georgian houses of Highgate until at last I reached the pride of Beverley; the Minster. Bathed in the glow of bright sunlight its mellowed stonework soared magnificently into the contrasting blue sky. For a time I just stood and stared at this huge edifice raised to God, my eyes following the lines of its twin towers which seem to stretch almost to heaven. But many visitors are surprised to learn that the Minster is not a cathedral as its dominating presence suggests, but 'merely' the Parish Church! For Yorkshire is so well blessed with such stunning ecclesiastical buildings that it can afford to pick and choose; York Minster is in fact Beverley's Cathedral and the seat of their Archbishop.

I wandered into the interior of this church which stands on the site of a monastery founded by St John of Beverley who retired here in the early eighth century. He was a local man who had been born at nearby Harpham in 640 AD, then rose to become the Bishop of Hexham and then of York. Following his death it became a place of pilgrimage which led King Athelstan here in 937 AD. Thankful for his success in battle he enhanced its status by creating a College of Secular Canons and granting it the Right of Sanctuary. After the Conquest the Normans continued to revere the holy site, a new church was built in 1170 but was later destroyed by fire, leading to the construction of the present magnificent building which dates from 1220.

In the quietness of the church I stood near the shrine of St John of Beverley, thinking of the thousands of pilgrims who once came here from every corner of the land, hoping that this holy man would intercede for them. It is said that the victor of Agincourt, King Henry V, was one of these; he believed his success over the French was due to the power of St John.

But these sacred bones have not rested in complete peace since they were first placed here almost 1300 years ago. In the year 1023 they were taken from the original burial site and put inside an elaborate jewelled shrine, in anticipation of his canonisation which followed in 1037. This was a fitting shrine for the revered saint but soon the turmoil of the Conquest came, then the disastrous fire of 1188 when the bones were thought to have been lost forever. However this proved to be wrong for in 1197 it was discovered that they had miraculously escaped the flames, so with a sigh of relief they were safely reburied for another century!

When the present imposing Minster was constructed in the thirteenth century St John's bones were once more enshrined in a place of honour behind the High Altar were they remained for the next three hundred years. But then came the horror of the Dissolution, in 1548 the shrine was destroyed and again the bones were lost. However in the relaxed atmosphere following the Restoration of King Charles II they were again found by a gravedigger; they had been saved by being carefully wrapped in lead. In the 18th century they at last found a permanent resting place in a specially constructed brick vault at the east end of the Nave which had an inscribed slab added in 1936.

From the shrine I continued my tour through this unique building; it was a stroll through thirteen centuries of turbulent English history illustrated in ornately sculptured stone, finely carved wood and glinting stained glass. Then before taking to the York road I followed in the footsteps of thousands of pilgrims and the more notorious Dick Turpin by enjoying the hospitality of one of Beverley's many ancient inns.

2

It was late afternoon when I drove west from Beverley, passing leafy suburbs which end in the sweep of green that surrounds its attractive racecourse. Yorkshire is of course a county that loves horse racing. Even those of us who have no interest in the sport cannot fail to have heard the radio announcer say, 'Now we have the racing results from Thirsk..' or perhaps Ripon, or Wetherby or Pontefract or York! But it is at Doncaster where·the famous St Leger is run that excited crowds from all over the world pour into the grandstands. This classic race takes it name not from a Christian saint, but from Colonel Anthony St Leger who first started the event on local Cantley Common in 1776. Then two years later it moved to the present course where, with the exception of two short breaks during the world wars, it has remained ever since. However it is here in the Wolds at Kiplingcotes that England's oldest horse race takes place. Some say it was founded in 1519 while others say it was as late as 1555, but all agree it is very old. It is run each March over a four mile course of muddy fields following a strict set of ancient rules. Often the horse that comes in second gets a larger prize than the winner, but of course this is Yorkshire!

A straight highway bordered by lush fields drowned in hazy sunshine, led me from Bishop Burton across the southern Wolds towards York. But just seven miles from the city centre near the banks of the Derwent, I saw one of those old fashioned road signs whose message was irresistible. Stamford Bridge it declared, pointing its weather-worn arm up a narrow lane that was overhung with a tunnel of foliage. As I drove slowly between the twisting hedgerows it was not just the miles but also the centuries which were tumbling away. For here where cattle now contentedly munch the lush grass, was started one of the greatest dramas in our history; a victory that was destined to turn so quickly to defeat.

When the year 1066 first dawned King Edward, known as The Confessor, lay on his death bed in Westminster Abbey, a building which had only been consecrated the previous year. He was a regarded as a weak ruler but a highly religious, gentle man, and was later to be elevated to sainthood. But the real power had lain with his father-in-law, the powerful Earl Godwin and his family who effectively controlled the country. As Edward lay dying he predicted that evil would soon befall his kingdom; a prophecy which seemed to be further underlined by the rare sighting of Halley's Comet a few months later. Just before his death on the 5th January, King Edward named Harold who was the late Earl's eldest son, as his successor. Such was the uncertainty of the period that Harold was crowned on the following day, when Edward was also buried.

But no sooner had the crown rested on Harold's head than opposition to his rule began to quickly materialise from two different factions who wanted the declining Anglo-Saxon kingdom for their own. These came from William, Duke of Normandy, who maintained that Edward had promised him the throne; and Harold Hardrada, the King of Norway, who had links with the Scandinavian settlers who now occupied much of northern England. Both of these two enemies were exploited by Harold's treacherous brother, Tostig, who having lost the Earldom of Northumbria because of his corrupt ways, now sought revenge. Thus King Harold, protected by his small army known as House-Carls, waited in anxious anticipation not knowing from which direction the blow would first fall.

It came from Tostig, whose forces began a series of raids on important ports on the south coast of England. They managed to plunder Sandwich, which brought a quick response from King Harold's army, But by this time his brother had continued his raids up the east coast, then hastened to Scotland where he was able to find sanctuary with King Malcolm III. However, now realising that his own army was inadequate, he then contacted King Harold Hardrada of Norway who agreed to mount a full scale invasion.

In September 1066 the Norwegian ships, carrying a formidable army, sailed first to the Orkney Islands then down the east coast of Scotland. After joining forces with Tostig's men the fleet continued southwards, leaving the coast at Hull to sail inland up the River Humber and into the Ouse. The army of about 9,000 men landed at Riccall just eight miles from the centre of York, where they camped.

At this time King Harold was in southern England, but the northern Earls led by Morcar of Northumbria brought their forces to York in an attempt to repel the Norwegian invaders. A short fierce battle took place at Fulford, but although the English fought gallantly they were no match for the larger army. The defeated Earls were forced to negotiate a peace treaty, agreeing to supply food and exchange hostages, if in return York was not sacked.

It was here in the village of Stamford Bridge where several roads met at an important crossing of the River Derwent, that the exchange of prisoners and supplies was going to take place. But the unsuspecting invaders did not know that King Harold, after learning of their presence, had marched his army over two hundred miles in five days. Taken unawares the Norwegians faced their opponents on the 25th September and a terrible slaughter took place. One of the epic moments recorded from the battle tells how a giant Norwegian stood alone on the small wooden bridge, holding back the English army with the ferocious swinging of his double

Monument commemorating the Battle of Stamford Bridge

edged axe. He was finally brought down by the upward thrust of a spear, planted by an enterprising soldier who had sailed beneath the bridge in a pig-trough!

The fighting continued for the whole day, by which time the invaders began to flee in disarray. An arrow had killed their king, Tostig's skull had been broken by an axe, and over 5,000 of the invaders lay dead. Those who remained alive were allowed to return home after a treaty had been signed that promised they would never attack England again. In triumph Harold marched into York where a great victory feast took place, but beneath the celebration was an underlying fear for he knew he had yet to face his other enemy, William, Duke of Normandy. This of course came at Hastings less than three weeks later when his exhausted army lost not only the battle but the kingdom. The gallant King Harold, who had reigned for a short but momentous ten months died just a few miles from the coast he had vowed to defend. His body was at first buried beneath a cairn of stones near the battlefield then later reburied in Waltham Abbey. But many Anglo-Saxons refused to believe their leader had really died. In the dark days that followed when the Normans devastated much of the north, rumours circulated that he had merely gone into hiding; one day he would return and free England from William's harsh rule.

With the roar of traffic on my right and the placid waters of the Derwent on my left, I stood in the village that has grown around the battlefield of Stamford Bridge. Here I read the words written on a simple memorial which recall the Anglo-Saxon's last great victory.

3

I looked out from the window of my hotel bedroom over the gardens and rooftops of York towards the Minster which lay half hidden behind the top branches of a sycamore tree. As the light breeze swayed these branches more of the gracious building was revealed, then as the breeze ceased it was tantalisingly removed from my vision. After ten minutes I could stand this suspense no longer. Although I was tired from the day's journey and hungry because I had not eaten since breakfast, I knew that I would not sleep soundly if I did not get a closer view. So summoning a reserve of dwindling energy I stepped out of the Edwardian doorway, walked through an archway of medieval stones (the hotel stood on the site of an ancient priory), then strolled into the centre of the city.

Darkness had fallen, the crowds had melted away and I almost had this noble church to myself. In a magical atmosphere of light and shadow I wandered along the deserted aisles. I looked where the rich and the holy had been laid to rest five centuries ago; their effigies embellished in red and gold. I knelt before the altar in the Zouche Chapel built in 1349 and dedicated to 'God, the Virgin, and all the Saints, especially St Mary and her sister Martha.' I gazed upwards in wonder at the elegance of sculptured ceilings and rounded arches, I ran my fingers over hardened oak carved by Norman hands, then I sat quietly watching the light dance like a kaleidoscope on the most remarkable stained glass window in the world. My tiredness and hunger were now almost forgotten; I had become entranced by the hypnotic holiness which has grown here in York.

Minster is an Anglo-Saxon word which means 'large church' and York Minster is the largest Gothic cathedral in the whole of Europe. This present magnificent building, cruciform in outline and with three superb towers, took 252 years to complete. King Henry III was on the throne when building first began in 1220 and the work continued through the reign of eight other monarchs before it was completed in 1472.

But Christianity had arrived in this patch of high ground between the Foss and the Ouse many centuries earlier. The Romans established their great northern capital of Eboracum here, which by 314 had its own Bishop. But when the legions withdrew from our shores the flame of paganism swept through the north, it continued for over two centuries until Edwin, King of Northumbria, became a convert to Christianity. In the tumbled stones of the former Eboracum he had a simple wooden church built where on Easter Day 627 he was baptised. It was from this seed that the present Minster grew; three churches having occupied the site before the Conquest,

York Minster

the last being destroyed by the invading Normans who were showing their disdain for Anglo-Saxon craftsmanship. They then erected a church which they considered to be worthy, this stood for 150 years before being demolished to make way for the present magnificent design.

However in more recent times York Minster has suffered from a series of problems. In 1829 a madman named Jonathan Martin deliberately set fire to the choir which caused considerable damage, then eleven years later the nave vault was also destroyed by yet another fire caused by a fallen candle. In 1967 came an even bigger shock for it was found that not only had death-watch beetles been gnawing away at the woodwork but the massive, 234 feet high central tower was in danger of collapse! Surveyors found that the 20,000 ton structure rested only on a shallow foundation of loose stones which was sinking into the ground. At a cost of over £2m, 30,000 tons of earth was removed from beneath the base then replaced with reinforced concrete.

No sooner had this work been completed than another disaster followed. On the 9 July 1984 the Minster was struck by lightning which some people said was a sign that God was unhappy with certain trends within the Church of England. The resulting fire destroyed all but two of the unique roof bosses in the timber framed central vault and almost spread to the central tower. But with resolute determination an army of builders, glaziers, artists and engineers quickly took on the task of massive restoration. By a tremendous effort this was completed almost a year ahead of schedule, the building being rededicated in November 1988.

As I sat in the hushed atmosphere watching the yellow light cast moving shadows on the ancient stones, my head was filled with this cavalcade of history which York Minster provokes. But I am told that if the experts were asked to decide what single feature makes it unique they would almost certainly say its stained glass. For it boasts 117 breathtaking coloured windows which contain over half of the total surviving medieval glass to be found in England.

Saint Bede tells us that stained glass came to Britain towards the end of the seventh century. It quickly became a powerful tool in the fight to spread the word of God among a largely illiterate society. Vividly illustrating the life of Jesus, events from the bible and the images of saints in sparkling coloured pictures, it had developed into an advanced art form by the late 12th century.

The glass was made by heating river sand and wood ash which was coloured by adding metal oxides to the molten mix. It was then blown into a balloon shape before being flattened to the thickness required. After being cut to shape it was coated with iron oxide and powdered glass, then reheated. The pieces were then linked together like a jigsaw puzzle around frames of lead soldered together to form the finished picture. Once the window was in position it was rendered waterproof by being sealed with a cement.

Waiting for the arrival of my evening meal in a secluded restaurant in the shadow of the Minster, I read of an incident that illustrates the powerful position which York enjoys. A medieval archbishop once claimed that the city was the second capital of England and therefore had precedence over Canterbury. The Pope at this time had to solve the dispute without upsetting either of his leading English clergymen. With great tact he declared that the Archbishop of York was the Primate of England and the Archbishop of Canterbury was the Primate of all England, which somehow seemed to settle the argument!

4

There had been a shower of rain during the night, the first rain for many weeks, but let me quickly add that it hardly dampened the pavements. As I stepped out of the hotel doorway, fortified for the day by a huge breakfast, the sky was now cloudless and the air pleasantly warm. I was happy that I could abandon my car for York is a city that must be explored on foot. Lorries and cars and coaches which have become the 20th century plague, are now firmly discouraged here. Inner city car parking has been made deliberately expensive for the city council wants to tempt motorists to use their Park and Ride system. Cycling, on the other hand, has been encouraged by the creation of a number of suburban cycle lanes which stretch into the city centre.

York was awakening as I followed the riverside pathway past up-market apartments which have been tastefully created from Victorian warehouses. Young mallard ducks disturbed by my footsteps, began to lazily stretch their wings as a motor-launch named the May Belle sailed by. When I crossed the cream coloured city walls I knew that I had reached York proper; a settlement once known by the Vikings as Jorvik, by the Saxons as Eofric, by the Romans as Eboracum, and by those who came before as Caer Ebruc. For that is what is so bewildering to a stranger about this unique city; so many different peoples have lived here and so many historic events have taken place here that it is difficult to decide where to begin. I then made my decision, I would follow no set plan but let fate rule my day. I then saw a sign which pointed toClifford's Tower; it seemed a good place to start.

Rising steeply upwards from flat ground is a grassy conical mound which has had its top removed and on which was built in 1345 Clifford's Tower. This is part of two Norman fortresses which once stood guard over the city on each side of the river; the other having been completely destroyed by the Danes. At the base of this dominant landmark I read the words on a plaque which commemorates one of York's most infamous episodes:

On the night of Friday 16 March 1190 some 150 Jews and
Jewesses of York, having sought protection in the Royal
Castle on this site, from a mob incited by Richard Malebisse
and others, chose to die at each other's hand rather than
renounce their faith.

This horrific tragedy, similar to the one which took place in Massada in the Holy Land, followed a period of anti-Semitic riots. The sheriff allowed the Jews to take refuge in the tower, but it proved to be only a temporary escape from the mob who were closing in. Determined not to allow themselves to be massacred they chose to kill themselves by setting fire to the tower.

I ascended the steep steps which lead to this elevated monument, then I wandered around its white walls which allow fine views over the city. In

Clifford's Tower

1644 the cannon balls of the Civil War did serious damage here, but the building was restored, only to be damaged again by an explosion thirty years later.

A famous historic character who would have been very familiar with this landmark was the highwayman Dick Turpin, but many of his renowned exploits owe more to fiction than fact. He was born near Saffron Walden in Essex in 1706, then in his youth became an apprentice butcher. However he found that cattle stealing was more lucrative, so he joined a gang of thieves who also became involved in smuggling and highway robbery. One of his colleagues in crime was another infamous and clever robber named Tom King. This less well-known highwayman found Turpin to be rather bungling and something of a handicap.

So the partnership ended with Turpin heading north into Lincolnshire and Yorkshire where he managed to stay just one step ahead of the law. However this ended in 1739 when he was arrested for horse stealing. He was convicted at York Assizes, then spent his last night here in the condemned cell in York Castle before facing the hangman the following day. Sadly I have to relate that the romantic tale of his exciting ride to York on his marvellous steed Black Bess, which we all loved to read as children is untrue. This was created by the author Harrison Ainsworth for his novel

Rookwood, then quickly became repeated by others until fact and fiction began to merge.

Another notorious man who was born here in York was Guy Fawkes. He was baptised on 16 April 1570 at St Michael-le-Belfrey church, his birthplace being a fine residence in Stonegate. His attempt to blow up both King and Parliament on 5 November 1605, as an act of defiance against religious intolerance, ended in failure. He died the following year after being cruelly tortured and his effigy has been burnt ever since on the bonfires which are lit throughout the land. There is, however, just one exception. The boys of St Peter's School here in York never burn a Guy, for as he was a former pupil they feel bound to respect his memory. Others too have at various times found sympathy with the Gunpowder Plot. A popular slogan written on walls during the Poll Tax demonstrations just a few years ago read: Guy Fawkes was right!

My walk then brought me into Castlegate, passing the splendid Georgian mansions of Castlegate House and Fairfax House designed by John Carr in 1759. Early morning shoppers were already crowding into the precinct of Coppergate which a plaque told me was: 'so called as early as 1378 and was perhaps one of the first medieval streets in the city to have a paved way. It was the scene of public markets and gatherings, proclamations and punishments'. It went on to relate how the Earl of Northumberland had been beheaded on this spot and that after the Restoration of King Charles II in 1660 an effigy of Oliver Cromwell was burnt here.

There was a time not long ago when Jorvik, the Viking name for York, was little known. However in recent years this has all changed for visitors now flock in to visit the Jorvik Viking Centre; a brilliant and unique heritage concept which has caught the imagination of the world. I joined the queue of people who were spilling out into the sunshine of Coppergate, all intent on stepping back in time.

In the tenth century, Jorvik was the Capital of the north of England, a rich and prosperous city which had been built up by the Vikings who first settled here in AD 866. But until archaeologists began excavating here in 1981 it was thought that all signs of Jorvik had long since disappeared. However they were astonished to find that deep down, preserved in the damp mud alongside Coppergate, lay the remains of whole streets of houses, workshops and warehouses. Alongside these were discovered the rubbish tips of the Viking families; their discarded junk of old shoes, boots, pins and thousands of other items became a fascinating Aladdin's Cave to the historians.

At last my turn came. I paid an entrance fee them I took my place in an open carriage that is rather like the ghost-train found in seaside fun fairs. But instead of being whisked into a world of horror I was taken on a journey through time. Using the marvels of modern technology not only are sights and sounds reproduced, but even the smells of yesteryear permeated into our time machine. Thirty generations of life in York glided by us in animated displays until we reached October 948 when time then stopped.

We had arrived in Jorvik where the townspeople were carrying on with a way of life few of us imagined ever existed. Here we saw the thatched buildings and narrow alleyways of Lundgate and Coppergate which lead down towards the River Foss. We saw Thorfast the bone carver making pins and combs from antlers; we saw wooden bowls and spoons being fashioned by Lothin, Snarri the jeweller selling his brooches and Svein's leather shop. And we had a fascinating glance into a Viking home where we saw the family chatting and working around an open fire, then we saw a moored cargo boat that had just arrived from Norway.

Achaeological detectives, engineers and many different types of craftsmen have merged their skills to bring this marvellous concept alive. Two of the original rows of buildings have been painstakingly reconstructed while two more have been left exactly as they were discovered.

At the end of the ride I arrived back in the 20th century. For half an hour I wandered through the Skipper Gallery where I saw over 500 objects from an amazing total of 30,000 which have so far been uncovered. These include amber beads imported from Denmark, a spur, pieces of woollen cloth, dice made from Walrus ivory and the fabulous Coppergate Helmet. But this magnificent headpiece is not Viking but Anglo-Saxon, it dates from the eighth century; made from iron and brass it probably gave protection to a nobleman who may well have been fighting the invading Vikings. What is known is that he was a follower of Christ, for the helmet is inscribed with: 'In the name of Jesus Christ, the Holy Spirit, God the Father and all we pray. Amen. Oshere of Christ'.

Before stepping out into the shops of Coppergate I struck myself a silver penny to spend. Unfortunately I was a thousand years too late for the dies used to produce this coinage were found during the excavations and belong to the age of King Athelstan!

5

One of the great joys of York, and there are many, are the large number of ancient churches which seem to hide up nearly every tiny street. Watched over by the Minster like a hen looking after her chicks, they provide a marvellous escape from the bustle of the town. Their pews are often filled by exhausted visitors who find they can no longer walk another yard without resting their travel-weary legs. If they are lucky they will also be able to have a cup of tea, for many of these churches are no longer used for religious services but have been put to other uses. This is because York is third only to London and Norwich in its number of parish churches, and dwindling congregations have made many of them redundant. Sadly we are never likely to hear again the collective feast of music which once resounded each sabbath from the bells of St Martin's, St Michael's, St Helen's, St Mary's, St Margaret's, St Cuthbert's, St Olave's and many many others.

'Would you please keep outside the barriers,' said a huge Irish navvy who looked menacingly in my direction. Sheepishly I obeyed, for I had tried to take a short cut past a deep muddy hole that had been dug on The Pavement. An army of his fellow workers wearing grim faces and hard hats, also nodded their disapproval, so quickly I escaped into The Shambles.

Once known by the far less attractive name of Fleshamels, this tiny medieval street with its gables which almost touch each other is the pride of York. It was mentioned in the Domesday Book and up to recent times remained a street of butcher's shops and slaughterhouses. However vegetarian visitors need not fear

The Shambles

for they are no longer greeted by the sight of blood soaked carcasses. Instead they can buy framed watercolours, guide books, that post card of the Minster for the folks 'back home, or just gaze out over a cup of steaming coffee at the passing crowds.

I walked over the gleaming cobbles which were sheltered from the sun by the overhanging upper stories, until I came to a sign often missed by browsing visitors. It reads: 'The Shrine of Saint Margaret Clitherow.' I stepped inside the tiny room which has been made into a simple chapel. Here Roman Catholic pilgrims come from all parts of England to light candles and to pray to this brave woman who died for her faith.

Margaret Clitherow who was born in 1555, was the daughter of Thomas Middleton, the Sheriff of York. In July 1571 she married a rich butcher named John Clitherow and came to live here in the Shambles. But three years later after a period of religious contemplation, she decided to become a Roman Catholic. Her Protestant husband accepted her decision, but this brought many problems as the authorities had outlawed the old faith. Her absence from the Parish Church aroused their suspicions which led to a series of raids on her home which eventually uncovered a chalice, vestments and other 'massing stuffe'.

She was charged with harbouring priests, but refused to plead as she did not wish to have her children and servants called as witnesses against her. This led to an automatic sentence of slow pressing to death under a weighted board; a penalty given to those who refused to plead when charged with acts of felony or treason.

'God be thanked I am not worthy of so good a death as this', were her last words. The terrible punishment was car-

Saint Margaret Clitherow

ried out on her pregnant body at Tolbooth Prison here in York on 25 March 1586. It is said that her remains were later rescued by fellow catholics who buried them secretly at an unknown site, but her hand is preserved as a relic in the Bar Convent. She was beatified in 1929 then canonised as one of the forty martyr-saints of England and Wales in 1970.

I wandered among the stalls of the open market which lie behind the Shambles, explored the delightfully named Whip-ma-Whop-ma-gate, then I decided it was time for some refreshments. I could not resist eating in Crumbles Tea Room in Goodramgate, having been tempted by a plaque outside which told me that it was part of: Our Lady's Row, Goodramgate. The oldest surviving row of houses in York built in 1316 in the churchyard of Holy Trinity. Here I replenished my depleted energy with a plateful of delicious cakes and an endless supply of tea.

Reluctant to move from this ancient hideaway I began to wonder, if given the choice, at what period in York's history I would most like to have lived. Would it be in Roman York, Viking York or perhaps Medieval York? After much contemplation I decided it was none of these for it would be Georgian York. During the 18th century the city had grown to become the social centre of the north. Fine, bright and spacious buildings were springing up, yet a rural atmosphere still prevailed close to the centre. The world was almost known, but not quite. An exciting age of mechanical technology was dawning yet the gloom, pollution and noise which it later brought had not yet arrived. There was also a more secure feeling about this period; barbaric tortures, internal warfare and religious persecution had almost disappeared. Yes, it would be Georgian York for me.

'Er, would you like anything else to eat Sir?'

The waitress had noticed that I had almost taken root in Crumbles Tea Room. I nodded 'No thanks', then red-faced I quickly departed from York's oldest house.

It was with bewildered resignation that I continued my afternoon stroll around the city, for it had become painfully plain that a person could spend a lifetime here and not see everything. I had just a few hours.

My path led me past the half-timbered exterior of St William's College which looks out over a green lawn. It is dedicated to the first Archbishop of York who just happened to be the great-grandson of William the Conqueror. The nearby Treasurer's House, in the shadow of the Minster, seemed to be sleeping in the hot sun. It was here, so I believe, that a ghostly army of Roman soldiers was seen in recent years, marching through the cellar!

Eager shoppers were crowding up Low Petersgate and Stonegate, seeking

Bootham Bar

out momentos of their visit to York. Slim young women with sun-tanned faces were buying herbs and creams from Culpeppers. An American man who looked as if he might be a professor was gazing into an antique shop, perhaps wondering how much that 17th century chest would cost to transport to California. His spell was broken by the chatter of voices; he turned to be confronted by a long line of smiling oriental girls who were following a lady guide in a floral dress. For two minutes he forgot the chest, he had become temporary enchanted by the small noses, large eyes and raven-black hair of the visitors.

I found myself near Bootham Bar which is not a pub as the name might suggest, but one of the ancient entrances to the city. Here I climbed the limestone steps which led me onto the wall, part of the 13th century fortifications that once protected York. Slowly I strolled along the elevated vantage point, looking down beyond the throb of traffic to the ancient landmarks that hide behind every corner.

These medieval walls replace those built by the Romans, which were banks of earth topped by a timber palisade. King Henry III ordered that these be strengthened, which led to the cream coloured stone being brought here from Tadcaster. The four main roads which enter the city were guarded by Bars; castle-like structures that were the strongest part of these walls. Bootham Bar guards the road to the north, Monk Bar and Walmgate Bar the roads from Scarborough and Hull, while Micklegate Bar looks out to the south. This remains the most imposing entrance for it is used by all visiting dignitaries including the ruling monarch.

My feet had begun to protest at the miles of pavements along which I had made them tread, they had decided my exploration of York must end. From a quiet corner I took a last long look at the central tower of the Minster soaring into the blue Yorkshire sky then reluctantly I turned around. But as I walked back to my car along a leafy riverside footpath I knew that soon I would return. For like the delicious chocolate bars which are made here, York is addictive.

Chapter Nine

York to Harrogate

I stop to see the battlefield where 4,000 Englishmen lie buried, then
I continue to Knaresborough and learn about the World's End. I
visit the Petrifying Well, see the chapel in a rock, hear about Saint
Robert and the weaver who printed his own banknotes. I visit
England's oldest chemist shop, see where Becket's murderers hid,
then disturb two lovers at the place where Harrogate began. I
admire Yorkshire's most elegant town, drink ghastly sulphur water,
learn of a mysterious disappearance then reluctantly end my
journey over windswept Blubberhouses Pass.

1

There is a handful of place names in England which, when come upon by chance, immediately send the blood rushing through our veins. On a bright sunny afternoon I came upon such a name down a quiet lane just four miles to the east of York. Having left the traffic behind me on the Harrogate road I drove at a snails-pace through a landscape of rolling golden hayfields till I was halted by the closed gates of a level crossing. After watching the little train chug its way into the distance I waited as the figure of a woman emerged from the nearby signal box on her way to move the twin barriers. It was then that my eyes saw the faded sign that identified this country crossing; it was Marston Moor.

I continued until I came into the village of Long Marston, hoping that I would see a sign that would direct me to this most famous battlefield of the Civil War, but there was none. The village appeared to be deserted, not a soul could be seen. I drove along its byways, stopped at the church which was firmly locked, puzzled, I wondered if I should head for Bilton or Hutton Wandesley. Then thankfully I was saved, for I saw a smartly dressed man strolling out of a cottage.

'It is surprising that something hasn't been done about Marston Moor,' he told me. 'After all it is one of the great milestones in our history. But at least there is a memorial on the roadside. Go back along this lane towards

Tockwith, you can't miss it. And there is a verge where you can park closeby.'

I thanked him, then five minutes later with a welcome breeze on my face I at last reached Marston Moor. The impressive memorial obelisk which was erected in 1939, looks out not on wild moorland as the name suggests, but on rich agricultural land contained by neat hedgerows. As I stared in silence across the sunlit fields I thought how odd that what today appears to be such a peaceful place, once witnessed terrible carnage and horror. For beneath these gently curving furrows lie the bones of 4000 Royalists and 300 of Cromwell's soldiers; Englishmen who died in this most futile and cruellest of wars.

The discord that caused the Civil War was rooted deeply in both power and religion. King Charles I, following the lead of his father, was an autocratic leader who sincerely believed in the divine right of kings. He paid only lip service to parliament, making his own, often unpopular decisions which he expected to be carried out without question. He was also a devout Anglican but was greatly influenced by his Roman Catholic wife, Queen Henrietta Maria. This led to him favouring Bishops whose allegiance lay with the High Church, in which many of the rituals and prayers closely followed those of the Roman Catholics. His supporters, the Cavaliers who in later years were to become known as the Tories, were mainly aristocratic landowners, squires and members of both the Church of England and the Roman Catholic Church. His radical opponents, the Roundheads, later known as the Whigs, firmly believed that parliament should have greater power than the king. They were often small business-men and strict Puritans of whom the dour country squire Oliver Cromwell, emerged as their leader.

After many years of bickering the inflexibility of the two sides slid them inevitably towards armed conflict. This came in October 1642 when the first major battle of the campaign took place at Edgehill, ending with an indecisive result. During the following two years the skirmishes and battles continued, casting a dark shadow over life in England. In April 1644 two Roundhead leaders, Lord Fairfax and the Earl of Leven, laid siege to York, the most important city in the north. Prince Rupert, the head of the Royalist forces, after winning a number of minor victories in Lancashire brought his army eastwards in an attempt to break the siege. The Parliamentary forces hearing of his approach, abandoned the city and came here to Marston Moor where they encamped in the assumed path of their oncoming opponents. But Prince Rupert after learning of their position, brilliantly outflanked them, proceeding to his main objective, the relief of York. This successfully accomplished he was then ready to meet the full fury of the Parliamentary Army.

Looking across the furrowed field from the monument towards a ditch, I could see where the Royalist army which consisted of 11,000 infantry and 6,000 cavalry, had been drawn up. Here, supervising the build up of these forces had stood commander-in-chief Prince Rupert with Lord Goring, Lord Byron and the Marquis of Newcastle at the head of three divisions. Turning around to look over Marston Lane I was now facing where the three opposing Parliamentary forces had drawn up their lines. On a high point I could see a tree known as Cromwell's Plump. Below this gathered about 28,000 soldiers led by Oliver Cromwell, with Lord Fairfax, the Earl of Manchester and the Earl of Leven as his commanders.

As the evening of the 2nd July approached, Prince Rupert, believing that no action would take place until the following day, began to eat his supper. But he was wrong, for taking him unawares Cromwell began the attack at seven o'clock. After this initial surprise the Royalists began to fight back and gained the upperhand, forcing Fairfax and his men to make a rapid retreat. At this stage it looked certain that Prince Rupert was going to be victorious, but then Cromwell began a brilliant military manoeuvre. He swept his men around to the rear of the Royalists, vigorously attacking the cavalry which quickly turned potential defeat into a great victory. Terrible slaughter followed with the Royalists surrendering or retreating in disarray. The battle was over in just two hours, but the Royalists were chased throughout the night with Prince Rupert reputedly hiding in a bean field.

The battle which took place here on that summer night in 1644 has found its special place in the history books, not because it marked the end of the Civil War, but because it was an important turning point. It led to the fall of York two days later and the loss of the Royalist hold on Northern England. The military phase of the war eventually ended in May 1646, to be followed by the execution outside Whitehall Palace of the autocratic King Charles I in 1649.

Looking down the deserted lane towards the village of Tockwith I was reminded of another, more recent conflict. For in 1941, Bomber Command began operations from RAF Marston Moor, an airfield that had three runways supported by over two thousand personnel. These meadows, where the clash of swords and the thunder of cannons once roared, then echoed with a different sound. It was the steady throb of the powerful engines of Halifax and Lancaster bombers, at times escorted by Hurricanes and Spitfires, intent on destroying the power of the Luftwaffe. One of the station commanders was Group Captain Leonard Cheshire, who later headed the famous Dambusters' Squadron then in civilian life brought hope to so many when he founded the Cheshire Homes.

2

I stood on the banks of the River Nidd at Knaresborough, sheltering from the bright morning sun beneath a sycamore bough and thinking what a perfect English scene lay before me. Hidden doves were cooing contentedly from the trees, red admiral and peacock butterflies in a feast of colour were sunning their open wings, while below me on the water the first visitors of the day had already taken to the little blue rowing boats.

'World's End is it?' said a lean young man to his friend.

Startled, I at first thought that perhaps he had been overcome by the magnificence of the view and thinking it unlikely he would ever see anything better, was suggesting some sort of suicide pact. But his friend's answer soon put my mind at rest.

'Good idea. I've heard that they've got some great new cask ale on sale brewed with honey.'

I soon discovered that what they were referring to was the World's End pub. Guarding one side of High Bridge it takes its name from the rather pessimistic prophecy of the town's most famous former resident, Mother Shipton. Crossing over the bridge I paid an admission charge then joined the visitors on Sir Henry Slingsby's Long Walk; a splendid riverside pathway, shaded by beech trees, which led me to Mother Shipton's Cave and the Petrifying Well.

Gazing into the dark entrance I half expected to see the face of an old crone with a red shawl and a black bonnet, perhaps calling out: 'Do come in. A problem of the heart is it? '

The tale of Mother Shipton's gift of prophecy starts in the late 15th century with her mother, a poor orphaned girl named Agatha Sontheil who lived here in Knaresborough. It seems that Agatha fell madly in love with a handsome youth, became pregnant, then like so many other young girls have discovered to their dismay, her lover would not marry her. However in his case there was a unique excuse for he revealed that he was not a mere mortal but a spirit, some say the devil himself. So instead he endowed her with supernatural powers, showing her how to heal, kill, control the elements and foretell the future. Naturally this raised some eyebrows in the town, she was accused of being a witch, but unlike the more unfortunate Pendle Witches she managed to escape with her life.

The birth of her baby daughter who she named Ursula, followed in July 1488, but this proved to be something of a disappointment. For the child was far from being beautiful, having a large bent nose covered in pimples, huge goggling eyes and deformed legs. Shortly afterwards Agatha sadly died in a convent where she had been given shelter, leaving her baby in the care of the parish.

However in spite of being born with great disadvantages, Ursula seems to have been blessed in other ways. She could read and write with distinction, and as she grew up it became apparent that she had also inherited supernatural powers from her mother. She is said to have married a man named Toby Shipton when she was 24 years old, but it is only in later life that her fame grew. For now known as Mother Shipton she would come to this cave in the dead of night to use her divine powers. At first she began to prophesy on purely local matters, then later she began to lay out in verse forthcoming world events that at the time seemed totally fantastic. These were first published in book form in 1663, having been copied from a manuscript said to have been found in a monastery. Her rhymed couplets fill page after page, many of her predictions have become reality, while others have obscure meanings which are open to speculation. The following is typical of her verse:

A house of glass shall come to pass
In England, but alas!
War will follow with the work,
In the land of the Pagan and Turk,
And State and State in fierce strife,
Will seek each other's life,
But when the North shall divide the South
An eagle shall build in the lion's mouth,
Taxes for blood and for war,
Will come to every door,
All England's sons that plough the land,
Shall be seen, book in hand:
Learning shall so ebb and flow,
The poor shall most learning know,
Waters shall flow where corn shall grow,
corn shall grow where waters doth flow,
House shall appear in the vales below,
And covered by hail and snow:

But happily the following prediction has proved to be untrue:

The world then to an end shall come,
In Nineteen Hundred and Eighty One.

However, it has been revealed that this world's end prophecy, which in

The tranquil River Nidd meanders through Knaresborough

some books is quoted as being 1881, was really a hoax, having been written by Charles Hindley of Brighton in 1873. But Mother Shipton's prediction of her own death in 1561 proved to be much more reliable. Having foretold the exact moment, she merely said goodbye to her friends, lay down in bed and died!

Close to Mother Shipton's Cave I looked at what for centuries has been one of Yorkshire's greatest curiosities, the Petrifying or Dropping Well. Here a stream trickles thirty feet over the edge of an overhanging cliff before flowing into the river. The water, which contains large amounts of carbonates and sulphates, has not only coated the crag with its white deposit but also 'turned to stone' a large number of objects which have been hung underneath, which include hats, teddy-bears and even underpants! The rocky pool formed by the water at the base of the cliff is known as the Wishing Well. I was told that to ensure that my wish would come true I should dip my hand in the water and then allow it to dry.

As I walked back to High Bridge, my hand drying in the sun, I was wondering how I would really spend my National Lottery prize which would be awaiting me next Saturday!

Knaresborough boasts one of the most splendid locations of any Yorkshire town, for it sits high on a hill overlooking this curving tree-lined gorge through which the river gently passes. On the opposite bank to Mother Shipton's Cave I strolled along Waterside, a lively riverside lane much-loved by visitors on sunny days. Here they eat lunch in small inviting cafes, hire rowing boats, exercise their dogs or merely sit on benches and watch the world go by.

'Please could you tell me the way to Saint Robert's Chapel,' I asked a young woman who was cleaning the doorstep of her cafe.

'Continue straight ahead until you reach Low Bridge, then its just five minutes walk along Abbey Road.'

I thanked her, then after making a diversion to look at the fascinating 200 year-old inn sign painted on copper at the Mother Shipton pub, I reached my destination. Keeping up the reputation which Knaresborough has gained for oddities this Chapel of Our Lady of the Crag, its correct title, remains one of the strangest in the land. Looking past a locked gate I could see a series of steps which lead not up to a building but into an ivy covered cliff face. For in 1408 a man known as John the Mason was granted a licence from King Henry IV to cut this chapel from the solid rock. A door, a small window and the effigy of a knight drawing his sword, overlooked by a cross, mark the entrance. I am told that it leads ten feet into the cliff up to a small altar, but unfortunately I was unable to gain access.

'You would need to go to the other side of town to the Catholic Church for the key,' said a smartly dressed man who lives in a nearby cottage. But I had little time and so much more to see.

Saint Robert of Knaresborough, whose cave lies a mile from the chapel, is not widely known today, yet during the 13th century he became one of Europe's most revered holy men. Robert Flower was born in York around 1160 to a wealthy family, but from childhood was intent on taking up a religious vocation. This he began as a novice Cistercian monk in Northumberland and then later in Fountains Abbey, but soon he decided that this life did not suit his temperament. He then joined a hermit who lived here in Knaresborough, but after a short period the hermit gave up his difficult religious path and Robert then began to wander around this corner of Yorkshire.

Quickly gaining a reputation as being a devout man of God, he was given the protection of a member of the powerful Percy family who had lands in the area. But others, including the Constable of Knaresborough Castle, were less sympathetic to his cause, making life difficult for him and hoping he would move on. However he gained more and more followers, which led eventually to the Constable giving in to public opinion and granting him a piece of land. Here Robert lived in a cave for the rest of his life, with a chapel dedicated to the Holy Rood being built by his brother nearby.

His devout example attracted many noble visitors including King John, whom he reprimanded for disturbing his prayers! Miraculous cures became attributed to him, he became the friend of the poor and of prisoners, and pilgrims flocked in to visit his humble cave. He died on the 24th September 1208, at first being buried in the chapel, but later his body was moved to a local priory that had been built because of his fame. Widely known as the Trinitarians, the monks of this Order of the Holy Trinity for the Redemption of Captives from the Holy Land, were often called Robertines.

St Robert's Cave gained a more sinister reputation during the 18th century, for in it was buried the body of a local man named Daniel Clark who had been murdered. In 1759 Eugene Aram paid the price for the crime, he was hanged at York and his body was then gibbeted. But since that time, like the case of Jack the Ripper, the crime has become the centre of much research and speculation. Some people believe that the bones found were not those of Clark and that Aram was wrongly convicted.

3

If Alice, instead of descending into Wonderland had come here to Knaresborough she would not have been disappointed. At every turn I discovered another strange and unique landmark which has a tale to tell. Looking up from the riverside to the top of a cliff face I noticed a grey turreted house which had a faded sign painted on its gable which announced: The House in the Rock. I was later told the history of this odd, four storey residence which lies on a magnificent vantage point overlooking the gorge.

Perhaps encouraged by the nearness of the Chapel of Our Lady, a local weaver named Hill, who lived during the 18th century, decided he too would like to cut himself a home from the solid rock. With the blessing of his landlord, Sir Thomas Slingsby, he began his back-breaking task in 1770 which was to last for sixteen years. So impressive was the finished house that the Duchess of Buccleuch gave Hill an array of flowers and shrubs to fill his garden. In return he named his new home Fort Montague, taken from the Duchess's family name.

Now living in such a splendid residence and having gained the friendship of many imminent people, the once humble weaver decided that he too deserved a title. So he began to call himself Sir Thomas Hill, Governor of Fort Montague. To further enhance his status he then, like the Bank of England, began issuing his own banknotes. But sadly this revealed his true financial position for they were only valued at five and a halfpence!

I puffed my way up Bridgate to the centre of the town, then discovered that I was lucky for it was market-day. Crowds of sun-tanned visitors were already spilling out into Cheapside. I joined this bustle, pushing my way between scores of stalls into the Market Place centred around the market cross where criminals were once publicly whipped. Traders, carrying on a tradition which stretches back six centuries, were shouting out to the crowds: 'Best tomatoes in Yorkshire', 'These strawberries are delicious', 'This dress would really suit you luv, its only a tenner.'

Above the noise of voices and traffic I could hear the sound of music drifting into the warm air. Around a corner I at last came to its source, a middle-aged man and woman who were appropriately playing old English tunes. The man, looking colourful in his flat-cap and red-spotted neckerchief, was heartily playing a banjo, while his wife, dressed in a long skirt and bonnet was accompanying him on her accordion. They brought a splendid splash of colour to the scene and their effort was being generously rewarded by a pile of coins given by passing visitors.

Ye Oldest Chymist Shoppe in England was half hidden by the mass of market stalls which had encroached almost to its doorstep. But I suppose

Ye Oldest Chymist Shoppe in England

that having been 'established in the reign of George I, 1720' in a building probably regarded as ancient when Henry VIII married his first wife, it has become quite accustomed to this inconvenience. I gazed into the small paned box-windows which are supported on what are known as Chinese Chippendale legs, that are a mere 235 years old. Here, where leeches, ringworm application and charms of quicksilver were once on sale, sophisticated cosmetics of today are on display.

I walked into the interior of this unique shop owned in 1720 by John Beckwith. Blending the past with the present, the lady assistant was dressed in a long floral dress and a mop cap while the male pharmacist wore a normal white overall. Here, among mortars and pestles once used to create portions for creaking Victorians I saw a mountain of perfumed beauty products which now tempt female visitors. But it is for its fragrant Lavender Water that this shop has become known to hundreds of customers throughout the world. Made faithfully to a secret formula from the past, the perfume is made only in small quantities then left to mature for several years in the ancient attic before being sold. I can think of no more appropriate setting for the creation of this most English of products.

Just around the corner from the noise of the market I strolled into a more tranquil world; among immaculately trimmed lawns and neat flower beds stand the remains of Knaresborough Castle, perched high above the river.

Here crowds tired by the hot sun, had escaped to sit quietly on benches, picnic on the emerald grass, perhaps play a slow game of bowls or just stare out from one of Yorkshire's most famous viewpoints. Lounging on the cliff edge I too stared out over the 100 feet deep gorge through which the Nidd has cut its meandering path. Linking the crags on each side of the river I could see the castellated railway viaduct, with the Parish Church beyond framed in a sea of green foliage. Turning around I looked again at the Keep and the scattered pieces of ancient masonry which cover this lush hillside. I then began to wonder how many of the people who were enjoying what is truly a peaceful spot are aware of its dramatic history.

Knaresborough was already old when Serlo de Burg, a follower of William the Conqueror built the first castle here, for the Romans had once lived on this strategic hillside followed later by the Saxons. But it was an event that began in December 1170, at the Castle of Bur in France, that was destined to link it with one of England's most infamous murders. King Henry II, who was staying there at the time, was in a raging temper caused by the actions of Thomas Becket. Eighteen years previously the King had made his friend Thomas the Archbishop of Canterbury, intending him to act as a mere puppet leaving the real ecclesiastical power with the throne. But as soon as Thomas became head of the Church in England his person- ality changed from being a light-hearted rogue to that of a stout hearted man of God. This led to a continuing bitter dispute between the two former friends as the King tried unsuccessfully to dominate the Church, leading to yet another raging tantrum.

'What sluggard wretches, what cowards have I brought up in my Court, who care nothing for their allegiance to their master! Not one will deliver me from this low-born priest!'

Four Knights, Hugh de Moreville, William de Tracy, Richard le Breton and Reginald Fitzurse, heard the King's rantings and decided to do some- thing about it. They secretly crossed the Channel by two separate routes, then met up at Saltwood Castle in Kent where they plotted Becket's downfall. This came on the 29th December 1170 when fully armed, they entered Canterbury Cathedral. Confronting the Archbishop with an intense passion that was typical of the age they began shouting and raving, accusing him of undermining the King. Well known for his hot temper he answered them with equal vigour, aware of what the inevitable end would be. In the darkened North Trancept a vicious blow from the sword of Richard le Breton shattered the skull of the man who would soon become revered as Saint Thomas of Canterbury. As the murderers in short lived triumph rode away from Canterbury, the skies darkened, lightning flashed and thunder boomed; it was as if the heavens were passing judgement on their sickening crime.

Fleeing north it was here at Knaresborough Castle where Hugh de Moreville was Constable, that the four Knights took refuge. Looking down from these ramparts on the green of the valley, they perhaps felt the first pangs of conscience for their murder of a great man. This eventually led them to Rome were they sought forgiveness for their sins from the Pope. As a penance they were told to go on an arduous pilgrimage to Jerusalem, from which none returned home alive.

Thirty six years after the death of Becket the castle witnessed a happier event when the corpulent King John brought his colourful retinue here to enjoy the hunting and to meet Saint Robert. The next century saw the good-natured but weak King Edward II on a visit here after he had given the castle to his favourite, Piers Gaveston. But it was as a prisoner of Henry Bolingbroke that the handsome and effeminate King Richard II saw the inside of these walls; later he was murdered at Pontefract.

It was the Civil War that brought the end of the castle as a fortress, for Knaresborough like many a northern town, had supported the losing side. After the Royalists met a decisive defeat at Marston Moor near York in 1644, cannon balls quickly soared over Kirkgate. When the smoke had cleared the castle which had stood triumphant for five centuries, remained only as a romantic ruin.

As I walked down the steep stone steps which lead back to the river I stopped to read a bright yellow poster which told me that another, more recent military event was soon to be celebrated on the Castle Top. The fiftieth anniversary of VJ Day would be remembered by street parties, fireworks and a thanksgiving service.

No visit to Knaresborough would be complete without a mention of another of the town's famous eccentric characters, Blind Jack Metcalfe, who was born here in 1717. When he was four years old he contracted smallpox from which miraculously he recovered, but it left him completely blind. However, with astonishing determination he went on to overcome his disability, living an amazing full life. He learned to swim, play the violin, guide strangers across the local countryside, and even established a horse-trading and carrier business. But it is as a road builder that he gained an unrivalled reputation throughout the north of England. Taking full responsibility for long stretches of new highway, he would choose the best line over the most difficult of terrain then design and build any bridges that were required. When he died in 1810 at the age of 93 he was buried in the village churchyard at Spofforth, where a fine tombstone was provided by Lord Dundas.

4

She was about eighteen and he was about twenty. She was wearing a brightly coloured gipsy skirt, had dark hair which rested provocatively on her shoulders and partly hid her smiling face covered in freckles. He was looking adoringly into her eyes, they spoke little, yet their body language said everything; they were obviously deeply in love. I felt ashamed that I was to be the one that would break their spell, but I had little choice. They had unfortunately chosen the ornate shelter that covers Harrogate's Tewit Well for their romantic rendezvous; a place that was high on my list of sites to visit for it is the spot where this elegant and appealing town really began. I coughed discreetly, they moved a little apart. This allowed me time to selfconsciously admire the fine architecture of the cupola and to discover with disappointment that the water is no longer visible. After completing a circuit of the well and taking a photograph I walked quickly away across the green lawns of The Stray, leaving the lovers to resume their embrace.

At the beginning of the 16th century Harrogate existed only as an area of wild, sparsely populated moorland which was part of the Forest of Knaresborough. It was only known by hunters who came here to bring down deer, and travellers who passed by on their way to Skipton. In 1571 Captain William Slingsby, a member of a prominent local family from Bilton, was riding alone across this isolated landscape when his eyes were drawn to a flock of birds. These lapwings, known also as peewits or tewits, seemed to be diving and screeching around a small depression in the ground. His curiosity aroused he veered his horse across to the spot where he discovered a well. Bending down to drink the water which was bubbling to the surface he was amazed to find that it had the same strong taste of minerals which he had sampled at a health resort abroad. He reasoned that this too must possess the same curative properties, so naming it the Tewit Well he eventually had the area around it paved and protected from animals by a wall.

The fame of the Tewit Well quickly grew, those suffering from many different types of ailments came here seeking a cure, while medical men arrived to give their professional views. When Doctor Timothy Bright compared it to a well that existed at Spaw in Belgium, he inadvertently created a title which would be later adopted by all such places. But at this time the Tewit Well was the only English Spa.

Following the publication of a book in 1626 which glowingly listed the many diseases which could be cured by drinking the water, people began flocking here in ever increasing numbers. At first Knaresborough was the nearest place where they could be accommodated, but many sought out lodgings closer to the well. Frugal hospitality was offered by a few cottages which existed in the immediate vicinity known as High Haregate, and those a short distance down the valley at Low Haregate. By this time other mineral wells were being discovered all around the area, including the famous Sulphur Well at Low Haregate which due to its strong fumes was known as the Stinking Spaw. By 1687 the first new hostelry, the Queen's Head, was built to accommodate those seeking treatment in the quickly expanding village then known as High Harrogate. An astonishing eighty eight different wells were eventually discovered, often containing completely different mixtures of minerals. These have been identified as strong sulphur, mild sulphur with alkaline salts, saline chalybeate, and pure chalybeate.

As I strolled along Slingsby Walk which was bathed in yellow sunlight, I began to think how fortunate Harrogate really is to be surrounded with such a multitude of gardens and open spaces. Montpellier Gardens, Prospect Gardens, Valley Gardens and The Stray convey a marvellous spectacle of colour. They also enhance the gracious 18th century architecture of the hotels and homes of the wealthy, which in turn highlight Harrogate's amazing transformation from a windswept hamlet into a fashionable Spa. But this came about not by chance but by astute forward planning. The pleasant pastureland known as The Stray because farm animals were allowed to 'stray' at will over its two hundred acres, was saved by an Act of Parliament in 1770. This stated that the 'land for ever hereafter remain open and uninclosed; and all persons whomsoever shall and may have free access at all times'. It is the type of document which brings a frown to the face of the land speculator and a smile to those who love our countryside.

A slim young woman wearing sun-glasses and sporting a gold coloured Gucci handbag was gazing into a shop window, perhaps wondering whether those shoes priced at £200 would really be ideal for her next sojourn to Nice. She had probably parked her BMW or Merc around the corner, having left an immaculate detached mansion just outside Ripon. Later she might join her friends for lunch in the exclusive Betty's Tea Room, followed by a peruse in one of the scores of expensive antique shops which hide in the leafy corners of this delightful town.

This air of genteel affluence discernible in the spacious streets of Harrogate today, began over two centuries ago when Georgian society came here to take the waters. Daniel Defoe was one of the first to record his observations of the rise of the Spa in his 'A Tour Through the Whole Island of Great Britain' written in 1724: 'We were surprised to find a great deal of good company here drinking the waters, and indeed, more than we found afterwards at Scarborough; though this seems to be a most desolate out-of-the-world place, and that men would only retire to it for religious mortifications, and to hate the world, but we found it was quite otherwise.'

But it was during the last century that the biggest expansion took place. The two former hamlets became linked by a parade of fine buildings creating a town which could boast to be the leading hydrotherapy centre in Britain. In 1826 the Harrogate Bath Hospital was built, followed by the Pump Rooms together with a host of up-market hotels and shops to cater for the wealthy visitor's every need. Following the building of the railway line in 1848 even more people arrived, including Charles Dickens who could not resist observing the antics of the many eccentric characters who had made Harrogate their home. The famous, including a host of foreign royalty, continued to be drawn here right up to the First World War which was to mark the slow decline of the town as a Spa. However when H.V. #Morton wrote The Call of England in 1927, he recorded that Harrogate was still using twenty five tons of peat each week for its popular Electric Peat Treatment. It was another forty years before hydropathic treatments sadly ended, but by this time Harrogate had other cards up its sleeve. Today as well as attracting the tourist it is one of our leading conference centres;

The Royal Pump Room

a place where young men in dark suits with lapel badges dash into hotel lounges to talk about sales projections and 'the way ahead'. It is also the home of the Spring Flower Show, the Great Yorkshire Show, the Cricket Festival, the Northern Antiques Fair..... and many more!

After admiring the towering obelisk which commemorates those who died for our freedom and reading a plaque unveiled last year to commemorate the fiftieth anniversary of D Day, I strolled down Parliament Street to the Royal Bath Assembly Rooms. Here I discovered that it is still possible to take the waters, for the Turkish Baths built in 1897 have survived. 'A total leisure experience with that unique Turkish feeling', I read from a brochure which also advertised 'massage and beauty therapy'. However, with the modesty in keeping with Harrogate's image I noted that at the mixed sessions 'Swimming costumes must be worn'!

I wandered into the part of this impressive building which houses the Tourist Information Centre, to find its interior still shines with Victorian grandeur. Its solid doorway is guarded by two busts, one was of Baroness Angela Burdett-Coutts 1814-1906, 'a wealthy philanthropist, friend of Charles Dickens, and a regular Harrogate visitor and benefactor', while the other is of the great writer.

'If you turn left, then walk for a couple of minutes you will come to the Pump Room Museum, the site of theOld Sulphur Well,' a softly spoken woman with a healthy complexion told me as she busily straightened a display of postcards.

Following these instructions I arrived at the museum which has a plaque outside which told me that: 'Doctor Edward Deane first drew the attention of the world to the strongest sulphur spring in Great Britain when he published his Spadacrene Anglica in 1626'. It then went on to tell me about Betty Lupton who became known as the Queen of the Harrogate Waters. She was the most famous of a group of women who dispensed cups of the life giving liquid to visitors. This she did for 56 years till her death in 1843 at the age of 83 years; her long active life, presumably resulting from sampling her own product.

I entered the Royal Pump Room, built in 1842 to enclose the Old Sulphur Well, then I paid my 75p entrance fee to a pretty, intelligent looking girl. I was then allowed to stroll in the footsteps of the famous, looking at a small collection of artifacts which chart Harrogate's unique history. These include a number of old bicycles, a photo of a founder member of the Cyclist Touring Club (CTC), George Henry Wray 1851 -1953, and a collection of old music-hall posters. A display of health products appropriately includes a tablet of Original Harrogate Sulphur Soap, while nearby rests a Bath Chair which may well have been left behind by an absent minded Victorian visitor. Some of the devices that were invented to administer the water treatments could easily be mistaken for instruments of torture. These included a peat bath used for the treatment tried by H.V. Morton over sixty years ago, and an ingenious shower which shot the health giving water at its 'victim' from all directions!

'Would you like to sample the water?' the girl asked me when I reached the exit.

I gave a reluctant nod as she handed me a small glass of the cloudy liquid. 'It's an acquired taste. Better to drink it fast,' she added.

With an uneasy smile I gulped the salty portion from the Stinking Spaw down then I spent the rest of the day walking the streets of Harrogate with my breath smelling of bad eggs!

5

A warm feeling of comfort and elegance greeted me inside the Old Swan Hotel. Guided by the soft glow of subdued lighting I looked into the Wedgwood Room where well-groomed women and grey suited young men were having lunch. Discreet waiters in white shirts and black bow ties, poured bottles of red wine or stood in silence while madam decided whether to choose that 'delicious strawberry gateau' or perhaps 'a small piece of cheesecake'. In the background could be heard the soothing sound of a piano appropriately playing a tune from the twenties; I had reached the soul of Harrogate.

Defoe may well have eaten here for 'The Sign of the Swan' was in existence by the early 18th century as a modest inn. But in 1840, at a time of optimism when the young Victoria had reigned for barely three years it was rebuilt to the present regal design. As the town continued to expand so did the progressive Swan Hotel, in 1878 it was purchased by the Harrogate Hydropathic Company who did not intend to be overtaken by that young upstart, Matlock Bath. They installed a resident doctor here, Richard Veale, who supervised the water treatment given to exclusive clients in an atmosphere of quiet luxury. The ambience of the hotel continued to attract the wealthy throughout the Edwardian period. Then in the aftermath of the Great War came the Roaring Twenties when in an attempt to forget the horrors of a lost generation, its ballroom resounded to the sound of the Charleston and the Turkey Trot. It was during this period, in December 1926, that an unexpected incident happened here that sud-

The elegant Old Swan Hotel

denly brought the hotel to the notice of the world; the mysterious disappearance of the Queen of Crime, Agatha Christie.

Agatha Christie was born in Torquay on 15 September 1890, the third child of Frederick Miller and Clarissa Boehmer. Her father was a wealthy American from New York who after marrying his British wife settled happily in Devon which he quickly grew to love. Agatha, together with her sister Madge and brother Monty, lived in the large family home of Ashfield. Here was employed a cook, a housemaid, a parlourmaid and a devoted nurse who looked after the children, often taking them for long country walks. But there was no governess at the house and Agatha did not go to school, so she received no formal education. Instead she was taught by her mother who held strong views about children's education, believing they should not be taught to read until they were eight years old.

Growing up in this settled but narrow middle class environment she became a shy, imaginative child, who was blissfully happy with her own company. She loved to read and create stories in her mind, and at the age of eleven took her first step into the literary world when a poem which she had written was printed in the local newspaper. But at this time came a sad blow to her idyllic childhood with the premature death of her father which brought with it inevitable financial problems.

However, when she reached sixteen her mother was still able to afford to send her to the traditional finishing school in Paris. Accompanied by her friend Dorothy Hamilton-Johnson, she slowly settled down to a new life in what was at this time the most exciting city in the world. There she studied language and art, showed an aptitude for music, and was trained in etiquette which helped to overcome her shyness. Her horizons were further extended when she later travelled with her mother for a three month holiday to Cairo, at this time full of eligible young men. After twice narrowly escaping marriage she returned home to Torquay, only to be swept off her feet by the handsome Archibald Christie, a dashing Lieutenant in the Royal Field Artillery. Their romance led to a formal engagement, then two years later on Christmas Eve 1914, to a quick marriage service in Bristol; hastened by the turmoil of the First World War.

Her new husband now joined the Royal Flying Corp, while the war gave her an opportunity to become a Voluntary Aid Detachment Nurse at the Torbay Hospital. In 1916, motivated by a light-hearted bet from her sister Madge, she attempted to write a detective novel in the fashion of Conan Doyle's Sherlock Holmes which she loved to read. Inspired by Belgium refugees she had seen in Torquay, her fertile imagination created the now legendary Belgium detective M. Hercule Poirot and his incompetent assistant, Captain Hastings. The Mysterious Affair at Styles took her just over a fortnight to write, but it was four years before she could find a publisher willing to put it into print. By this time she was a mother; her daughter Rosalind whom she named after one of Shakepeare's great characters, having been born in 1919.

Her first book brought her a mere £26 for serialization rights and no royalties as it did not reach the minimum sales target of 2,500 copies. But its modest success had motivated her to continue writing. A steady output followed, she acquired an agent to represent her interests and then in 1926 with the publication of The Murder of Roger Ackroyd, came the break-through she desired. The twists and turns of the plot together with its surprise murderer made it a sensational success, being immediately hailed as a classic detective story. However, in the midst of this new found fame when the eyes of the world were upon her came two tragic episodes which were to shatter her life. Her mother who had played such an important part in her early cloistered life, sadly died, to which was added the shattering discovery of Archie's love for another woman.

On the evening of the 3 December 1926 there followed an event which proved to be as baffling as any mystery story. At this time she seemed to be in reasonably good spirits, having to some extent come to terms with the dramatic happenings in her life. As was usual she dined alone at Styles, her Sunningdale home which had been named after her first book, for now she saw little of Archie at weekends. Later she wrote two letters, one to her husband and another to her secretary, then after kissing her sleeping daughter she told a servant she was going out for a drive.

But Agatha Christie did not return home to Styles that night, then early the next morning her bull-nosed Morris car was found by a gypsy boy off a lane in Berkshire. Its lights were turned on and the bonnet was up; it had apparently been abandoned. The police who came to investigate found that it was undamaged yet could find no tyre tracks on the grass. Inside the car was a fur coat and a small suitcase which appeared to have bursted open, scattering a number of items of ladies' clothes on the seat. They also found Agatha Christie's driving licence which confirmed she was the owner of the vehicle, but she seemed to have completely vanished.

Colonel Christie was informed of his wife's disappearance by Superin-tendent William Kenward who was put in charge of the investigation. A mammoth search quickly followed, extending across the Berkshire coun-tryside from Newlands Corner where the car had been found. This involved hundreds of police and volunteers, a spotter plane, bloodhounds and divers who searched a local lake known as the Silent Pool. Then came a number of baffling sightings which brought with them conflicting evidence to what had really happened; clues which would have puzzled even the great Poirot. A farm worker claimed he had started the car for Mrs Christie in the very early morning. He said that she had appeared cold and distressed, but had driven away in the opposite direction from the place where the vehicle had been discovered. Then two other men said they had seen her walking along a local road, she had asked them which direction it was to Petersfield.

When the story hit the news headlines on the following Monday morning it caused a national sensation. Although the search was continuing it had so far proved fruitless and the police were looking at a number of wide ranging possibilities. Had Agatha Christie been kidnapped or even murdered, had she committed suicide in some hidden place or was she merely lying injured and had still to be found? As the days went by the mystery seemed to deepen. A newspaper offered a reward of £100 for anyone who could solve it and her husband increased the figure to £500. However this did not stop the police listing him as a possible suspect. After all he was on the brink of leaving her, so he had the most to gain from her disappearance for it solved a lot of his problems.

It was Saturday the 4 December when Mrs Teresa Neele, an attractive 35 year old woman with shingled red hair signed the register here at Harrogate's Hydropathic Hotel. Although alone she quickly engaged in conversation with her fellow guests, relating how she was visiting from Cape Town and in spite of not wearing evening clothes joined in the lively dancing in the evening. During the following week she mingled freely with the other ladies, played games, sang at the piano and went for walks across The Stray. Appearing relaxed and happy, she also visited the fashionable shops of the town, buying a wardrobe of new clothes.

The first suspicions that Teresa Neele and Agatha Christie were indeed the same person were raised by hotel guests who had seen her photograph in the newspaper. They lightheartedly pointed out to her that she bore a striking likeness to the missing writer, which unperturbed she agreed, going on to discuss the mysterious disappearance. However it was a part time musician, Bob Tappin who played in the hotel band, who finally decided to inform the Harrogate police. They sent a detective around to the hotel to watch her movements, with the hotel staff being told to carry on their duties as usual. But in the meantime the press had got wind of the story, which brought an avalanche of reporters north. One of these managed to confront Teresa Neele, addressing her as Mrs Christie, she answered his questions quite naturally, mentioning she probably had amnesia.

By this time Colonel Christie had been told that a woman answering the description of his wife had been found in Harrogate, so he was immediately taken to Yorkshire to discreetly observe Teresa Neele. Having been told her assumed name he would have been almost certain this was his missing wife, for the name of the new woman in his life was Nancy Neele. In an atmosphere of subdued excitement he waited with Superintendent McDowell here in the elegant lounge of the Old Swan Hotel. At last the slim figure of a woman wearing a pink dinner dress appeared before him, and he gestured to the policeman that she was indeed his missing wife.

The astonishing reunion was remarkably civilised with Agatha Christie telling other guests that this was her brother, even though they were well aware of his true identity. The couple calmly ate dinner together, in spite of the massive presence of the press outside and the obvious interest of the guests. They spent the night in a suite of rooms then departed the next morning by car, after using two decoys to try to put the reporters off the scent.

So what lay behind this astonishing episode in Agatha Christie's life? The explanation put forward by her husband was that she was suffering from loss of memory and concussion, while others said it was brought about by stress. But many of her fans believe these solutions do not answer the host of questions that, like clues from her books, are raised by the strange affair. Although she gained a massive amount of free publicity this is unlikely to be the reason behind the event, for it did not fit in with her shy, retiring nature. Some feel a more likely explanation is that she was cleverly combining a real-life test for one of her future books, with revenge on her husband.

In 1928 she was divorced from Archibald Christie, who shortly afterwards married Nancy Neele; the couple lived happily together for the next thirty years. Two years later, although retaining the name Agatha Christie for her future detective novels, she married a young archaeologist named Max Mallowan who rose to become one of the most imminent scholars of his generation, receiving a knighthood in 1968. Over a fifty year period she wrote an astonishing ninety-four books which became worldwide best sellers, making her one of our wealthiest writers. These include the ever popular Murder on the Orient Express (1934), Death on the Nile (1937), Ten Little Niggers (1939), A Pocket Full of Rye (1953) and the Three Blind Mice (1950), from which was adapted London's longest running play, The Mousetrap. She also wrote six romantic novels using the pseudonym Mary Westmacott.

The dapper Hercule Poirot made his final appearance in Curtain (1975), to be followed by that loveable eccentric, Miss Marple, in Sleeping Murder (1976). These books had been written earlier but held back until the career of their creator was coming to an end. Agatha Christie, who was now officially Lady Mallowan, died on the 12 January 1976 at the age of 85. She lies buried in a country churchyard at Wallingford in Oxfordshire, but part of her lasting memory remains here at The Old Swan Hotel in Harrogate. Her celebrated disappearance was recreated once more for the film Agatha. This starred Vanessa Redgrave and Dustin Hoffman, and was made on location around Harrogate.

Leaving the splendour of the hotel I stepped out into the bright sunlight. As I walked back to my car alongside the flowery gardens I passed a pub that seemed a perfect antidote against Harrogate's classy image; it is named Scruffy Murphy's. I could well imagine what Compo would say if he came this way.

'Hey up. This seems about right, dus think?'

6

In the falling light of early evening I drove westward from Harrogate, soon exchanging the fresh greenness of meadowland for the rugged brown of the Pennine hills. As I ascended the twisting road of Blubberhouses Pass, like a man returning home from a sumptuous banquet, I was filled with a marvellous feeling of contentment. For blessed with the hottest summer for centuries I had feasted on the very best of Yorkshire.

With the distant profile of Pendle Hill in my windscreen some of the lasting images of this unforgettable journey came flowing back. I remembered the spacious streets of James Mason's Huddersfield, the sadness and the triumphs of the Brontë Sisters in Haworth, and bracing Ilkley where the locals have a bit o' brass. The almost overwhelming beauty of the Dales; Malham Cove and Gordale Scar, the Three Peaks, Wharfedale and Wensleydale and remote Swaledale. The rugged isolation of the Tan Hill Inn, the haunting beauty of Fountains Abbey, the hidden corners of Richmond, and the windswept freedom of the heathery summits of the North York Moors.

My first view of the North Sea at Staithes, the magic of Whitby which I saw from its clifftop church, the laughter of Scarborough in the hot sun and the shriek of sea birds at Flamborough Head. The ageless charm of The Wolds villages, the glory of Beverley and the majestic splendour of York. The half-forgotten battlefield of Marston Moor where so much English blood was shed, the prophecies of Mother Shipton at Knaresborough, and the green elegance of Harrogate.

Although I have seen so much on this journey my only regret is that I have also missed so much. However, this is inevitable – for a man could spend a lifetime exploring Yorkshire's broad acres and still yearn for more.

Index

A

Abbot Huby's Tower	90
Aire, River	36
Airedale	33
Airedale Terrier	35
Ampleforth	101
Arkengarthdale	82
Ayckbourn, Alan	139

B

Bamforths	5
Beck Hall	52
Bede, Saint	160
Belvedere Gardens	138
Beverley	152
Beverley Minster	153
Beverley, racecourse	155
Bingley	33
Birkbeck, John	61
Bishop Burton	155
Blackstone Edge	19
Bolton Abbey	42
Bolton Priory	43
Bootham Bar	169
Boulby	111
Braine, John	33
Bridlington	148, 151
Brontë Country	27
Brontë Society, the	29, 135
Brontë, Anne	136
Brontë, Branwell	28

C

Caedmon	124
Calder, River	13
Captain Cook Memorial Museum	128
Carroll, Lewis	116
Castle Hill	6
Chapel-le-Dale	66, 69

Christie, Agatha	188
Clapham	59
Clapham Beck	59
Cleveland Plain	107
Cleveland Way, the	103
Clifford family	44
Clifford's Tower	161
Coast-to-Coast Walk	131
Cook, James	111
Cragg Vale	19
Craven Museum	45
Cringle Moor	107
Cromwell, Oliver	171

D

Dales Way, the	41
Dane's Dyke	147
Defoe, Daniel	183
Dobson, Bob	20
Dracula	125

E

Edale	2
Edward the Confessor	155
Eskdale	128

F

Fawkes, Guy	163
Filey	143
Flamborough Head	130, 139-143-169
Lighthouse	144
Foss, River	164
Fossdale Beck	78
Fountains Abbey	55, 90
Freeman, Henry	126
Fylingdales Moor	133

G

Gaping Gill	62
Gardale Scar	54
Gargrave	47
Giggleswick	56
church	58
Goathland	133
Gordale Scar	54
Great Ayton	107
Green Howards, the	85

H

Halifax	13
Gibbet	16
Piece Hall	15
Harold, King	155
Harpham	154
Harrogate	170-191
Harty, Russell	56
Hauxwell, Hannah	82
Hawes	75
Haworth	28
Heaton, Neil	107
Hebble Brook	13
Hebden Bridge	23
Hebden Water	24
Helmsley	102
Herriot, James	80, 83
Hilda, Saint	122
Holme, river	3
Holmfirth	1-21
Holtby, Winifred	151
Hornsea	151
Horton-in-Ribblesdale	72
Hubberholme	73
Huddersfield	6

I

Ilkley	23-63
Moor	40
Ingleborough	66
Ingleton	62

J

Jones, John Paul	145
Jorvik Viking Centre	163

K

Keighley	38
Keld	80
Kilburn	100
Kingsley, Charles	49
Kirk Beck	48
Kirkby Malham	49
Knaresborough	173, 176, 178
Knaresborough Castle	179

L

Laughton, Charles	139
Leeds	1
Littondale	73
Long Marston	170
Lord's cricket ground	99
Lord, Thomas	97
Lydgate	2
Lyke Wake Walk	106

M

Malham	51
Tarn	51, 54
Malhamdale	48
Margaret Clitheroe, Saint	166
Marks, Michael	46
Marston Moor	170
Mason. James	9
Metcalf, Blind Jack	181
Moors Murderers	2
Morton, H.V.	145, 184
Mytholmroyd	18

N

Nidd, River	173
North Western Railway	70
North York Moors	89-129

O

Old Peak	130
Old Sulphur Well, Harrogate	185

Oldham 1
Olicana 39
Owen, Bill 5

P

Pendle Hill 192
Pennine Way, the 52
Penny Hedge Ceremony 128
Penyghent 68
Pickles, Wilfred 17
Priestley, J. B. 35
Priestley, J.B. 74

R

Raistrick, Dr Arthur 44
Ravenscar 130
Reeth 83
Ribblehead Viaduct 67, 71
Ribblesdale 72
Richmond 64-109
Rievaulx Abbey 104
Ripon 92
Robin Hood's Bay 130
Rochdale Canal 23
Rombalds Moor 37
Rudston 148
Rudstone, church 149
Rye, River 104

S

Saddleworth Moor 2
Scarborough 132, 134, 136
Settle 55
Settle-Carlisle line 71
Shambles, The 165
Shipton, Mother 173
Skipper Gallery 164
Skipton 44
    Castle 45
Sowerby Bridge 18, 23
Spencer, Thomas 46
St Robert's Cave 177
Stainforth 72
Staithes 110

Stamford Bridge 155, 156
Stoker, Bram 126
Stoodley Pike 21
Sutcliffe Gallery 121
Sutton-under-Whitestonecliffe 100
Swaledale 79

T

T'owd Genn Memorial 4
Tan Hill Inn 81
Tewit Well, Harrogate 182
Thirsk 97
Three Peaks 64
Tite, Sir William 7
Todmorden 1-33, 41
    Moor 21
Top Withens 25, 27
Towngate 4
Turpin, Dick 154, 162
Twaite 80

V

Vale of Mowbray 84

W

Wensleydale 75, 79
West Riding 4
Weyland, Valerie 87
Wharf, River 39
Wharfdale 43
Whernside 67
Whitby 110-147
    Abbey 119, 122
Wyatt, Sir Thomas 137

Y

York 148-169
    Minster 158
Yorkshire
    Dales 42-87
    Terrier 35
    Wolds 143

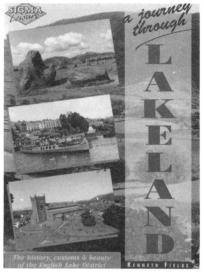

Also by Kenneth Fields:

JOURNEY THROUGH LAKELAND: the history, customs and beauty of the English Lake District

"...a most enjoyable diary, wide ranging in its coverage and appreciative in its comments" – THE KESWICK REMINDER. £7.95

JOURNEY THROUGH LANCASHIRE: the history, customs and beauty of Lancashire

"Packed with whimsy & wonder" – THIS ENGLAND. £7.95

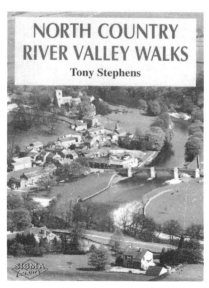

NORTH COUNTRY RIVER VALLEY WALKS

This book, by northern writer Tony Stephens, covers 500 miles of walks in 5000 square miles of stunning countryside along river valleys with diversions to higher ground to reach the source of the river or to admire the wide panoramas of river systems from a lofty vantage point. All of the famous rivers are featured, including the Calder, Lune, Ribble, Swale and Wharfe. £7.95

Companion volume, also £7.95, with a further 250 miles of walks:

PEAKLAND RIVER VALLEY WALKS

More books about Yorkshire

DISCOVERY WALKS IN THE YORKSHIRE DALES: The Northern Dales

DISCOVERY WALKS IN THE YORKSHIRE DALES: The Southern Dales

Brilliantly illustrated, vividly described, these books by walks leader David Johnson are real eye-openers for all those even remotely interested in why the countryside looks the way it does - "... most useful as well as entertaining" – YORKSHIRE HISTORY QUARTERLY.

Each volume: £6.95

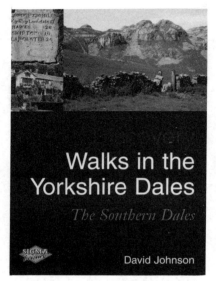

SOUTH YORKSHIRE WALKS: 30 Classic Routes

Martin Smith's book on South Yorkshire offers many delightful rambles "...ideal for both morning strolls and all-day hikes" ALL SPORT AND LEISURE MONTHLY.   £6.95

TEA SHOP WALKS IN THE YORKSHIRE DALES

Clive Price has devised the 30 walks in this book to explore the unique landscape of the Dales, crossing high moorlands and following riverside paths. Enjoy picturesque villages and ramble through ruined medieval abbeys,

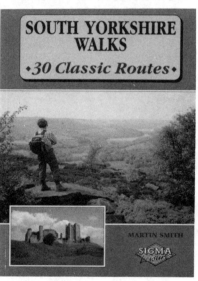

such as Fountains, or visit the ancient castles of Middleham and Bolton. Yorkshire is a county renowned for its hospitality and baking, so to round off each walk is a specially selected tea-room, where you can sample the best gateaux - sinfully smothered in cream from the local cows!   £6.95

TOWN & VILLAGE DISCOVERY TRAILS: Yorkshire Dales

From simple village walks to longer adventures around larger towns, this book is a pure education! Many of the towns and villages are recorded in the Domesday book, and each has a story to tell. Walker and writer, Elizabeth Fowler has taken all the excellent photographs and provided clear maps to accompany the trails.   £6.95

WHARFEDALE TO WESTMORLAND: historical walks through the Yorkshire Dales

Aline Watson's book traces the 120-mile route followed by Lady Anne Clifford some 300 years ago. Sections are described, together with short circular routes.   £6.95

YORKSHIRE DALES WALKING - ON THE LEVEL

Another "on the level" book by writer and photographer Norman Buckley has all the pleasures of the dales without the climbs "..a great buy" ILKLEY GAZETTE.   £6.95

YORKSHIRE DALES WALKS WITH CHILDREN

This book guides walkers, their children and their families through the Yorkshire Dales. It contains over 20 circular countryside walks between 2 and 5 miles long, well-distributed across the Dales, mostly within the boundaries of the National Park. A check-list

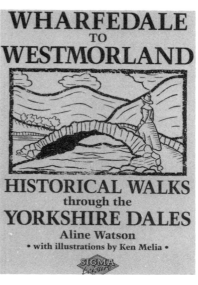

of things to spot on the walk are given, along with notes to parents about points of interest to discuss with the children on the way round. Stephen Rickerby, a geography teacher, is well-qualified in keeping children entertained! £6.95